VERSE-BY-VERSE
Bible Study of Genesis

David R. Bradley

Copyright © 2024 David R. Bradley

All rights reserved.

No part of this publication may be reproduced, distributed, or transmitted in any form or by any means, including photocopying, recording, or other electronic or mechanical methods, without the prior written permission of the publisher, except in the case of brief quotations embodied in critical reviews and certain other noncommercial uses permitted by copyright law.

Acknowledgment

I'd like to thank all of the Christian ministry leaders that have been so influential in my life. Fellow pastors, Sunday School teachers, church music leaders, youth ministers, etc.

Dedication

This book is affectionately dedicated to my wife, Cynthia. For her love, friendship, encouragement, and support. I knew when I met her, an adventure was going to happen.

Table of Contents

GENESIS
    Introduction 1
CHAPTER ONE
    The Creation 9
CHAPTER TWO
    Creation of Mankind 17
CHAPTER THREE
    The Temptation 25
    The Protoevangelium 32
CHAPTER FOUR
    Cain Murders Abel 37
    The Family of Adam 44
CHAPTER FIVE
    The Wickedness and Judgment of Men 51
    God's Covenant and Instructions to Noah 58
CHAPTER SIX
    The Great Flood 65
CHAPTER SEVEN
    Noah's Deliverance 69
CHAPTER EIGHT
    Covenant of the Rainbow 75
CHAPTER NINE
    The Tower of Babel 81
CHAPTER TEN
    Promise to Abram 85
    Abram's Failure in Egypt 89
CHAPTER ELEVEN
    Abram Trusts God 93
CHAPTER TWELVE
    Abram's Choices 99

CHAPTER THIRTEEN
    Abrahamic Covenant Confirmed   105

CHAPTER FOURTEEN
    Failure to Wait upon the Lord   113

CHAPTER FIFTEEN
    The Sign of the Abrahamic Covenant   121
    Nothing Is Impossible With God   125

CHAPTER SIXTEEN
    Abraham Intercedes for the Righteous   131

CHAPTER SEVENTEEN
    God Delivers the Righteous From the Judgment   137

CHAPTER EIGHTEEN
    Abraham and Abimelech   145

CHAPTER NINETEEN
    God's Provision and Protection   151

CHAPTER TWENTY
    Abraham's Greatest Test   157

CHAPTER TWENTY-ONE
    Death of Sarah   163

CHAPTER TWENTY-TWO
    A Bride for Isaac   169
    Isaac Marries Rebekah   175

CHAPTER TWENTY-THREE
    God Chooses Jacob   179
    Live For the Eternal Not the Temporal   185

CHAPTER TWENTY-FOUR
    Renewal of the Covenant With Isaac   191

CHAPTER TWENTY-FIVE
    Isaac Blesses Jacob   199
    The Stolen Blessing   204

CHAPTER TWENTY-SIX
    Jacob's Dream at Bethel   209

CHAPTER TWENTY-SEVEN
    The Deceitful Wedding – Jacob Marries   215
    The Battle of the Brides   221

CHAPTER TWENTY-EIGHT
    Honesty Is Honorable   227
CHAPTER TWENTY-NINE
    Afraid? Trust in the Lord   233
    Confronting in Love   239
CHAPTER THIRTY
    Dealing With Crisis   245
    Wrestling With God   250
CHAPTER THIRTY-ONE
    Reconciliation – Humility & Forgiveness   255
    Reconciliation – Rejected   260
CHAPTER THIRTY-TWO
    The Effects of Sin   265
    Jacob Gets Right With God   270
CHAPTER THIRTY-THREE
    God Keeps His Promises   275
CHAPTER THIRTY-FOUR
    Joseph: Picture of Christ   281
CHAPTER THIRTY-FIVE
    Lineage of Judah   289
CHAPTER THIRTY-SIX
    Joseph: From the Pit to the Palace   297
    Dealing With Temptation   302
CHAPTER THIRTY-SEVEN
    Joseph: From Prison to Prominence   309
CHAPTER THIRTY-EIGHT
    Pharaoh's Dream   315
    Famine in the Land   321
CHAPTER THIRTY-NINE
    Joseph Tests His Brothers   327
CHAPTER FORTY
    Rebuilding Trust   337
    Passing the Test   342
CHAPTER FORTY-ONE
    Joseph's Final Test   347

CHAPTER FORTY-TWO
    Redemptive Love   355
CHAPTER FORTY-THREE
    How Do We Know God's Will?   363
    How Do You View Life   369
CHAPTER FORTY-FOUR
    Do You Keep Your Word?   375
CHAPTER FORTY-FIVE
    Passing On the Truths   381
CHAPTER FORTY-SIX
    How We Live Now Not Only Affects Our Future, But Others as Well   389
    Forgive One Another   398

GENESIS

Introduction

Lord, as we study the book of Genesis, the truths that are there. The people and the events. That the Word will come alive to us so that we might make application in our lives. Lord, we want your Word to change us. We know that all of your Word is profitable. It is given for our instruction. Help us to learn from this book each and every chapter.

As we begin this lesson, a study on the book of Genesis, it is not only the first book in the Bible but, a lot of times, it is the first book that the book attempts to read. Because it is at the beginning. The book Genesis is the beginning. God makes known how everything comes about. God is the creator. He speaks, and there is the world and the people. We see some famous events. Creation, The Fall of Man and the Flood, the tower of Babel, the offering of Isaac, Jacob's dream, Joseph being sold into slavery. The people God chooses a people for himself. Abraham and his descendants. We call them the Jews. Not only are there some famous events in this book, but there are famous people. Adam and Eve, Enoch, Noah, Abraham, Isaac, Jacob, Joseph. The book historically covers a long period of time stretching from the creation of man all the way to the death of Joseph in Egypt. My prayer for us as we go through this study. It will be a long one but a very exciting study because there are so many great stories and truths in it that, first of all, we see God as the creator and the redeemer; He is the Sovereign Almighty one who loves man, provides for man, and deals with man. We will see that as we go through. Then, we will see man as the creature who is the crown of all creation. Out of all that God created, man is the best thing. But we see the fall and how God deals with man. And finally, the third thing as we go through the book is God's redemption plan. This is the story of the Bible. It starts in Genesis, and we see how the perfect God brings sinful man back to Himself. Through His provision, we call him Jesus Christ; in Genesis, He is called the seed of a woman. Seed of Abraham, seed of Isaac, seed of Jacob, seed of Judah. As we look at this book, we see the lives and the events as we go through it. In some parts, we will go into a lot of detail, and in other sections, we will go through more quickly. My prayer is that we will understand them and make applications in our lives so that we can conform to the image of our Savior, Jesus Christ. Let's begin with Prayer.

What comes to your mind when you hear the word "God"? Who is God? What does the name mean? What does that title mean to you? Some people might answer like this: "God is a kind word. A helping hand. God is truth. The mystery of life we greet. Issac Ivanov said, "God is a convenient invention of the human mind." Gabriel Green, president of the Amalgamated Flying Saucer Club of America, says, "God is the electromagnetic field surrounding the earth of which everything is composed." Colleen Ping says that, "God is part of us that cares for a child that is starving in another country." So, how would you answer?

Is God a feeling, a force, a kind deed, or is He the all-powerful creator of the universe dealing with man in grace, mercy, and justice? This lesson, as we start the book of Genesis, we aren't going to get a definition of God. But we will see His power and His majesty. It says that in the beginning, God created the heavens and the earth. To study the book of Genesis is indeed monumental. It is a long book with 50 chapters. It is powerful with the events and truths in it. Many people believe it is the most important book in the Bible because it is the foundation of all the rest of God's revelation. The book is the beginning and the understanding of the creation. Mankind, sin, and the Fall. The Flood. Salvation. Languages. The Covenants. So many things. As we look at this book, what we are going to do in the months to come is to:

1. Get the big picture. We are going to see how this revelation fits together. However, the book is very simple to put together. I will show that in this lesson.

2. We will get details. We are going to go through this book verse by verse, passage by passage. Some things, we will actually slow down more and dig it and go through them so that we will understand it not only but how they can affect us and relate to us.

3. We will go through chapter by chapter. There are some areas we will go faster through, but we always see the context and what God is trying to reveal to us.

Our goal is:

1. We want to see God. His character. His actions. The majesty of our God. He is the creator. The redeemer. The Sovereign one who shows grace, mercy, and justice in dealing with humans. Genesis confronts us with the Living God.

2. We want to see ourselves. We want to see man. The creation. Man is the crown of all creation. Man is not the end of some evolutionary process that we just happen to be there now. You will see that as we go through it. You will see the fall and God's plan of redemption of Mankind. You are going to see the results of the Fall and how God uses people throughout history to carry out his plan.

3. Understand the events and truths from the book. There are so many famous things in the book of Genesis. We also want to see the book theologically. What can we learn? How

can we become more like Jesus Christ through reading and studying this book?

All Scripture is given by the inspiration of God. All Scripture is profitable. It helps us mature. It helps us to serve. So we want to know what's in this book for us.

So, let's begin with a little background. Who wrote the book? When? Why? How is the book put together? The book is called Genesis. Which is really a Greek title. The word Genesis means "beginnings". That's what the book is about. If you had a Hebrew Bible, the book wouldn't be called Genesis. But "Bereshith" or "B'resheet" which means "in the beginning." In fact, in many of the Hebrew books, the title of the book is the first 2-3 words of the book. Genesis is the foundation of the Bible. In our Christian Bibles, the OT is divided into four different parts. The Law, The History, The Writings, and The Prophets. The Hebrew Bible, the OT (Tanakh), is not divided that way. It is divided into three parts. The Torah (Law, which is the Pentateuch), Nevi'im (Prophets), and K'tuvim (Writings). In the Hebrew Bible, the NT is called the B'rit Hadashah.

Moses is the author of all five books of the Pentateuch (the first five books of the Bible). Jesus recognized Moses to be the author of Genesis. Moses is the man who led the nation of Israel out of Egypt. The first five books really fit together. Genesis is the beginning and the Fall. In Exodus (Sh'mot) is the Redemption. Leviticus (Vayikra) is the Communion. Numbers (B'Midbar) are the guidance. And Deuteronomy (D'Varim) is the instruction. All those books fit together. God has a plan. Moses is the lawgiver. He is set apart by God. He is a special man. He grew up in Egypt up to the age of 40. He had been trained in all the wisdom of the Egyptians. Then, he lived for 40 years with his own people. Then, at age 80, God brought him back to lead out the nation of Israel. All five books of the Pentateuch were probably written at the same time, which was at the end of Moses' life around 1440 B.C.

How do we know that Moses (Moshe) wrote the book of Genesis? The Torah itself tells us that Moses is the author. Several other books indicate that Moses is the author of

Genesis. And even Jesus quoted verses from Genesis and attributed them to Moses. How did Moses put all this together? Have you ever thought about it? Because Moses wasn't there at the creation, the flood, or with Abraham. Well, the Bible tells us that God is the one that gives revelation. 2 Peter 1 says that "holy men were moved by the Holy Spirit as God spoke through them and gave revelation." So anytime that a person gives a direct revelation from God, whether it is Moses, Peter, Paul, James, John, etc., it is God's direct revelation through them giving them that revelation. Probably during Moses' time, people knew all the stories from the past. The old traditions which had been passed down. Remember, people lived a lot longer back during the days of Noah. In fact, there were people during Noah's day who probably knew Adam personally. In the next lesson, we will get into all these time periods and generations and the "gap" theory (which I don't believe).

When we look at this book, we see God using Moses to write down revelation so that we might know the beginnings. The age-old question of how did everything get started? How did our solar system and our world begin? Well, the truth is that God has given us His revelation. Now, there are people who reject it. And even really smart scientists who reject God's Word. But folks, in Chapters 1 - 2, we have the creation story as God wants us to know it.

Chapters 1-11 are the early history of the human race.

Chapters 12 -50 are the early history of the Jewish race. That's it. That's the outline for the book of Genesis.

By the way, when Abraham crossed over into the Promised Land (Israel) from the Ur of Caldez (Iraq), he became known as a Hebrew. Which literally means one is crossed over the Tigris and Euphrates Rivers. That's why the early descendants of Abraham were called Hebrews. Later, they became known as Israelites because they were descendants of Jacob. Then later, after that, they became known as Jews because they were descendants of the Southern Kingdom called Judah. (Y'hudah)

Chapters 1 -11 cover a long time period. From the Creation, Fall, Flood, and Division of the Nations. There's no way to really know the age of the earth. There are people who say it was billions of years. Conservative creationists today hold the time of the earth to be only 6,000 -15,000 years.

Chapters 12 - 50 cover only a 300-year time period. Which is the life of Abraham, Isaac, Jacob, and Joseph.

When you think about the book of Genesis, there are really only two ways to look at the book.

1. Some call it a myth. They say it is a great little story, but the stories are just made up to teach a lesson. Adam and Eve were symbolic to show how it could have all started, but really, they were only meant to teach a theological hypothesis.

2. Others hold to the book of Genesis historically, which is the way I do and hope you do, which is that the events recorded in this book are true and the people were actual people. Shown not only what actually happened but also teaches theological truths. Not even an event that happened to Abraham, Isaac, Jesus, or anyone else in the Bible is recorded there. Certain things are included in the Bible for a reason. God's revelation of what He wanted to tell us.

As we go through the book of Genesis, we are going to highlight four major things:

1. We are going to look at God's character. All the way through the book.

2. We are going to see man and the creation, Fall, and relationship with God. All the way through the book.

3. We are going to see God's redemption plan. It starts in Chapter 3:15. It goes through the entire Bible.

4. We are going to see Man's responsibility. (to make known God's plan of redemption to others)

From Paradise to Prison (Joseph in Egypt) is the book of Genesis. What a powerful book. We are going to see a lot of great things in the coming months. Every lesson. Don't miss one lesson. It's good stuff.

Read Genesis 1:1. In the Bible, the word "heavens" is plural in the beginning. There are three beginnings in the Bible.

John 1:1: "In the beginning was the Word, and the Word was with God, and the Word was God." That's the eternal beginning. God has no beginning.

Then, there is the beginning of creation. Genesis 1:1: "In the beginning, God created the heavens and the earth." That's creation.

And then in 1 John 1:1, "That which was from the beginning, which we have heard, which we have seen with our eyes, which we have looked at, and our hands have touched - this we proclaim concerning the Word of life." This talks about Jesus—His incarnation.

Back to Genesis 1:1. Notice there is no explanation for God. Where He came from. Moses didn't try to provide any philosophical or scientific evidence for God's existence. Moses presents God as Sovereign and Holy. God created the heavens and the earth, everything. Do you know what this does? It refutes atheism because it is God. It refutes pantheism because God is separate from His creation. It refutes polytheism because there is only one God. It refutes humanism because God is the center and creator of everything, not man. And it refutes evolution because God created, not evolved. "In the beginning, God created (Bara in Hebrew) the heavens and the earth." Bara means to create. (and almost always means out of nothing). Never used for man. Only exclusively for God as the subject, indicating that only God can accomplish this activity.

This word Bara almost always means that there wasn't anything there out of which God created everything. This is one of the ways that God has made Himself known, and that is through His creation. Romans 1:20.

CHAPTER ONE

The Creation
Genesis 1:1-31

Last time in our overview of Genesis, we saw that the summary statement of the Bible is found in Genesis 1:1: "In the beginning, God created the heavens and the earth." Exodus 20:11 says, "For in six days the Lord made the heavens and the earth, the sea, and all that is in them..." God is the creator. We are going to study Chapter 1, which is about creation. Chapter 1 is sort of an overview of what God says about the beginning. Not only our world but man and himself. Then, we will begin studying Chapter 2, in which God goes into detail about the creation of mankind. The way that the Hebrew writers almost always write is to first give an overview of a story, then come back and give you the details of the most important aspect of the story. We will also talk about the Gap theory. Is there a billion-year gap between Genesis 1:1 and Genesis 1:2, as some people think? I don't, but we need to look at this theory in order to be prepared to answer questions that people ask. Then, we are going to talk about the days of creation. Are they literal 24-

hour days, or were they long periods of time as some people think? I don't, but we need to look at that theory also.

The book of Genesis is actually called Bereshith, which means "In the beginning." In this revelation from God, we see the beginning of all things. The creation of the heavens and the earth, man, plants, animals, birds, fish, the Fall and sin, the languages, covenant, etc. It, indeed, is a book of beginnings. Remember, as we go through this book, we are going to focus on four key things:

1. God and His character. The God who loves, provides, protects, and judges.

2. We will see mankind. The creation and the Fall are made in the image of God, but at the same time, they are fallen.

3. We will also see God's plan of redemption. God, who so loves us, brings man back to Himself through His Son, Jesus Christ.

4. Man's responsibility. We are to not only know God but to make known to others God's plan of salvation. Why would God choose a people, the Hebrews, to announce and proclaim, reveal to mankind this savior, messiah that God would send to the world? Remember, the outline of the book of Genesis is very simple.

The first 11 chapters are about the early history of the human race. The creation, fall, flood, and divisions of the nations. Then, chapters 12-50 are the early history of the Jewish race because God chose a man, Abraham, then Isaac, Jacob, and Joseph. If you can remember that, you got the book. There are so many great things we are going to cover.

Read Genesis 1:1. This is the summary statement. The rest of chapter 1 & 2 is the details of this verse. Verse 1 is the beginning of creation. God (Elohim) created (bara) everything. The Hebrew name for God is El, and here it is Elohim, which is a plural form that is used for honor and majesty. And remember that bara is only used with God as its subject. The word is used most often for the creation of the universe and the elements out of nothing. God places the emphasis on earth because that is where He placed people. Then, we will talk about evolution, macro, and microevolution, which I don't believe, but we need to be able to answer questions that people will ask us. Next, we will talk about whether we are creationists, theist evolutionists, or progressive creationists. What are we? We will talk about all those things.

Read Genesis 1:2. In Hebrew, as in your KJV, NIV, NASB translate the word Hayetah as "was." Gap theorists will incorrectly translate it as "became." Did God create the earth formless and void, or did something happen after His creation, and it became formless and void, as the Gap theorists think? So basically, the question is: is this the original creation, or did something happen to the earth, and it got all messed up, so He re-created it? The proponents of the Gap theory say this is where the dinosaurs lived and died off and where there were these pre-Adamic people who weren't really human, such as the Neanderthal Man; this took billions of years, and this is where the so-called ice age happened. And then it was formless and void, and God said, "Oh no. I've got to fix it again." Which is verse 3. But I don't hold to that theory. I believe in the traditional view that this is God's first creative act; therefore, Verse 2 doesn't reflect a negative concept but rather an unfinished beginning. Why? The Hebrew language supports the traditional view of "was," and theologically, it supports the traditional view in Exodus 20:11: "that in 6 days God created the heavens and the earth and all that is in them." And also because there was no death before the fall of man. So how do you have a pre-Adamic race of people dying until you have sin in the world? You can't. I believe that this is an original creation. I also hold to a young earth. Not billions of years old.

There are five aspects to each one of these six days.

1. The introduction – "and God said."

2. The command – "let there be."

3. The fulfillment – "and it was so."

4. The evaluation - "and it was good."

5. The conclusion – "and the evening and the morning were the first day." (second, third, etc.)

It is plain that God has a plan and a purpose for His creation. It is ordered. It's not a product of some random arrangement.

Read Genesis 1:3-4. Notice we aren't talking about light from the sun. That doesn't happen until the fourth day. Here, God is talking about some light source. But He doesn't tell us where it came from. This is the first of three separations. The light from the darkness. Then, the sky from the water. And finally, the land from the sea. This is a literal light from darkness. But all through the Bible, light is always good, and darkness is always evil.

Read Genesis 1:5. Here, 'Day' in Hebrew is "Yom," which is a literal 24-hour solar day or daylight. 1900 out of 2000 times in the OT, "Yom" means 24-hour day or daylight. Only 100 times (5%) does it mean the Day of the Lord. And when the word "Yom" is used and it has a cardinal or a numeral adjective such as 'first,' 'second,' 'third,' etc., it ALWAYS means a literal 24-hour day. A Jewish person reading this would only interpret "Yom" as a 24-hour day. Especially since it says, "The evening and the morning were the first day." in verse 8, it says, "The evening and the morning were the second day." In verse 13, the third day. In verse 19, the fourth day. In verse 23, the fifth day. In verse 31, the sixth day. Every time, it means a literal 24-hour day. Jewish people divide their time into evening and morning. For example, a Jewish person would say that right now, it is Monday night because it is after 6:00 p.m. when the sun goes down. And tomorrow is Monday day. 'Yom' here in Genesis 1 is not a long period of time. It isn't millions of years in some evolutionary process.

So when Moses wrote this book, He wanted the readers to understand that God created everything in six literal days. Exodus 20:8-10. Follow the pattern of God, working six days and resting on the seventh.

Read Genesis 1:6. Here, God is separating the water from the water. He is putting in the sky (air) between the atmospheric waters and the waters of the earth.

Read Genesis 1:7. Apparently, there was water covering the earth at this time, and this canopy of cloud-covered water encircled the earth. Some scientists think that this canopy of water over the earth is why people lived so long because it shielded them from the sun's radiation. Then, after the flood, which released this canopy of water, people died much sooner.

Read Genesis 1:8. God called this expanse 'heaven.'

Read Genesis 1:9-10. The Hebrew word for earth is 'berets.' It means the ground. This is the separation of ground and water.

Read Genesis 1:11. Herb that yields send, a fruit tree that yields fruit *according to its kind.* An apple tree doesn't produce oranges. But apples. Things reproduce after their own kind. Cats make cats. Dogs make dogs. Cats don't become dogs. They don't evolve into something else. God is trying to show us that He created and the creation is orderly and perpetuates itself within God's established laws. Not evolution. This is what the Bible says. I believe it. It is the authority. It is the Word of God. Notice God begins with plants, not with seeds. God produced a functioning, mature creation. There is all this speculation on how old the earth is. Some scientists believe the earth is billions of years old. Even though 2/3 of the ways to determine the age of things they don't use. Only the ways that guess the earth to be really old. But we see here that God created the world, the mountains, etc., mature. Adam, when he was put on this earth at the perfect age of 36, how old did he look? He wasn't a baby, was he? How long did it take God to make him? He took a little dirt from the ground, and there he was. Just because the mountains look old doesn't mean they are.

Read Genesis 1:14-19. Before this, God separated the darkness and the light. And now God is going to put something in the sky that is going to do that. This will give regular and harmony to the times and the seasons of the earth. The stars are created and appointed by God to serve the earth. God is in control. He is Sovereign. God did it all. The creation gives glory to God. This is day four.

Read Genesis 1:20-23. Again, we see here that the birds and sea creatures were created by God, who told them to multiply the earth according to their own kind. No macro or micro evolution here. This is day five.

Read Genesis 1:24-25. This starts on day six. Again, we see the phrase "according to its kind." Frogs don't grow up and become birds, which grow up to be cows. This statement occurs ten times in this chapter. Creation is orderly and perpetuates itself within God's established laws. Not evolution. And it was good.

Read Genesis 1:26. God the Father takes the form of a Spirit being. The Holy Spirit takes the form of a Spirit being. The Son of God takes until his incarnation. Spirit being. When the Bible here talks about man being made in the likeness of God, we are talking about that aspect of man having a mind, will, a moral conscience, a concept of eternity, to think abstractly, to be able to understand, to worship God we are talking about our spirit. Animals don't have that. Birds don't have that. Fish don't have that.

Inside us, God has put the concept of eternity. That there is something more than our physical bodies on this earth. You and I are made in the image of God. That alone shows your value. There is nothing in this whole world that equals you. You could take every possession or resource in the world, and you could measure it against one human being and say, "Would this one human life be worth all the money of the world, all the oil, all the gold, and the answer would be NO.

Your life is worth more than anything that could possibly be. God said let's make man in our image. He didn't say let's make man God. We aren't God. We are finite and dependent on God. There will never be another person exactly like you. God made you exactly the way you are. His goal is to convince you to be like Him.

"Let us make man in our image, according to our likeness." This shows us the Trinity.

Read Genesis 1:28. Man was created to rule the earth, the animals, the birds, the fish, etc. The earth is God's. He created it. But he has given us dominion to be good stewards of God's property. God tells man to be fruitful and multiply. Reproduce. That is why he created males (Ish - man) and females (Isha - out of man).

The word man (Adama - which means ground). God took from the ground and formed the Adama. It is interesting to note that Eve wasn't named until after the Fall. Because she was "the mother of living." And God saw everything that He had made, and it was "VERY GOOD."

CHAPTER TWO

Creation of Mankind
Genesis 2:1-25

Open your Bibles to Genesis 2. We are continuing our study of the Book of Beginnings. We studied the 6 days of God's creation of all things. We also saw the crown of creation. Man is made in the image of the living God. Man set apart to rule and have dominion over all the earth. In verse 31 of the last chapter, we see that "God saw everything that He had made, and indeed it was very good." In Genesis Chapter 1, we see, in a sense, an overview of the creation story, which is a true account of the beginning of the universe and the world. As we move into Chapter 2, we are going to see the details of creation (at least what God gives us), but the focus will be on the creation of man. Have a basic understanding of the Sabbath. Then, we will see the responsibility that God gave to Adam in the garden.

One of the things that we see in our society is that people live for the weekend. They say, "I can hardly wait till Friday night. I got the whole weekend to do nothing." They work hard all week and look forward to this time of rest. Holidays and vacations, too. Some will say, "If Adam and Eve had not fallen into sin, we wouldn't be working. We would have all our days off." Well, the truth is, and we are going to see it in this passage, that God gave man the responsibility to work before the Fall. Man was appointed to keep and take care of the garden. Work is not a result of the Fall. It is done for the glory of God. Question – How do you view your work? For the glory of God or a necessary evil that you have to do? We are going to see that because of the Fall, work is different.

We have seen six literal days. Evening and the morning, days one, two, three, four, five, six. Well, there is one more day. And that is the seventh day. We see it in Chapter 2. God rested from His labor. It is called the sabbat (the Sabbath). Many people will ask you – When is the Sabbath? Are we supposed to keep the Sabbath now? If people work on Sunday, are they breaking the Sabbath? Is there a Christian Sabbath, so to speak? Well, we are going to see all that as we get into this Bible study.

Read Genesis 2:1-3. In verse 1 is the summary statement.

The heavens and the earth and everything connected to them (animals, fish, birds, man) were finished. Then, He makes the statements. Read Genesis 2:2. Some people will ask, "How could God get all that done in 6 six days? Why would He take six days? Couldn't He just say, "Let there be..." And it will all be there, right then?

Wasn't it really just long years? (2 Peter 3:8 – "But, beloved, do not forget this one thing, that with the Lord one day is as a thousand years and a thousand years as one day." Peter is **not** saying that a day equals 1000 years and a 1000 years equals a day. He doesn't equate them. In fact, Peter says, "A day is as *a* thousand years." Peter is saying that time doesn't affect what God promised. When God makes a promise, no matter how long it takes, He is going to do whatever He says. It doesn't matter whether 30 years have passed, a thousand years have passed, or two thousand years have passed. He could do it in one day, that normally could take a thousand years if He wanted to. He can do anything He wants to do. Time is not an issue. Time doesn't affect God's promises. He always keeps His Word. He always does it in His perfect timing. A thousand years could go by, and that is no more than a day concerning what He is going to do. This passage in Peter is talking about Jesus Christ's return to judge the world.

We are going to look at the Sabbath in just a minute, in Exodus 20:8-11, for a clue of possibly why He decided to create in 6 days. Genesis 2:3 says that "God rested on the seventh day from all His work which He had done." The word rested is a Hebrew word where we get the word Sabbath from. The Hebrew word literally means to "cease." It doesn't mean to rest like 'whew. I'm so tired I need to sit down." The word means "to stop." Read Genesis 2:2 using the word 'stop.' Read Genesis 2:3. God blessed the seventh day. Blessed means "to make it favorable." Good day. Then it says here that "God sanctified it." That is a very special Hebrew word, quardaz. Literally has the idea of "Holy and set apart." Because He stopped creating (bara) and making or forming (asah). God created everything and then formed it. Then, on the seventh day, He stopped his creating and forming. He set apart that day.

By the way, when people say to you, "You shouldn't work, buy groceries, eat out in restaurants, etc. on Sunday because that is the Sabbath." You need to remind them that the seventh day is Saturday. When God tells Moses in Exodus 20:8 with the fourth commandment to work six days and rest on the seventh. Now why? Here is what God says in Exodus 20:11: "In 6 days the Lord made the heavens and the earth, the sea, and all that is in them, and rested (ceased) the seventh day." So we see that even the nation of Israel came and got the laws at Sinai; God said, "Work six days. Rest on the seventh." It is the pattern that I gave you. The Sabbath is a day that you rest, enjoy, and worship. Sabbath was made for the man. The Pharisees said, "On the Sabbath, you can't walk, you can't knock dirt off yourself, you can't do anything." The Pharisees turned it into a day of bondage. But Jesus said, "Wrong. It is a day of relaxation. Joy. Worship." You got to have a day off.

By the way, only one of the Ten Commandments is not restated in the New Testament. And that is the Sabbath. What we find in the NT is that we worship not on the Sabbath day as the Jewish people did. We worship on the First day of the week because Jesus Christ rose on the First day of the week. 1 Corinthians 16:2 when Paul says, "When you come together on the first day of the week (Sunday). The Lord's Day (don't call it the Christian Sabbath), then, is sanctioned by the apostles as the proper day of worship. It is a clear distinction between old Judaism and new Christianity.

The principle is this - you need a day of rest each week. If people work seven straight days over and over, they will wear out. They will destroy themselves. All of us need at least one day off each week. I take Saturday off. Now remember, I am always available to you church family. But I also need to spend time with my family and in rest. Now, on your day of rest, take time for worship. And in our society, we come together as believers on Sunday. It is a good thing to do.

In Hebrew, what they usually do is first give you the overview and then give you the details. Genesis 2 is the details for Genesis 1. Because Genesis 1 was the overview. In Genesis 2, the details are on the most important part of creation, which is mankind. Read Genesis 2:4. In Hebrew, there is a little statement called a "toledoth." Which means, "This is the account." It is found in 4, 5, and 6 places in the book of Genesis. Every time you see it, it's like a stopping place that says, "Ok, now I'm going to give you some more information." By the way, did you notice that this verse marks the introduction of the personal name of the God of Israel, Lord God? YHWH Elohim. (YOD, HE, WAW, HE). It derives from the verb "to be" (hayah). Up to this point, only "Elohim" translated God, indicating the transcendent God of Creation, has been used, but here, the personal name occurs, introducing God in His redemptive capacity. It is the appropriate time for the appearing of God as redeemer, at the very moment that man appears in history.

Read Genesis 2:5. Most scholars say that Moses is talking about plants in the garden that have to be cultivated by man in order to keep them growing. But we just don't know. Read

Genesis 2:6. Apparently, there was this great sprinkler system with this water coming up from the ground. Maybe because of the water canopy, a lot of dew came up at night. But we just don't know. The best that we can understand is that it does this all the way up until the time of Noah before it rains.

Now, we are going to see six things in this section.

1. We will see the creation of the male (ish) first.

2. Then, the place to live. That's the garden.

3. Then, we will see a description of the area.

4. Then, we will see the responsibility God gave the man. (adamah)

5. Then we will do the special command.

6. The creation of the female (isha).

Read Genesis 2:7. The Lord God *formed* man. It means that God shapes the man from the dust of the ground. The Hebrew word for ground is adamah. His name is 'dirt.' There is no evolution at all here. God creates the man. God breathes life into him. God is the life-giver. When you think about a person, the Bible says we are divided into two parts. Material and immaterial. The material part is the body. And before the Fall, it would have lasted forever. After the Fall, it decays, it corrupts, and dies. Then God raises it up and gives us a body that lasts forever. There is also an immaterial part of a person. In the Old Testament, the words 'soul' (nephesh) and 'spirit' (ruach) are almost used interchangeably. They are used back and forth. In the New Testament, they are never used back and forth. There is a soul and a spirit. They are two different words. In the New Testament, it talks about how we are a body, soul, and spirit. In our immaterial part, there seems to be a distinction between the soul and the spirit. We might talk a little about that in Genesis 3 when we will talk about the Fall. Have you looked at a dead person in an open casket during a funeral? They just don't look the same. Do they? The part that makes a person a person is the soul, and the spirit that's inside is gone. We are material and immaterial. We are formed and shaped in the image and likeness of God with a will, discernment, feelings, morals, and a knowledge of eternity. We are special and unique.

There are really only three views about how we came about.

1. Evolution – everything came from a single cell that started with a Big Bang explosion and changed into something else, which evolved into something else over billions of years.

2. Theistic Evolution – in which God created some things, then let them go and evolve up, and every now and then, He steps in and changes a few things around.

3. Biblical view of Creation – that God supernaturally brings all things into existence.

Read Genesis 2:8. The Hebrew word for garden (gan) means delight. The Greek word for garden is (paradisas). God created this great place to live and put the man there. Read Genesis 2:9. Two trees are mentioned here. The 'tree of life' gives life. This is the tree when we get over in Revelation 22:2: "In the middle of the street of the holy city, the New Jerusalem, and on either side of the 'river of life,' was the 'tree of life' giving its fruit forever... Then there is the 'tree of the knowledge of good and evil.' It is a tree that tells you right from wrong. And we are going to see that God's plan for using that tree was so that people would know right from wrong. Because He is going to put the man there in this garden, in a state of innocence. We are going to see how that works. One tree gives life. The other one gives something else.

He describes the area in Genesis 2:10-14. Four rivers are mentioned going out of Eden. Pishon, Gihon, Hiddekel (Tigris), Euphrates. Where was this garden? If the Tigris and the Euphrates rivers are in the same place now as they were, then it is Southern Iraq (Mesopotamian region – the fertile crescent).

But remember, the Flood probably changed everything around. So, more than likely, we just don't know.

Genesis 2:15. Here's point four. The responsibility God gave the man. Tend the garden. This is the work that was part of God's plan from the beginning. It was necessary for man's good. Many people grumble and complain about having to work. But folks, I just love what I do. By the grace of God, I get to be a pastor. I get to work in His church. I get to come here and study His Word, then teach it to you folks. It's great! And I hope that you feel the same way about the work that you get to do.

Genesis 2:16-17. Now the command. "of every tree of the garden you may freely eat; but of the tree of the knowledge of good and evil you shall not eat," Notice the Scripture doesn't say it is an apple tree. God set this up so that mankind would learn right from wrong. And what He wanted man to do was learn right from wrong by doing right. Don't eat from this tree. If I don't eat from this tree, I learn right from wrong because I did right. If you eat from this tree, you learn right from wrong by doing wrong. That is why it is called 'the tree of knowing of good and evil.' Then God says in Genesis 2:17, "For in the day that you eat of it you shall surely die." In Hebrew, it literally says, "Dying you shall die." Dual aspect. When he ate the fruit from this tree, did he die physically? No. Not immediately. But he did die spiritually right then. His spiritual death resulted in physical death. There is a dual death mentioned here. The wages of sin is death. We come into this world as babies spiritually dead. Romans 5:12. Because we are made in the likeness of Adam, everything comes after its own kind; we come just like Adam, dead as a fallen human being. That's why Jesus said, 'In order to come into the kingdom of God, you must be born again. You must be made spiritually alive. And unless something is changed, you lose friends, family members, neighbors, co-workers, classmates, etc. will be separated from God forever. The Bible calls it the second death. So that is why we must have a relationship with God, which comes by faith in Jesus Christ, and we are born again.

Marriage is God's idea. It is a divine institution. God, Himself, united the first family. That alone should demonstrate the importance of marriage. God made the woman for the man. Read Genesis 2:18. This is the first time that God said "it is *not* good." Everything else God said it was good. God said, "It isn't good that man should be alone. I will make him a helper suitable for him." In Hebrew, the word helper means 'one who gives aid.' Like a nurse. Suitable refers to the opposite. It means that where he is lacking, she will fill up. And vice-versa. The husband's strengths become the wife's, and the wife's strengths become the husband's.

Read Genesis 2:19. God brought all the animals and birds to Adam so he could name them. Hippopotomas. Duck-billed playtemus. Do you see the dominion? Animals aren't naming the man. The man is naming the animals. I think God is showing Adam that there is nothing like him. He is alone. Read Genesis 2:20. Nothing matched Adam.

Read Genesis 2:21-22. She came out of the man. She is a part of him. She has the same flesh and blood, a being with equal faculties and likewise "in the image of God." Adam was designed to be fulfilled only when completed with the divinely given partner. God personally made (banah) which means built, the women. God made the woman for the man. God brought her to the man. A partnership is made.

Read Genesis 2:23. And Adam said "Va va va voom." God recognizes the uniqueness of the woman as a perfect mate derived from his own being.

Read Genesis 2:24. A famous verse in the Bible. Both Paul and Jesus quotes it. Here, marriage is interpreted as a new relationship bound by mutual oath. God's intention for husband and wife was monogamy. An inseparable union. Leave the mother/father relationship and go to the husband/wife relationship. One flesh means one physically, one spiritually, one emotionally, and one intellectually. From the day you are married, you are no longer you. You can longer say "this is what I am going to do." Because it is not you any more it is you and the other person together. You now say "this is what I think we are going to do."

Genesis 2:25. Signifies moral innocence.

CHAPTER THREE

The Temptation
Genesis 3:1-13

In this lesson, we will be looking at the Fall in Genesis 3. The results of the Fall have passed to all. And all have sinned and come short of the glory of God.

If you think about our world today, it is a lot different than what we read about here in the garden before the Fall. There is sin, death, corruption, sickness, disease, and failure in every area. We live in a Fallen world. What happened? Sin entered the world. According to Romans 5:12, "Sin entered the world through one man (Adam), and death through sin, and in this way, death came to all men because all sinned." We come into this world sinful people. We come into this world, fallen people. We are dead in our trespasses and sin. That is why people can't save themselves. The wages of sin is death, and we all have sinned and come short of the glory of God. That is why we need a Savior. That is why God sent Jesus to be the Messiah. The question that arises before we get to Genesis 3 is: Where does sin enter the universe? We are going to see how sin enters the world. But we are going to see this creature coming and trying to make the woman doubt God's love and God's Word. Isaiah 14:12-14. Ezekiel 28:14-17. In those two places, we see a creature, an angel called Lucifer, the one who guarded the throne of God, the one in which it was said that no unrighteousness was found in him, is the one we see in Isaiah saying the 5 I wills. "I will ascend to heaven, I will raise my throne above the stars of God, I will sit enthroned on the mount of assembly, on the utmost heights of the sacred mountain, I will make myself like the Most High." Here is a being who decided that he would be like God, and God removed him. And sin entered the universe through Lucifer, who we call the devil. And sin entered the world through man, whom we call Adam.

Genesis 3. This is the saddest chapter in the whole Bible. After this, nothing is the same ever again. That is until Jesus Christ comes and makes the new heavens and the new earth. The eternal state and all those in rebellion, including Satan and his demons, and rebellious men and women will be separated from God and from us forever. And we will serve Jesus Christ forever and ever.

Read Genesis 3:1. It says that the serpent was more crafty. The word crafty doesn't necessarily mean something bad. Of course, here in this passage, it is bad. But it really means cleaver. How do you picture the serpent? Think about it right now. First of all, he is not coming slithering up Because that is part of the curse. There is no telling what this creature looked like. Do you think that when this creature talks to her, she says, "Whoa, I never heard a snake talk before?" No. She said, "I'll talk to you." The whole scene is different than we can imagine. This creature may have been a very beautiful creature, somehow upright, more clever than any of the animals which the Lord God had made. The serpent is some creature being possessed by the devil with a plan. The plan is to get man to rebel against God. The devil's plan isn't for people to be bad, bad. It is just for people to reject God. The devil's plan for unbelievers is for them to never trust Christ. He doesn't care if they go to church all their life as long as they don't put their faith in the finished work of Jesus on the cross for their sins. The devil's plan here in Genesis is to get these newly formed people to rebel against God: The God who created them and everything in the universe, the God who put them in the garden, the God who blessed them, the God who protected them, the God who takes care of them They are in a state of innocence Satan is saying "I am going to get them." That is his plan.

We realize that after God casts Lucifer out of heaven, He allows him access to the earth. And there will be a time, and you read about it in the book of Revelation, that the devil will be cast away forever into the lake of fire, Eternal separation. Notice the first aspect: Who does the devil come to? He comes to the women. You see, man was created first and talked with God, got all the instructions, and had been there longer, so to speak. Notice what the devil says: "Did God really say, 'You must not eat from any tree in the garden'?" Do you see what he is doing? He is raising a doubt. You see, what the devil wants you to do is doubt God about anything. He wants you to doubt God's love, And he wants you to doubt God's Word. "You know, if God really loved you, he would let you eat from any tree, including that one right there. Why do you think he is holding that one back? If he really loved you, he would give you everything you wanted. What's the problem?"

Read Genesis 3:2-3 The woman replied to this talking serpent, "We may eat fruit from the trees in the garden, but God said 'You must not eat fruit from the tree that is in the middle of the garden, and you must not touch it, or you will die.'" Did God say not to touch it? No. She added to God's Word, didn't she? Are we supposed to add or take away anything from God's Word? No. Of course, Adam may have told her not to touch it. We just don't know.

Read Genesis 3:4. Now, this is the second one. The devil says, "You will not surely die." 'God hasn't told you everything.' Don't you get it? God is lying to you. Now, listen, there is a reason God won't let you eat from that tree.' 'You're not going to die.' 'How well do you know him?' 'If God really loved you, he would give this fruit to you.' And we doubt God today in the same way. "If God really loved me, I would be happily married." "If God really loved me, I would have a good job." "If God really loved me, I would have a more reliable car and a newer house." "If God really loved me, he wouldn't allow my teachers at school to give me all of these tests and homework." And some people will tell you, "God wants you to be happy. Just go ahead and do it. Even though the Bible says not to."

Read Genesis 3:5. Think about that for a moment. Is that a true statement? Did God tell them if they ate the fruit that, their eyes would be opened, and they would be like Him, knowing good and evil? No. She thought, 'Hey, the reason God doesn't want me to eat this fruit is because I will be like him. And He doesn't want any competition.' 'You mean all this time he has been doing good stuff for us, but the truth is he just doesn't want us to touch that tree because we will be like him. Then, there will be three gods. No wonder. He must not really love us. He hadn't been telling us the truth.'

That is exactly what the devil wants you to think today. Satan wants you to think that God doesn't love you. You can't trust the Bible all the time. Folks, doubt brings discouragement, and discouragement leads to distrust, and distrust leads to disobedience.

Sin always looks a lot better than it really is. All those beer commercials at the Super Bowl, everybody is so happy. Hey, what a party! It looks a lot better than it really is. The devil always misrepresents the truth. John 8:44 "...he was a murderer from the beginning, not holding to the truth, for there is no truth in him. When he lies, he speaks his native language, for he is a liar and the father of lies."

What if she had said, "Excuse me! First of all, I trust God. He has never lied to me before. He has always provided for me. He has always protected me. And I think He loves me. I am going to trust Him. Second, if that's true, why don't you eat it and become a god? You eat it first."

Well, what happened is the saddest portion of the Bible. Read Genesis 3:6. She saw three things.

    1. She saw that it was good for food. She was hungry.

2. The fruit was pleasing to the eyes. It looked good.

3. It was desirable to make her wise. She wanted to be like God.

This is the temptation. The lust of the flesh. The lust of the eyes. The pride of life. To resist temptation, we must pray for strength to resist, run away from it, and just say no to it. Don't give in to temptation. When you do, it then becomes a sin. You see it, you want it, to take it, then you try and hide it.

She also gave some of the fruit to her, who was with her, and he ate it. In Hebrew, it implies that Adam was there. He should have said, "Honey, don't touch it or eat it." But he didn't. He wanted to be like God, too. There is a difference here. She sinned by being deceived. He sinned knowingly. 1 Timothy 2:13-14. That's why it is by one man, Adam, that sin entered this world. The woman had a decision to make. Either listen to this being and disobey God or not. Adam had a very powerful decision to make. Follow his wife or follow God. He made a choice. Are we going to be influenced by what other people do, or are we going to obey God's Word?

At that exact moment, the man and the woman died spiritually. As a result, they began to die physically. There is guilt and loss of fellowship immediately.

Read Genesis 3:7. This is the guilt. They now knew right from wrong. It wasn't as the devil had promised. And never is. It always costs you more than you think. It will always take you further than you realize. Notice that their relationship with God and with each other has changed. They tried to cover up themselves. This is a picture of a man sinning and trying to hide it. It never works. All throughout history, man has tried to cover up his sin by his own efforts. Rather than go to the living God and confess. Rather than go to the provision that God has, which is Jesus Christ. Man says, 'I can do it. I can clean up this myself. I can do this what I am supposed to do.'

Read Genesis 3:8. This is the loss of fellowship with God. Hid themselves? How ridiculous is that? Trying to hide from the Almighty God, the creator and sustainer of the universe.

They had been talking with God every day. They have had a great time with him every day. God walks in the garden with them. This apparently is a normal thing. What is the problem? They are guilty of disobedience. Sometimes in your life, your friends who are fired up for the Lord are growing, then suddenly they aren't. All of a sudden, they are in church. Something is wrong. They died spiritually, they have broken fellowship with God, and now they are dying physically. The wages of sin are death and separation from God. Notice two things in this verse.

1. God is coming for the man. He is a God who seeks out man. It isn't man who seeks out God. God seeks to bring man back into fellowship with Himself.

2. Man has lost his fellowship with God. And there is guilt and fear.

Read Genesis 3:9. And God called to the man, "Where are you?" Do you think God really didn't know where they were? No. God wanted the man and the woman to come out from behind the tree and say, "We have some bad news. I blew it. It's not her fault. I should have known better. I am supposed to be in charge of this. I should have known better." God wanted them to talk to him and confess their sin. God, of course, he knew they were hiding over there behind that tree. Because he is God. He knows everything. He actively offers us his unconditional love. If God didn't come after man, no man would be saved. Salvation is all of God. God uses His Holy Spirit to convict man and to bring man unto Himself. Thank God that He came after you.

Read Genesis 3:10. The man answered, "I heard you in the garden, and I was afraid because I was naked, so I hid." There is shame involved with sin. Of course, Adam and the woman hid because they disobeyed, not because they were naked.

Read Genesis 3:11. This is another rhetorical question because God knows everything. What God wants Adam to say is 'yes. I ate from the tree. I messed up. I'm sorry.' Until you realize that you need a Savior, you won't come to Jesus Christ.

It is the first step to reconciliation. If you are a born-again Christian and you are saved, then at one point in your life, where you said, "I can't save myself. I can't do it. I can't be good enough to please God. I realize that I have fallen short. And my only hope is Jesus as my savior. I come to Him.

Read Genesis 3:12. Adam didn't confess to God. God wanted Adam to confess and tell the truth. But he blames the woman. Defective woman. Adam also blames God for giving him the woman. Adam is blaming God for his troubles. Pride caused the Fall of mankind. It is the root of most sins.

Read Genesis 3:13. God then goes straight to the woman. She didn't confess to God either. God wanted the woman to confess and tell the truth. But she blames the serpent. Pride. Blaming others. Making excuses.

We must admit our wrong attitudes and wrong actions and apologize to God. Don't try to get away with sin by blaming someone else.

The Protoevangelium
Genesis 3:14-24

We are going to see a negative and a positive. The negative is going to be the curse, the curse on the man, the woman, Satan, the serpent, and the earth. The positive is the cure. And that is going to be the seed of woman, who is going to come and save all of us.

Read Genesis 3:14. Somehow, God cursed that animal (serpent), whatever it was. Because it was God's choice of doing things, He is a sovereign God who can do anything He wants to do. Whatever that animal looked like before the Fall, we don't know, but what it looks like now, we do know, and it does slither on its belly. Now God turns to the one who ultimately behind all of this, who is Lucifer, the son of the morning, the one who guarded the throne of God, the one in Isaiah 14 and Ezekial 28, the one that took 1/3 of the angels with him, one of the most powerful being ever created, that said "I will be like the most high.", Satan, the devil, the accuser, the father of lies, etc. He has about 30-35 names in the Scripture.

Read Genesis 3:15. In a very limited form, there is the Gospel. It has been called "the Protoevangelium" in Latin since the second century. It means the "first preaching of the gospel." It says here that there is going to be a conflict between the seed of the serpent and the seed of the woman. And ultimately, He will crush the head of the serpent. And you, the serpent, shall bruise His heel." What we see there is this. There are the descendants who follow God and those who don't. There will always be a conflict between those who are believers and those who are not believers and, of course, a conflict between believers and the satanic forces. Also involved in all of this is the seed of the woman, who is the Messiah, the savior to come. The seed is possibly a veiled first announcement of the virgin birth because biologically, in conception, the seed (sperm) is delivered by the man; but in the miraculous conception of the Messiah, the seed was the woman's, the result of her being overshadowed by the Holy Spirit. Jesus Christ, as the seed of the woman, will ultimately defeat Satan and his seed. Yes, Satan bruised Christ, but He couldn't keep Him in the grave. He was resurrected and won the victory; it is finished. It was a crushing blow to Satan, and the ultimate devastating of Satan by Christ will take place when He makes his second coming and then throws Satan and his followers into the lake of fire for the final crushing blow.

This passage in verse 15 is the beginning. The OT is what we call progressive revelation. That is, as you go through the OT, you see more and more information about the Messiah. All we can find here in this verse is that He is going to be the seed of the woman. But how is the woman going to know when the Messiah is going to come? Well, after a number of years, God chose a man named Abraham from the Ur of Caldees. And God says, "Through you, all the nations will be blessed." So now he is not just the seed of a woman but the seed of Abraham. So, God's revelation is now getting more specific. Then, through Isaac, Jacob, Judah, David, etc., all the way down until exactly the right time, according to Gal. 4:4, "God brought forth His Son born of a woman." That's the seed of woman. And Paul says in Galatians, this seed is Jesus Christ.

Read Genesis 3:16. How many of you ladies have had babies, and it hurt? God tells the woman here in this verse that it is going to hurt to have babies. Why? We don't know. But some have thought because, in pain, God sent his son, Jesus Christ, to suffer for us. But look back on this verse, there's more. The word "desire" is only used three times in the OT. One time in here in verse 16 and 2 times in Chapter 4. It literally means the desire to rule. God is saying that women are going to desire to rule over their husbands. It is a negative word. Then God says that the man is going to take charge over or boss (it doesn't mean leadership in this verse), which is also a negative word.

When the wife and the husband try to push each other around, you will have great conflict. So, how can this part of the curse ever be overcome? Well, you see it in the book of Ephesians where people who know Christ as Savior, and you find the command in the power of God for the husband to love his wife as Christ loved the church; we find that in that passage for a woman to come under the authority of her husband as unto the Lord. And for the husband to love his wife. It is the only way it can work. Because the curse has put in one sense that battle within her relationship.

Read Genesis 3:17-19. God commanded Adam not to eat of the Tree of Knowledge of good and evil, but he heeded the voice of his wife instead of obeying God. Here is both a curse on the man and a curse on the earth itself. Thorns and thistles are now part of gardening and farming. Now, work is going to be hard. It was not as easy as it had been in the garden before the Fall. God tells Adam that he was taken from the dirt; his name means dirt, and he will return to dirt when he dies. Our physical bodies decay when we die. However, when Jesus Christ returns, one day, He will raise our physical bodies up off the ground once again. The curse will remind us of sin every time we see a snake, every time there is a baby born, every time there is conflict in a family, every time you labor in your work, every time somebody dies. Do you realize that every time there is a funeral, it shows the curse of sin?

Read Genesis 3:20. Adam has always, up to now, called the woman Isha. But now he calls her Eve, which means "mother of the living one." Because there is hope of life and eternal life because the seed (Messiah) will come through the woman.

Read Genesis 3:21. This is one of the most eloquent object lessons ever given to man. The picture will start here in this verse and go all the way through to Christ. Man tries to cover up his sin. (remember, Adam tried to cover his sin with fig leaves) But God here had to kill something, the shedding of blood, which was the first sacrifice of atonement for man's sin. The death of the innocent for the guilty. Which was a prefiguring of the death of Christ on the cross as a propitiation of man's sins. Notice that God furnished the skins, fashioned the garments, and clothed Adam and Eve. God did it all; they did nothing. God acted in grace and mercy. God is giving them a symbolic way of saying, "If you want to approach me and have fellowship with me, then you must have come through a sacrifice. And this is just a picture of the one that is going to come later to pay for your sins. But here is an innocent animal dying in your place, the shedding of blood, to cover your sin until the seed of the woman (Messiah) comes and crushes the head of the serpent.

Read Genesis 3:22. If they had eaten of the Tree of Life, then they would have lived forever physically in a fallen condition.

Read Genesis 3:23-24. God drove them out of the garden and put cherubim (winged creatures on the ark of the covenant, also sewn into the tabernacle curtain; in Ezekial 10:20, the cherubim are described as having four faces - lion, ox, man, eagle and four wings; who celebrate God's holiness and power) at the east (only means outside the garden) of the garden who had a flaming sword to guard the way to the tree of life. Only through God's redemption in Christ does man have access again to the Tree of Life.

CHAPTER FOUR

Cain Murders Abel
Genesis 4:1-13

At the end of Chapter 3 we saw God's provision for the man and the woman. The sacrifice to cover their sin. The death of that animal, the shedding of the blood. Well, as we get into Chapter 4, we are going to see the first two sons, or the first two sons that are mentioned here, Cain and Abel. We will see how they approach God. Cain approaches God one way, and Abel approaches God another way. And it is a picture of how a person is able to approach God. How do you come to God? Well, our goal is to continue to grow in the grace and knowledge of our savior, Jesus Christ, as we study His Word.

Here is the most important question that a person must answer. How do you get to heaven? What does a person have to do to eternal life, to be with God forever? Sometimes, we ask people, and we get answers like this:

Try to live a good life, be a good person, and live by the golden rule; others say you have to keep the Ten Commandments, and others say you have to join a church. No. None of those will do it. So, how do you get to heaven? How does a person approach the living God? Well, it is by faith. We are going to see that in Chapter 4.

There is a man named Tom Monahan, who is the owner of Domino's Pizza and the Detroit Tigers. A few years ago, I read an article about him in the paper. Here is what it said. The accumulation of wealth bothered him spiritually. He stated, "I have always understood that some of the Bible verses talk about how it was hard for the rich man to get to heaven." And he knew that he was a rich man. So this is what he started doing. He started saying three rosaries a day, ate only bread and water twice a week, and no longer goes to work in his 2 million office complex. Mr. Monahan is on his quest for holiness. On his quest to earn his way to God by limiting the food that he eats, praying a certain way, and no longer enjoying his office building. He is trying to approach God based on his works. But he still feels empty inside. But the truth is that the only way to please God is by putting your faith in Jesus Christ. His son came to this earth, born of a virgin named Mary, lived a sinless life, was accused of being a criminal even though he had done no wrong, was given a death sentence, died on the cross, was buried in a tomb, and was resurrected three days later, and because God was satisfied with his blood sacrifice for the payment of our sins, which was perfect and forever, and you and I have been reconciled with God if we believe and put our faith in Christ you will have eternal life with God in heaven when your life is over on earth. We approach God on the basis of Jesus by faith. We are going to study about Adam and Eve's (Havah) two sons, Cain (Kayin) and Abel (Hevel). One comes to God by works, and the other comes to God by faith. And we can learn a lot as we look at this portion of Scripture.

And it is all through the Bible until you get to Jesus. Animal sacrifices being done over and over, covering sin, all a picture of the coming sacrifice of the Messiah. It all shows that one day, a redeemer would come and pay for the sins of mankind. And without the shedding of blood, Hebrews 9:22, there could be no forgiveness.

Secondly, I want you to see that the sacrifices in the OT covered the sins of mankind. They did not pay for them. You see, Jesus Christ fulfilled all of this. He was that sacrifice that all of the OT sacrifices pointed to. And Jesus didn't cover man's sins; he paid for man's sins. Some people will use the word "atonement." They will say that "Jesus atoned for our sins." That is an inaccurate word. And church people use it all the time. The word atonement comes from the Hebrew word "Kippur" (Lev. 23:25), which means covering. Jesus didn't cover our sins; he paid for our sins. John 1:29. He is the lamb of God who takes away the sin of the world. He is the final sacrifice for sin, forever. God allowed the killing of animals in the OT to be used as sacrifices to cover sins until the seed of the woman, the Messiah, would come. Jesus was the Messiah. (Mashiach).

Read Genesis (Bereshith) 4:1 Adam had relations (yadá in Hebrew) with his wife Eve. (KJV - knew, NIV- lay with, NASB - had relations) Adam experienced Eve in the most intimate relationship between a man and a woman, the sexual bond. And she conceived and birthed a baby whom they named Cain (Kayin), which might have meant acquired. I bet it hurt. Why? No epidural in those days. Because God said, it would remember. Eve exclaims that "she has a baby with the help of the Lord." Either she acknowledges that God is the source of life, or she thinks this baby is the seed of the woman. Of course, he wasn't because Cain (Kayin) was conceived by Adam, which is just a seed of man (sperm). Not the seed of woman conceived by the Holy Spirit, which actually will happen 4 thousand years later. But she doesn't know that.

Read Genesis 4:2. She had another son. Abel. (Hevel) which means vanity. Notice it doesn't say she conceived again. So maybe they were twins. Don't know for sure. Then, later in this chapter, we read that she conceived again and birthed Seth (Shet). How many kids do you think she had? Probably a bunch. They lived a long time before the flood. 900+ years. Notice there is quite a bit of time span in this verse. First, these boys are born, and then the verse says they were working adults. Two different career choices. Which is ok.

Read Genesis 4:3-4a. In the course of time (NASB, NIV) or process of time (KJV), which means at the end of the days. (yowm) (mem vav yowd) Same word as Genesis 1:5. Which probably meant at the end of the work week, which was the seventh day. And the men (not boys anymore) bring their offerings to God. Do you think this is the first time in these two men's lives that they ever brought an offering to God? How many times do you think they have done it? Do you think Adam made sacrifices for God? What would Adam take? Some kind of animal, don't you think? I am going to do what God did. Cain brings <u>some</u> of the fruit of the ground, but Abel brings the firstborn and their fat, which was the <u>best</u> of his possessions. One brother wanted to please God and had an attitude of faith, and the other brother was discharging his duty by his works. So, how is God going to respond to this? I think we have a picture of a person approaching God by the sacrifice and another person approaching God by the works of his hands.

Read Genesis 4:3b. The word "had regard" (NASB), "respect" (KJV), or "favor" (NIV) is best understood in Hebrew as 'gazed upon favorably.' When Abel brought that animal up there, God said, "Looks good." But verse 5.

Read Genesis 4:5a. God had no favor when Cain showed up with turnips or whatever it was. Why? What is the difference? Hebrews 11:4 says, "By faith Abel offered to God a better sacrifice." The only way you can come to God is by faith. It is never by work. Over and over throughout the Bible, it is faith. Secondly, Abel's sacrifice was a better one because of the blood. You can't get blood out of a turnip. Right? What is the picture? There has to be the shedding of the blood. There has to be death. There has to be the substitution of one taking your place or one dying in your place. All of the <u>sin</u> sacrifices in the OT were mandatory, and from animals that they slit their throats and killed them. Had to. It was the picture of the Messiah coming to die in our place. The grain offerings were voluntary acts of worship recognizing God's goodness and provisions.

Faith is obeying God. Faith is taking God at His Word. Cain wanted to do his own thing. The problem is you and I don't approach God in the way we want to. We approach God in the way He says to approach Him.

Read Genesis 4:5b. Cain was very angry because God didn't have regard for his careless offering. Who is he angry at? He is angry at God. It is not a good idea to get angry at God because He is all-powerful, and we aren't. Who else is Cain mad at? Abel. Why would he be mad at Abel? He was jealous. 'Why would you take his and not mine? Just because he has an animal, and I brought the fruit.' God says, 'You know what to do. What is right.' Today, we know what is right. And there are consequences if we don't obey. Then we get mad at God. And get mad at all the other people who didn't do wrong. But we see the grace of God. Because God could have killed Cain for his wrong attitude and wrong sacrifice just like that. (Snap!) But look what God does.

Read Genesis 4:6. God says, 'Why do you have a bad face? Why do you look all upset and mad?' What is God trying to do? God wants Cain to say, 'I blew it. I wasn't thinking. I apologize. I know I need an animal sacrifice. I will go get one. I'm sorry. Forgive me.' That's what God wants.

Read Genesis 4:7. God tells Cain that if he does right, God will give him another chance. If Cain does what is right, he will be happy. If you do what is right, the joy will return. Folks, if we do what is right, there is joy in the Lord. Then God tells Cain if he doesn't do what is right, sin is crouching at the door of your life and is about to jump all over you. The word 'desire' here is the same word as in 3:16, which means if you remember to rule over you. God is warning Cain that sin is near and wants to rule over him. In our lives, we have a pull to do wrong. It is called the flesh. Also called sin. And its desire is for us to live ungodly. God then says in verse 7 that you must overcome this sinful nature. Cain must do what is right. What is Cain supposed to do right now? Confess the wrong and go get the proper sacrifice. But what does Cain do? We don't know. It's over. The obvious conclusion is he didn't do it.

Read Genesis 4:8. (NIV) The Greek Septuagint, the Samaritan Pentateuch, and the Ancient Syriac add this phrase: "Let us go out to the field." Cain deliberately and deceitfully planned to kill his very own brother and did so. Cain probably thought he didn't need an animal sacrifice. "It was a waste of good animals, personally." "Who do you think you are, Abel? And Able might have told his brother, 'If I were you. I would go get the proper animal sacrifice like God said." 'Who do you think you are telling me what to do? Hey, I'm just telling you what's right.' 'You don't tell me anything. I am the older brother.' And while they were in the field, Cain rose up and killed his brother. And Cain probably said, "Hey God, you want blood. I'll give you some blood." Cain killed his brother out of anger and jealousy because his works were evil. It is a picture of the unrighteous and the righteous. The believer and the unbeliever. It is a picture of mankind. People approach God by faith in the blood sacrifice of Jesus Christ, and people try to approach God through their own works, the fruit of the ground.

Read Genesis 4:9. God knows what happened. God wants Cain to confess that He killed him. But what does Cain say? 'I don't know.' Which was an outright lie. He was a liar. Plus, he was a murderer. Then Cain says, 'I'm not my brother's keeper. I don't have to keep up with my brother." He was challenging the right of God to ask these questions. He wasn't showing respect to God. But folks, God is God. He can ask any question he wants. And we had better answer Him every time. Are you and I are brother's keeper today? Yes, we are. How are our friends and family going to know about salvation unless we tell them? We also should help people with physical needs. Here at First Southern, we have a food pantry in which we help folks (especially our own brethren) with a bag of groceries if they need a little helping hand. And third, we must help build up one another spiritually. Equipping the saints to do the ministry. We are responsible for one another. Our purpose is to serve the living God and touch others in His name.

Read Genesis 4:10. Now God moves from His grace to His judgment. Death cries out to God. Because human life is precious to God. We are made in the image of God. All through the Bible, both OT beginning after the flood and in various passages in the NT, God has given man the responsibility to put to death a person who has killed others. Why? Because of the value of human life. If someone kills another person and we just let them be locked up in prison, then you are saying that this life that was taken is not that valuable. In the Bible, if you accidentally killed someone, the family had the right to kill you immediately. But if you ran to a city of refuge (Six cities – three on one side of the Jordan River and three on the other side) and if you made it there, you would call for the elders of the city and confess to them that you accidentally killed a person, they might let you inside the city gates, and then the situation is examined, and if it was determined to be an accident, then because life was so valuable, you had to live in this city of refuge until the high priest dies, which may be a lifetime, then you may go back to your hometown. But if it was determined that you killed that person on purpose, they would turn you over to the victim's family right then.

Read Genesis 4:11-12a. God says that now the ground, which is soaked with his brother's blood, will be cursed and will not yield its produce for him. He isn't going to be able to grow anything, which was his living.

Read 4:12b. God says he would become a fugitive from God.

Read Genesis 4:13. Cain says that his punishment (Avon), or literally his iniquity or sin, is greater than he could bear. Notice he doesn't plea for pardon or express regret. He was a selfish person who was about to be driven from his home to live the life of a nomad.

The Family of Adam
Genesis 4:14 - 5:32

Continuing our study of the book of beginnings, which is Genesis, we studied about two sons of Adam and Eve, named Cain and Abel. We saw their worship. We read that one came by faith, and the other came by works. We saw God's response. And we saw in the last lesson of Cain and Abel in the field, and Cain, being angry, killed his brother. We are going to start the lesson by seeing the curse on Cain. We saw God cursed the earth, on the serpent, the man (ish), and the woman (isha). We are going to begin by reading about how Cain seeks to live apart from God. We are going to see a couple of things.

1. The consequences of sin.

2. We will see what the world was like before the flood, seeking to live apart from God.

As we begin, let me raise a few questions for us.

1. What was God's punishment for Cain?

2. Who is Lamech? And what did he do?

3. How should we view our time on the earth?

We find in the Bible that the church is supposed to affect the world. We, as believers, when we gather for worship and for training, then scatter out into the community, we are actually supposed to affect our community. We are supposed to be, as Jesus would say, the salt and light of this world as we go with the message of Jesus Christ. But one of the problems that seems to happen a lot is that the culture affects the church instead of the church affecting the culture. Think about our culture. Three things always jump out to me:

1. Me first. Our culture promotes the idea of looking out for #1.

2. Things and possessions. Our culture is very materialistic.

3. Instant gratification. Our culture wants everything right now.

If you stand in line at McDonald's for longer than a couple of minutes, you get upset. That's how we are. Well, the same type of attitudes have come into the church life also. So many Christians, when they are looking for a church, ask, "What do your church have to offer me?" Not gifts and talents that I have to offer. Where is the Bible being taught? How can I grow as a Christian? How can I serve as a Christian? But what can you offer me and my family? My first attitude. Also, many churches are materialistic. They are always needing money for something. They also try and tie in a lot of programs and activities. We have to be careful in this area. Thirdly, many Christians want spiritual growth to be instantaneous. They want a seminar or a weekend retreat. Something I can go to give me something to make me mature. Instead of a lifetime growing process. Maturity occurs over a period of time. So, the world is affecting the church in a sense instead of the church affecting the world.

As we continue with Genesis 4, we are going to see the life of Cain. What the world is like, and how it goes away from God. In review, remember that the blood sacrifice that Abel brought by faith is the picture of the coming Messiah, the substitute who is going to pay for mankind's sins. This was the foreshadowing of the seed of the woman.

Read Genesis 4:13. This is Cain's response to God after God lays down the punishment. Notice that the LORD is all capital letters. This is the personal name of God. Whenever you see LORD in all capital letters, it is the Hebrew word YHWH (YaHWeH). It is the ever-existing, all-powerful God. Cain isn't saying that his punishment is too great to bear, but he is saying that his sin, my iniquity (awoni in Hebrew) is too great to bear. He is saying that his sin is too much, but we see God's grace. What could God have done? God could have put him to death just like that. (snap). But God doesn't. Why did God let Cain live? We really don't know. Some people might suggest that Cain was repentant. But I don't see it in Cain's words in verse 13. But maybe Cain's life is a picture of one who rejects God and seeks to live away from God. And what life is like for those who reject the living God?

Read Genesis 4:14 We see four things.

1. Driven from the ground.

2. Hidden from your presence.

3. Restless wanderer on the earth with no home.

4. Be killed by others.

Read Genesis 4:15. God said, "No, that's not true. I'm going to let you live this way the rest of your life." Over and over in the Scriptures it says that sin has consequences. Whatever you sow, you reap. When you sin, what happens first of all? We break our fellowship with God. It affects others. Our fellowship with others. There will be discipline from God. There is no joy. And no peace.

When people have sin in their lives, one of the first things they do in a local body is they quit coming to church. They stop meeting with their fellow believers. They not only lose fellowship with God but also with other believers. If you have sin in your life, you may think you can hang around other believers, but it doesn't work. So, the first thing they do is not necessarily what they are supposed to do, but they stop participating in church activities. No joy and no peace. What should a person be supposed to do when they sin? Confess it.

The Greek literally means to tell on yourselves. (homolegao) Cain is worried that if someone would find him, they could kill him. Who could find him? The only people we know about so far are Adam and Eve. Could there be others? Yes. Probably lots of distant relatives by now. We will see at the end of this chapter that Adam and Eve have another son named Seth. How old do you think Adam was when he had Seth? 130 years. (Genesis 5:3) What do you think Adam and Eve were doing all those years before? Probably having other kids. God says in verse 15 that He will deal with anyone who messes with Cain. Seven times a lot.

All the way through the Bible, vengeance belongs to who? Always belongs to the Lord. When people do you wrong or say things, you don't have to get them back. God handles all those kinds of things. Also, note in verse 15 that God will put a mark or sign on Cain so no one would kill him. What do you think it was? You think God wrote "do not kill" on his head. We really don't know what it is.

I think God put something on him that basically said, 'This person is under the curse of God; don't get near him.' He was a marked man. We see the grace of God allowing Cain to live. Well, now comes the spread of civilization. Cain is going to leave. We are going to see a pattern here. A contrast. Cain will be going out, and he and his offspring will be moving away from God. Then we are going to meet Seth, and his offspring began calling upon the name of the Lord. One is a picture of the fallen world living their own lives, and the other one is a picture of those who believe and seek to live for God. Look at the culture beginning in verse 16.

Read Genesis 4:16. Do you know what Nod means? It means wandering. God said that Cain would be a wanderer, and so he left and settled in Wandering. This world is characterized by polygamy, violence, and aggressiveness. Look what it says in verse 17.

Read Genesis 4:17. Where does Cain find a wife? All we have studied so far is about Adam, Eve, Cain, and Abel. Well, why do you assume there are only three people on the earth just because we have only read about it right now? If you read Genesis 5:4, it says, "Adam had other sons and daughters." Cain had to find a wife from one of his family members. And had a son named Enoch. Read Genesis 4:18-19. Wait a minute. "a man shall leave his father and mother, and the two shall become one flesh." (Genesis 2:24) How do you become one flesh with two people? It won't work. But Lamech (the seventh in the line after Cain) says, 'I will do what I want to do. I don't want to listen to any rules.' We live in a world today that says, 'I want to do my own thing.' 'If you want to believe that Bible stuff, fine. But I have my own life to live the way I want.' Here, we see a picture of the Fallen world moving further and further away from God.

Read Genesis 4:18-22. These people are developing many skills but notice they are leaving out God. Read 4:23-24. Now we read a little poem from Lamech, the polygamist who has now killed a man and is boasting about it. He is saying, 'I am so important that if anything happens to me, it will be avenged worse than Cain.' A man of pride.

Read Genesis 4:25. Seth is born. His name means 'substitute.' He is probably not the third son but an important person because he represents the replacement of Abel, the lineage from which the seed of the woman would eventually come. Read Genesis 4:26. These people would be the ones who call upon the Lord. (the seventh person after Seth would be Enoch, who in Genesis 5:20 says, "he walked with God.")

Genesis 5 is the Genesis boot-hill. It is the death chapter. This is the genealogy (not a complete list because 'father of' can also mean 'was the ancestor of' or possibly just the firstborn is listed) of Adam through Seth's lineage. Not Cain's. Now, most people, when they come to a generation listing, will just turn the page, but in this lesson, I want us to see some things in this chapter that we can learn from. Notice that God wants us to remember that people are important to Him as individuals, not just races or nations. That is why God refers to people in this chapter by name, mentioning their life span and descendants. God's love is for each and every one of us. It is clear that God's command is not to eat of the tree of knowledge of good and evil, for when you eat of it, you will surely die. It has come true because as soon as Adam and Eve disobeyed and ate from that tree, they died spiritually and began to die physically. We see that here in this chapter. Death. The first four verses are a review of the creation of man and woman in God's own perfect image, and then sinful Adam has children in his own imperfect image. Then, in verses 5-20, we see the cycle. A person lived, had offspring, and then died. Same thing over and over. To show the result of the Fall. Did people really live that long back then?

Yes, according to the way the Hebrew is written. Literal years. When you see the word years preceded by an actual number, such as 930 years, it means literally. Not symbolically, as some might say. Also, the Greek Septuagint points out that these were literal years. Remember, the rain hadn't fallen yet, so probably the waters above the earth (the canopy) protected them from the harmful radioactive waves of the sun. Because immediately after the flood, people lived fewer years. Adam lived 930 years. Seth lived for 912 years. Noah lived 950 years. But then, after the flood, Abraham lived 175 years. Isaac lived 180 years. Jacob lived 147 years. Joseph lived 110 years. Moses lived 120 years. Etc.

But there is also hope of life in this chapter in two men. Enoch and Noah. Men who walked with God. In verses 22-24, we see Enoch, the man who *walked* with God. The Septuagint translates this as "Enoch was well-pleasing to God." He had a relationship and a special fellowship with God. He chose to live for God. We, too, chose to live for God. When you put your faith in Christ and then live the Christian life, you are choosing to walk with God. What do you think it means "and God took him away"? In Hebrew, it literally means "God translated him." Which means taking it from one place and putting it in another place. Where do you think He took him? I don't know. It doesn't say. But he (and Elijah) didn't experience physical death.

Also, a whole generation, those alive at the rapture when we will meet Christ in the air, will experience such a translation. (1 Thess. 4:13-18) My hope is that the rapture will come soon because it could happen at any second, and I won't have to experience physical death. Wouldn't that be great! In the midst of a chapter where there is death, death, death, there is the hope of life. And in the times when all of us have experienced loved ones dying, there is hope of life because of Jesus Christ. And one day, you will be with your loved ones again.

Then, lastly, in verses 25-32, we will see Noah, who also *walked* with God (Genesis 6:9). In verse 29, the name Noah is similar in sound to the Hebrew word meaning "to comfort."

We are going to study Noah building the ark, which is chapter 6 of the next lesson. That will be a very interesting chapter.

CHAPTER FIVE

The Wickedness and Judgment of Men
Genesis 6:1-8

In this passage, we are going to find the reason for the Flood. Why did God bring judgment? We will read that the wickedness of man was great and that man was continuously evil. So, if you think about the theme of this section, it is that God deals with the wickedness of man. How does He respond? It is really two-fold. 1. God brings judgment. 2. The grace of God. The passage and some of the verses are some of the hardest in the Bible. Especially since it is hard to understand just what is going on, we will see that in verses 1-2. There is a lot here that we can make an application.

There are two major views concerning end-time events. There are some who believe that things are going to get better and better. And that the Christians are going to take the message of Christ through the entire world. And the world is going to get Christianized. Then Christ is going to return. Then there is a second view that the end times will not get better but actually get worse and worse. And that the message as a whole is rejected, wickedness gets worse and worse. Then Christ is going to come and judge the world. Which of these views is the Biblical truth? Well, Jesus himself gave us some information in Matthew 24-25 about the end-time events. Jesus said, "As was in the days of Noah, so shall it be in the coming of the Son of Man." How things were in Noah's time will be the way things will characterize the end times.

In this lesson, we get a picture of what things were like in the days of Noah. The brief description that we get is the world just before He judged it with the Flood, and the key statement is "the wickedness of man was great upon the earth." There are some who teach today that man is basically good, and put in the right circumstances and the right environment, crime and sin will be eliminated. The Bible teaches just the opposite: there is none righteous, no not one. All have sinned and come short of the glory of God." "All are like sheep gone astray." Each one is one way; there is none that seeks God. No one does good. In this lesson, as we look at Genesis 6, we see the world as it was during the days of Noah, and wickedness was great on the face of the earth.

As we begin, let's review where we are and what we have studied so far because we will begin a new division of the book. Genesis is a powerful book. It shows God as the creator. Remember, you can divide the book of Genesis into two parts.

chapters 1-11 deal with four big events. The Creation (1-2), Fall (3-5), the Flood (6-9), and Division of the Nations (10-11). Then, chapters 12-50 go into detail about four people – Abraham, Isaac, Jacob, and Joseph.

So we have moved to a section that is famous. The whole idea of the Flood. And there are people who will say things like, 'Was there really a worldwide flood? Did all that really happen?' In the next three chapters, we are going to see this event, the Flood. Now, let me just remind you of a summary. God created the heavens and the earth in 6 days. He created the man; then

He created the woman out of the man; he placed them in the garden with instructions to take care of it. To eat from all the trees except one, the tree of knowledge of good and evil. We then studied that that failed; they ate from the tree, they ran and hid from God, He found them, and in His grace and mercy, He had a provision for their sin. He said that the seed of the woman would crush the head of the serpent. And God actually said that coming through woman would be a preview of the Messiah; the one who is to come will deal with sin. So, in a sense, right there, Adamah and Isha were looking forward to the one that God was going to bring. Now, when they had their son, Cain, she probably thought he was the Messiah. But they found out very quickly that Cain wasn't the Messiah because he killed his brother. Then, they had another son named Seth. And then eventually came Noah. And then, through Noah's son, Shem, come the Jewish people, beginning with Abram.

Now let me just show you about Chapter 6. There is a lot in this chapter. We are going to study the first eight verses of this lesson, which is the whole reason for the Flood. Then, we will get into verses 8-10, which are about Noah and his family. Then, beginning verses 13-22, talking about the building of the ark. The question will be, "Could they build a boat that would hold all the animals? Why are they going to get them on the boat? And if they get them on there, will there be any room for food? Did dinosaurs go on the boat? How long were they on the ark? (over a 1 and 10 days). How big was the boat? By the way, they could have gotten all the animals on with 2/3 of the boat empty. We are going to talk about all this when we get to it. Don't miss the next episode of "Bereshith".

Well, let's begin by reading the first two verses of Chapter 6. These are probably the most difficult passages in the OT, if not the entire Bible. Let's see what it says. Read Genesis 6:1-2. "and they took *wives* for themselves" – literally, in Hebrew, it says, "and they took them, for themselves." Now, let me go on and read a couple of things. Especially verse 4. Read Genesis 6:4. Who were these mighty men? These so-called 'sons of God, daughters of men, came together, and their offspring were mighty men." "Nephilim actually means 'giants'. And many people will ask, "What is going on?" So we want to talk briefly about 'who are the sons of God and daughters of men?' Now, there are three major views. And I want you to just understand what they are.

Now, the first view is that the sons of God refers to believers and the daughters of men refer to unbelievers. Such as the offspring of Seth and the offspring of Cain. Remember, in Chapter 5, there is a division. A godly line goes through Seth, and an ungodly line goes through Cain. Here are a couple of questions. Why did the godly people get to be called the sons of God, and why did the ungodly people get to be called the daughters of men? Why the daughters? The second question is: Where do you get these giant people? If they are just believers and unbelievers coming together. Then, in verse 3, the Lord (Adonai) basically says, 'I'm not going to put up with this.' Now, does He mean He isn't going to put up with believers marrying unbelievers? So, some will say that believers marrying unbelievers wouldn't have produced these giants.

Then, the second viewpoint is that maybe "the sons of God" are noble men (kings) marrying more than one woman. (daughters). That's what is wrong. Polygamy. And that is why God said, 'I am not going to put up with this.' The only problem with that is it doesn't really answer 'who were the giants.'

Then, it takes us to the third view, which is probably the most controversial view. This view believes that the Sons of God were angels. Some angels came to the earth and took the form of people because angels can do that, and took human women, had sexual relations with them, and bore offspring. And God said, "I am not going to put up with this." The title "sons of God" in Hebrew is 'bene elohim.' It is used about eight times in the OT. Every time it is used, it is used to refer to angels. Every time. Job 1:6, Job 2:1, Job 38:7, Psalm 29:1, a couple of places in the Proverbs. Also, it would explain the Nephilim (giants). Half angel - half human. Now, the Bible says that angels don't reproduce themselves. There was a set number of angels. But that doesn't imply that angels couldn't take human women for themselves. Remember when the angels went down to Sodom? What did the people in Sodom want to do with them? Have sex with them. And finally, turn to the book of Jude, verse 6. This mentions an event about some angels (demons) that did something wrong. And many scholars tie this together with Genesis 6. Pretty weird? Good stuff, though? Isn't it great? Jude is saying, "God has taken some angels and bound them somewhere because they didn't do what they were supposed to do." Now, what did they do? Many scholars would say this is talking about when some angels (demons) came down to the earth and had sex with people. Now look what Jude says in verse 7. Now, in Sodom and Gomorrah, what was the strange flesh that the people were having sex with? Homosexuality. What would be the strange flesh of an angel? Human beings. So this view is that angels came to the earth and had sex with human women and produced these giants.

Now, there is a book that was written about 200 years before Christ came to the earth called the Book of Enoch. It wasn't a Canonical book. It isn't a Biblical book. It doesn't have the same authority. But there was the tradition and the thought that there were angles at a point in time that had sex with human beings. You know that Jude quoted Enoch. In the book of Enoch, it says this: "Angels saw beautiful women and said, "let us take them for ourselves." So you search the Scripture yourselves. Go to 2 Peter, and Jude, and Genesis. Find every place that the sons of God are used in the OT, and see what you can find. As bizarre as it seems, most conservative scholars would say this is probably dealing with angels with people. Now, what does God say about this?

Read Genesis 6:3. God is basically saying, "I'm not going to let this go on. I'm not going to put up with the pollution of the human race." If the human race gets totally polluted, how can the Messiah come? This verse goes on to say that God is going to give man 120 years, and then the judgment is going to come. 1 Peter 3:20: "God was patient as he waited for Noah as he prepared the ark."

Read Genesis 6:5. How were the things in the days of Noah? Wicked and evil. We never have to teach people to do wrong. We are born with a sinful nature. We have to teach people to be right. Now watch as we bring this to a close. Two things. God's pain and God's plan.

Read Genesis 6:6. The Hebrew word for sorry has the idea of regret, hurt, and grief. Now, these are anthropomorphic things. Giving characteristics to God as a human being. God knows everything. This evil behavior didn't surprise Him. But it is the idea that God saw the wickedness of man, that he was evil, and that he was sorry that the people chose sin and death instead of obedience, which led to a relationship with Him.

Do we actually realize how much our sin grieves God? Most of the time, we don't even think about it. But remember, sin caused the Fall of the entire human race. Do we realize that sin costs God His Son? That because of sin and the wages of sin is death, God demonstrates his love towards us, that while we were yet sinners, Christ died for us. God loved us and sent his son to be the satisfactory payment for us. 1 John 4:9-10. Do you realize that sin breaks fellowship?

First of all, immediately with God, and then with fellow believers. Do you realize that when you sin, you put yourself in a position in which you will not gain rewards? Even if we do something good, we do it in the flesh because we have broken our fellowship with God. Sin grieves God. That's the pain. Now, look at the plan.

Read Genesis 6:7. God says he will exterminate man, animals, creeping things, and birds. Could God say this: "Ok. I have looked out there; I made these people, and I love these people, even though they reject me totally. So what I am going to do is just forget it. I am going to pretend they didn't sin." Could God do that?

NO. Because of his character, He is a just and righteous God. God must judge these people because of their sins. And by the grace of God, the sin of mankind was ultimately judged on Christ on the cross. In the midst of God's grief over man's wickedness and evil thoughts, saying, "I am going to blot out this," look at verse 8.

Read Genesis 6:8-9. Now we know that God is going to tell Noah to build an ark and get on in order to save his life. Did God do that because Noah was righteous, blameless, and walked with God? No. Read verse 8 again. By the grace of God,

He chose Noah. (Chen - first time used in the OT). Why did God choose you? That you get to be a child of God? Is it because God found you righteous? Or was it by grace that you are saved through faith in Christ? Noah found grace in the eyes of the Lord. It is the grace of God that we, too, have salvation. By the grace of God, we have eternal life.

By the grace of God, we live. By the grace of God, we have the power of the Holy Spirit. By the grace of God, we have spiritual gifts. By the grace of God, we get to meet with other believers. By the grace of God, we have his revelation.

God's Covenant and Instructions to Noah
Genesis 6:9-22

In the next few chapters, we are about to see one of the most famous events in the Bible, and that is the Flood. Chapters 6-8 are about God's judgment upon the earth. And He brings a worldwide flood, not a localized flood, to destroy sinful man. In the last lesson, we saw God's pain and God's plan. His pain was that He was sorry about mankind's continuous sin (verse 5), and his plan was to destroy man. Genesis 6:6-7. Then, in verse 8, we see that Noah found grace in the eyes of the Lord.

First of all, we know that God is perfect, holy, and righteous. That is the character of God. In contrast, we all have sinned and come short of the glory of God. So, God is perfect; we are sinful. How in the world are we going to get to God? A lot of people will say, well, just do the best you can, and God will love you. It is the lie of the devil. Well, you can't do good. And God already loves you.

Now, we want to think about two things.

First of all, what is the righteousness of man? Filthy rags.

And the second thing to think about is that the standard we are dealing with is not just being good but being perfect. Never sinned one time. So the truth is we can never measure up. Think about it. If we sin, what do we earn? We earn death. If we do good, what do we earn? Filthy rags. So that means that we can never measure up. God is perfect. Man is sinful. So here's the question: How can a fallen person be right with God? How can a man be righteous? Of course, the answer found in the Scripture is by faith. When a person puts their faith in Jesus Christ, when a person trusts in God's provision for salvation, God gives that person righteousness. That is an incredible truth. Romans 4:5. Now, the reason I have reviewed that Scriptural teaching is a man named Noah was called a 'righteous man." In Genesis 6:9. He was a righteous "man that found grace (Chen in Hebrew) in the eyes of the Lord." Grace is an un-merited favor.

We have eternal life because by the grace of God, He reaches down and brings us to Himself through His Son, Yesuah. (Jesus)

Now, he is going to tell us about this man, Noah. Read Genesis 6:9-10. There are three things that are said about this man, Noah.

1. He was a righteous man. This doesn't mean that he never sinned. It means that he was a believer. He loved God. Righteousness comes from faith.

2. He was blameless. Literally has the idea of maturity. He was growing in the knowledge of God.

3. He walked with God. (Enoch was the other man who walked with God). He maintained a very close, personal relationship with God. We, too, are to walk worthy of our calling. Ephesians 4:1.

And the question is: are you righteous? Are you blameless and growing in your faith? And do you walk with God in a close relationship?

There are three aspects of righteousness.

1. The righteousness of God. He is perfect. He is a holy God. He determines right from wrong. The law is the character of God. The law is perfect. What's wrong with the law is we can't keep it.

2. As sinners, we need to be made righteous. You can't have a relationship with God unless you are righteous. And that comes simply by faith.

3. As believers, we must pursue righteousness.

Matthew 6:33: "Seek ye first the kingdom of God and His righteousness." We ought to be men and women seeking to live a godly, righteous lifestyle in the midst of a fallen world. Do other people see the difference that Christ has made in your life?

Remember when the people came up to Jesus and asked, "What is the top commandment? There are 613 commandments in Mosaic law, and Jesus replied, "Love the Lord your God with all your heart and all your soul and love your neighbor as yourself. On these two commandments, all the other commandments hinge."

Read Genesis 6:11. The word corrupt means to decay. The world was decaying. It reads in the Hebrew that the earth is corrupting itself. Sin always destroys. Sin will kill you. The wages of sin is death.

Read Genesis 6:12. We say it is pretty bad now. What do you think it was like back then? Do you think it was worse than it is now?

Read Genesis 6:13. Judgment is coming.

Read Genesis 6:14. God said make for yourself an ark (tevah in Hebrew). The way of grace. It was the escape from the judgment. The ark is a picture of Jesus Christ. Because in Christ, we escape from judgment. This was a gigantic barge. Like a shoe box. Flat bottom. Squared sides. It was huge. Bigger than modern ocean liners. It had three levels. It wasn't this cute little boat with animals sticking out of it like you see in children's books. It was made of Gopher wood. This must have been a hardwood. Noah was to make the ark with rooms. The Hebrew word here for rooms means "nests." Or compartments. Noah was to cover it inside and out with pitch, a tarlike substance used to make the ark watertight. The Hebrew word for pitch (kapor) was also used for 'covering,' which we take and use as the covering of sin.

Now for six questions:

1. How big was the ark?

2. Could all of the animals fit on the ark?

3. Did all the animals get on the ark?

4. How could Noah get all the animals?

5. How long were they on the ark?

6. How could they make it?

Read Genesis 6:15. Question one: How big was the ark? A cubit was the length from your elbow to the tip of your finger. About 18 inches. So the length of the area was 300 cubits 450 ft. A football field is 300 ft. long. So the ark is 1 and ½ football fields long. Its width was 50 cubits, which is 75 ft. wide. (which is a ½ football field) Notice this is exactly six times longer than it was wide. The same ratio is used by modern shipbuilders. Which is very stable on the high seas. Its height was 30 cubits, which is 45 ft. tall. (5 story building) This ark was huge. And Noah and his three sons are going to build this, probably miles from any body of water. And it is going to take them 120 years. This isn't a project that you do in your garage on Saturday afternoon.

Read Genesis 6:16. God told Noah to put windows on the top. Ventilation. And only 1 door on the side. There is only one way in and one way out. Who tells them to get in? God. Who shuts the door? God. Who tells them to come out? God. Who opens the door? God. This is a picture of God's provision for their salvation. Their deliverance from the judgment to come. Jesus is our door. He is our salvation. It has three levels. People have figured out the mathematics of this ark. It had over 100,000 square feet. It has 1,400,000 capacity cubit feet. It could easily hold 14,000 tons. It would hold 522 box cars of cattle if you wanted to put that many cows in it.

Second question: could all the animals fit on the ark? Yes. Well, people have figured that there are 18,000 different species of animals. The average size of all the animals is about the size of sheep. They could have put 120,000 sheep easily onto it with room to spare. What they would have filled up if you put all the known species on the ark would take up about 150 box cars out of the 522 box cars. Not even 1/3 of the space is available. And maybe many of the animals were babies and not even fully grown.

Read Genesis 6:19. The point is the ark is a safe place to deliver and to save. To keep them alive. Two of every kind. So they could repopulate the earth. Read Genesis 7:2. Seven of every clean animal. Clean animals were for sacrifice.

Third question: Did all the animals get on the ark? Yes. Read Genesis 6:17. The Hebrew word for flood here is "Mabul there," which literally means the destruction of water. This is the only place that it is used. It is only used to describe this flood. It is never used to describe a normal local flood that you might have in your town. Only to describe this flood in Genesis.

Read Genesis 6:18. A covenant (berit in Hebrew) is a promise. God has obligated Himself through this pronouncement to maintain His commitment to Noah if Noah obeys God.

Fourth question: How could Noah get all the animals? It would be impossible for Noah to round up all of these animals. Read Genesis 6:20. "Every kind shall come to you to keep them alive." A migration of animals came. This would have been incredible. This was a supernatural work of God. Noah built the ark by faith. Hebrews 11:7. Has it rained before? No. But he believed in God.

Fifth question: How long were they on the ark? It rained for 40 days and 40 nights. (Genesis 7:4) The water rose 150 days. (5 months) (Genesis 7:24) Then, in Genesis 8:4, the ark rested on Ararat in the seventh month. Then, in Genesis 8:5, the mountain top is visible in the tenth month. Then, in Genesis 8:13, the water is dried up after almost a year. Then, in Genesis 8:14, God said to go out of the ark. This was at the one-year, ten-day point they were on the ark.

Sixth question: How could they (8 people) make it on that ark all that time? Genesis 8:1. God remembered them. God cared for them. Whose job was it to keep all those animals alive? God. It was all he could do was to keep the place clean. Ha. Maybe some of those animals went into hibernation for a year. God keeps everything in order.

CHAPTER SIX

The Great Flood
Genesis 7 (Bereshith 7)

Last lesson we studied God's prediction in chapter 6, His literal prediction of the coming judgment on the earth. That He will bring a worldwide flood. In this lesson, we will study the fulfilment, the literal fulfilment, in chapter 7. This sets a prophetic pattern that is followed throughout the whole Bible. Earth was no longer the perfect paradise that God had intended. Humanity forgot about God. People didn't trust and obey God. Except Noach. Noah was a righteous man, which means he believed and had faith in God. Noah walked with God, which means he had fellowship with God. And by the grace of the Lord, God promised to save him and his family, which was a covenant (Berit). Noah had three sons, Shem, Ham, and Japheth. (Yefet) So Noah and his sons took their wives on a cruise. Abraham, David, and Jesus descended from Shem. God, in His grace, provided a way of salvation from His judgment. God provides us with a way of salvation from His judgment, too, through Jesus Christ. He is our provision.

In the last lesson, we studied chapter 6 and learned that the ark took how many years to build? 120 years. And it was how long? 300 cubits (450 ft.) How wide? 50 cubits (75 ft). How high? 30 cubits (45 ft). And that scholars have estimated that almost 125,000 animals could have fit into the ark. And we read in Genesis 6:20 that the animals came to Noah. 2 of every kind, male and female. And we read that Noah did all that God commanded him to do. He was obedient and put his trust in the Lord. He believed that the Lord would send a flood of water on the earth to destroy all air-breathing animals, birds and people except Noah and his family.

Read Genesis 7:1. Only Noah had been righteous or a believer in God. The people in Noah's time did not accept God's words, which Noah preached to them for 120 years while he was building the ark. The people did not agree with God that they were living corrupt and evil lives. The people didn't trust in His promise to send the Deliverer. They didn't believe that God would destroy the world with a great flood. God waited patiently for 120 years for them to change their minds, but they didn't. So God tells Noah, who did believe, to get into the ark with his family. God saved Noah because he agreed with and trusted in God.

Read Genesis 7:2-3. Take 2 of every unclean animal, male and female, and seven *pairs* of clean animals, male and female, into the ark with him to repopulate the earth when the flood is over. The clean animals were to be used as a sacrifice after the flood was over in chapter 8:20 and also for food after the flood in chapter 9:3.

Read Genesis 7:4. After seven days, God says he is going to send rain for 40 days and 40 nights to blot out everything from the face of the land. Fish weren't in the ark. The number 40 was chosen to convey a sense of fullness. Noah opened the window of the ark after another 40 days. (Genesis 8:6) Forty days was the period of the embalming of Joseph. (Gen. 50:3). Moses was forty days on the mountain. (Ex. 24:18). The spies spent forty days in searching Canaan. (Num. 13:25). The Israelites wandered for forty years in the wilderness (Num. 14:33). Moses twice fasted and prayed for forty days. (Deut. 9:9, 18). The Jews were forbidden to inflict more than forty stripes (Deut. 25:3). Goliath defied Saul's army for forty days. (1 Sam. 17:16). Elijah, strengthened by food from the angel, fasted for forty days (1 Kings 19:8). Nineveh was allowed forty days to repent. (Jonah 3:4). Ezekiel bore the iniquities to Judah for forty days. (Ezekiel 4:6). The Lord Jesus fasted for 40 days (Matthew 4:2). Christ appeared during a period of 40 days, teaching the Apostles about the kingdom of God (Acts 1:3).

Read Genesis 7:5. Noah obeyed the Lord.

Read Genesis 7:6. Noah was 600 years old when the flood came. He lived a total of 950 years.

Read Genesis 7:7. Noah and his family entered the ark. (tevah) But everyone else in the world continued to live their own sinful lives until it was too late.

Read Genesis 7:8-10. The flood came just like God said. God never tells a lie.

Read Genesis 7:11. In a Biblical Jewish year, there were 12 months of 30 days length, making a total Biblical year of 360 days. Rain began to fall on the 17th day of the second month, called Bul (also called Cheshvan), using the Civil calendar, which would have possibly been in November. (Remember God added a Religious calendar in Exodus 12 (Pesach lamb to be slain in Egypt) in which He rotated the months. Bul became the 8th month.) Notice that water came from 2 places. A great downpour from above (the vapor canopy over the earth) and subterranean waters from below the earth (springs erupted or possibly earthquakes and volcanic eruptions).

Read Genesis 7:12-15. Noah, his family, and the animals all went into the ark through the 1 door. This was the only way anyone could be saved from the flood and God's wrath against sin. Jesus Christ is the "one way" of salvation.

Read Genesis 7:16. After they were all inside, God shut the door. God himself shut them inside the place of safety. When God shut the door, it was too late. Those outside the boat now had no way to escape God's anger because God had shut them out. When God decides it is time to punish the world, there is no escape from Him.

Read Genesis 7:17-24. This was no ordinary rain. This was a deluge. The water rose for 150 days (5 months). It was higher than 15 cubits (20 ft) above the mountain tops. Ararat mountain range was 16,000 ft. (more than 3 miles up). The Hebrew word kol is translated as <u>all</u>, which adds to the impression that the Flood was a universal phenomenon. No one could have escaped the catastrophe except those in the ark. God is all-powerful! He is supreme and sovereign! God has control over all the earth, the rain, the wind, the sun, the moon, the stars, everything! He made all things and controls them all! He alone is almighty! Nothing is impossible to Him! God can do anything! God is holy and righteous. He is a God of love, but He is indeed a God of wrath against sin!

CHAPTER SEVEN

Noah's Deliverance
Genesis 8

We are seeing one of the most famous events in the Bible and of all time, the Flood. God brings His judgement to the world, which is found in Genesis 6, 7, and 8. We have seen that the sin of man was great, and the wages of sin is death, so what does God do? He judges the world. And in the midst of this judgment, we see the grace of God. And the great truth is: all have sinned and come short of the glory of God, and because the wages of sin is death, there is supposed to be judgment, and in the midst of judgment, there is the grace of God. The grace of God in Jesus Christ.

Well, we see in this passage, in the midst of this judgment upon the earth, we see the grace of God. Noah was chosen by God. He was commissioned to build a big ark, this big boat, for the salvation of his family and the animals. And we saw last time that that Flood came. Noah's family was told by God to enter the ark through the one door. God brought the animals to Noah, and God shut the one door. And the water came. From both below the earth, possibly in the form of fissures, and upon the earth, it rained for 40 days and 40 nights, possibly from the water canopy that surrounded the earth at that time. Then, the water rose for 150 days. (5 months). It was higher than 15 cubits (20 ft) above the mountain tops. Ararat mountain range was 16,000 ft. (more than 3 miles up). And that ended chapter 7. And now we are going to see the next 120 days. Because they were on the ark 1 Jewish year and ten days. (370 days + 7 more days before it started to rain) We are going to see Noah and his family get off the ark along with the animals. And we are going to see what Noah does next.

When you think about God, he is so great. He is a gracious God. He is a God who answers prayers. He is a God who takes care of us. Sometimes, we have gone through trials and problems, and we have prayed, and we got answers. And God takes us right through those times. And when that happens, we thank Him and praise Him. And we say, "Thank you, God. You take care of us." In the Bible, we think of David, who praised God. And even in the book of Jonah, I preached about Jonah this afternoon at the Presbyterian Manor nursing home. In Jonah chapter 2, Jonah is in the belly of the great fish, and he is praying to God. Now, most people think he is praying to God to get him out of there. But he isn't. His prayer is a prayer of thanksgiving. Thanking God for saving his life by having the fish swallow him because he was drowning. When we go to Genesis 8, we see Noah getting off the ark, and the first thing that he does is build an altar to God, worshipping Him and thanking Him for his salvation. It was a burnt offering, which means total dedication. And we will study that in just a minute.

Remember in chapter 7 that Noah and his family, along with the animals, entered the ark (tevah) in the 600th year of Noah's life, the second month, called Cheshvan or sometimes called Bul, using the Civil calendar, which would have been possibly in November. And the seventh day. And really, the ark is a picture of Jesus Christ, the Messiah whose name was Yesuah. It is a place of salvation. The only place that they could be delivered would be to be in the ark. The only place that you and I can be delivered is to be in Jesus Christ. And we are in Christ, by faith. Go back and look at Genesis 7:21-22. There is the judgment. Genesis 6:5 says that the Lord saw that the wickedness of man was great on earth and that every intent of the thoughts of his heart was only evil continually. So He decided to wipe it out. That is a powerful thing.

Let's begin now with chapter 8. Let me break it down for you. In verses 1-12, the flood waters begin to go down. After that, in verses 13-19, they leave the ark. Then, in verses 20-22, we see Noah (Noach) in his act of worship.

Now when you see Noah, what do you think about him? Pretty good guy, right? I mean, he is the one who found grace in the eyes of the Lord, but he was also a righteous and blameless man. He obeyed God. And the first thing that he does when he comes off the ark is to worship God. But wait until we get to chapter 9. Noah does something that not only affects himself but affects his offspring for years to come. One thing about it: no matter how good you are, we all have sinned and come short of the glory of God. All of us have fallen short. Even Noah. He fails. And every one of us has failed. Don't put your confidence in people. Because you will be disappointed. Put your confidence in Jesus Christ, and you won't be disappointed.

Read Genesis 8:1. Look how he starts off this passage. "God (Elohiym) remembered Noah." The Hebrew word for remembered is 'wayyizkor', which means concentrated effort. God remembered his covenant. Chapter 6:18. His covenant or promise was that He was going to get Noah into the ark and keep him safe. The wonderful thing is God remembers and keeps every promise that He makes, including the prophecies that are coming in the future.

Read Genesis 8:2. This is a general statement about God stopping the rain, the underground springs, and everything.

Read Genesis 8:3. The best that we can understand here is that the water rose for 150 days (5 months). Then it began to decrease.

Read Genesis 8:4. The ark rested on the mountains of Ararat on the seventh month (Nisan or, sometimes called Aviv), 17 days. Which is 150 days, the water decreased.

Read Genesis 8:5. The water decreased until the first day of the tenth month. (Tammuz) Then, only the tops of the mountains were seen. So now they have been on the boat for eight months. Can you imagine what it would have been like being on that ark for eight months, through storms and high seas, all that rocking back and forth, with all those animals who need a bath? The smells. Eating the same food every day. No opportunity to just drive over and get a Big Mac. Being cooped up with the same people day in and day out without cable TV.

Read Genesis 8:6-7. Noah waited 40 days (now it is the month of Av), opened the window, and sent out a raven. And it says, "It kept going to and fro until the waters had dried up from the earth." So, I guess it finally found something to land on. Don't know.

Read Genesis 8:8-9. So Noah then sent out a Dove to see if the waters had receded from the face of the ground. But the dove came back because she couldn't find any place to land.

Read Genesis 8:10-11. Noah then waited another seven days and sent out the dove again. But this time, she returns with a what? - it doesn't say olive branch. It says "freshly plucked olive leaf."

Note: Olive trees don't grow at high elevations.

So it says in verse 11 that Noah "knew that the waters had receded from the earth." But noticed he didn't get off the ark even though he knew he could. Why? Because God is the one who put him on the boat. Who is going to get him off the boat? God.

Read Genesis 8:12. Noah waited another seven days and sent out the dove again, but she didn't come back.

Read Genesis 8:13. It is now Noah's 601st year, in the first month (Tishri or, sometimes called Ethanim), in the first day.

It's not quite a year that they have been out there. Notice that Noah moves something so he can look out. And he saw that the surface of the ground was dry. But he didn't leave the ark.

Read Genesis 8:14. It is now the 27th day of the second month (which is Cheshvan or Bul), which is the same month that they started this journey. And the earth was dried. 370 days after the flood started, they entered the ark one week prior to the beginning of the rainfall.

Read Genesis 8:15-17. Finally, God says, "Go out of the ark." Notice what it says at the end of verse 17. "be fruitful and multiply on the earth." Sounds just like what God said to Adam and the woman in the garden. Genesis 1:28. Why? Because Noah and his family are starting the population over.

Read Genesis 8:18-19. God obeyed and got off the ark. He was a righteous, blameless man. He was righteous because he was a believer in God. Blameless because of his spiritual maturity and obedience to God. Are you characterized as a person who obeys the Scripture? Have you committed to live daily according to His Word in God's power?

Now, this begins the third Dispensation (oikonomos) or stage, which is a distinct and identifiable administration in the development of God's design for human history. The third Dispensation is called the Dispensation of Human Government.

The first two dispensations revealed were: Innocence (Adam to the Fall) and Conscience (Fall to Flood). There are seven dispensations in all. We are currently in the sixth Dispensation, which is the Church Age.

The third Dispensation begins here and goes to Abraham. God Himself instituted civil government after the Flood. God reveals that evil is to be restrained through civil government and through the punishment of it.

Read Genesis 8:20. The first thing that he did when he got off the ark was build an altar to the Lord and take every clean animal and clean bird (up to 5 pairs of each) and offer a burnt offering. He responded to God. This was a voluntary act of worship. An expression of devotion, commitment and complete surrender to God. The sacrifice was totally consumed. In reality, that is what we should do also. God so loved us that He sent His Son to die for us as our substitute. In His grace and mercy, He has provided a way of salvation for us. We should offer our complete surrender to Him. Romans 12.

Read Genesis 8:21. What does it mean when it says that "God smelled a soothing aroma"? This is a figurative way of saying that the Lord takes delight in his children's worship of Him. And God accepted this offering of expiation and thanksgiving. He said to himself in his heart to never again destroy every living thing as I have done. Also, note that the answer to mankind's sin isn't judgment. Because there was still sin after the Flood, the answer to man's sin is the Savior.

Read Genesis 8:22. Notice that the seasons will continue "while the earth remains". The earth will not be eternal. Its final destruction is described in Ps. 102:35 and quoted in Heb. 1:11, 12. II Peter 3:10.

CHAPTER EIGHT

Covenant of the Rainbow
Genesis 9

Open your Bibles to Genesis 9. We will see two aspects in this lesson. 1. God gives a command to man. 2. God's covenant (berit in Hebrew) to man. We first saw the covenant in Genesis 6:18: "But I will establish my covenant with you..." Then, remember we saw back in Genesis 7:21 that God said in his heart: "Never again will I curse the ground because of man, and never again will I destroy all living creatures as I have done." Now, in chapter 9, we will see what this covenant is all about. In chapter 9, we are going to see the value of human life.

When we look at Chapter 9, we see the value of life. Remember that the flood is over. Noah has stepped off the ark. God has judged the world. Every creature died except Noah, his family, and the animals that God brought to him to put in the ark. God, in His grace, chose Noah to build the ark. God kept him safe. And when Noah came off the ark, the first thing that he did was to build an altar. He worshipped God.

OUTLINE

Genesis 9:1-7 - God's command. Which deals with man and the animals. And man with man.

Genesis 9:8-17 - God's covenant. Which is, in a sense, God's second covenant. There are seven major covenants. (Adam, Noah, Abraham, Moses, restoration, David, new covenant) This Noahic one is an unconditional type of covenant or divine promise to never again will all life be cut off by the waters of a flood.

Look back in Genesis 8:20. This was a picture of total sacrifice. Noah is saying to God, "I dedicate my life to you." Now, let's see what God says to do.

Read Genesis 9:1. God (Elohiym) blessed. The word blessed in Hebrew is Barak. This word can be used in two different ways. Whenever it is used - man Barak God, it always means man praises God. Whenever it is used -God Barak man, it always means a blessing. Now, look at God's instructions. "Be fruitful and multiply, and fill the earth." Does that sound familiar? Genesis 1:28 during the creation story. But here it is different. Look at verse 2.

Read Genesis 9:2. Now it seems that the animals, birds, and fish will be afraid of man. Now watch this. Verse 3. Read Genesis 9:3. The Best that we can understand is that before the flood, they didn't eat animals. Genesis 1:30. (God gave green herbs to eat) Now, since they have come off the ark, God says they can eat the animals, too. This is not a contradiction with Deut. 14:3-21. That passage deals with the Jewish people. Perhaps strict food laws were given to the Jewish people to make them distinct from other nations whose food was often closely associated with idolatry. By the way, Jesus removed the clean-unclean distinction from food altogether. (Mark 7:19).

But notice there are some restrictions to eating the animals. Verse 4. Read Genesis 4. God says that life is in the blood. Don't eat the blood of an animal. God is saying you can eat the flesh but drain the blood out first. The blood belongs to God. God is saying life belongs to me. The blood of man belongs to me. And the blood of animals belongs to me. Leviticus 17:11 says blood is life, and the blood is what makes the covering of sin. This is a picture of Jesus Christ's shed blood. The life that was shed to pay for the sins of mankind. The principle of blood atonement is God's divinely ordained remedy for the problem of sin. The Scriptures insist that atonement for sin is not possible apart from the shedding of blood. The giving of the life of an innocent to atone for the guilty.

Now, what about the life of a person? God is going to look at it in two ways. 1. What if an animal kills a person? 2. What if a person kills another person? Watch what he says in verse 5.

Read Genesis 9:5. This says that God requires the lifeblood of an animal if it kills a person and that God requires the lifeblood of a person if he/she kills another person. This shows how valuable people are to God because we are made in the image of God.

There is a big debate about capital punishment today. Some people will say, "So what if this guy killed seven people? Let him live in jail. Don't take his life." But God says the only thing that can match those lives is his life. Now, the Bible makes great provision, especially when you study the Mosaic law, that when a person accidentally kills someone, they had a provision to protect those people. But whenever a person murders someone on purpose, they should be put to death. It begins here: it is found before the Mosaic law, under the Mosaic law, and after the Mosaic law.

Read Genesis 9:6. The man in this verse isn't an individual. It means the government will incorporate Capital Punishment. This isn't vengeance. It is justice. It shows the value of life. Remember, there are three institutions that God put together. 1. Marriage & family. 2. Government. Which helps man to control himself. Make laws, rules, regulations. (Romans 13:1) 3. The church. The Body of Christ, which God had set apart.

Read Genesis 9:7. God repeated his command to fill the earth. Next, God reminds Noah of the Covenant that He is going to make with him.

Read Genesis 9:8-10. Who are Noah's descendants? Everybody. Including us today. This covenant is unconditional. We don't do anything. God does it all. The breadth of this covenant is with Noah, his descendants, and every living creature, including the animals and birds that were on the ark.

Read Genesis 9:11. God says I establish His covenant with us: "Never again shall there be a flood to destroy the earth." The Hebrew word for flood here is Marbul. It is only used to describe this worldwide flood. It is never used to describe little, local floods. Now, God is going to give us a sign of the covenant.

Read Genesis 9:12-17. Apparently, before the Flood, there wasn't any rain, so people probably hadn't seen a rainbow before. So now God says that whenever it rains, the rainbow will be seen in the clouds, and He will remember (or keep his promise) to not destroy the earth by a worldwide flood again. Beginning in the next verse, verse 18, we are going to get a closer look at Noah and his sons. We are going to see righteous Noah sin. (by his drunkenness.) And tied into Noah's failure is his son, Ham's failure. Scripture never minimizes sin, even by those who are committed to God.

Read Genesis 9:18. Who do you think of when you hear about Canaan? The Canaanites. The Land of Canaan. The land that God told Abraham to go to. That was the land that God was going to give to him. Descendants of the Canaanites included 6-7 different peoples. Jubusites, Hivites, *electric lights.* Haha. You never know who they are going to be.

Read Genesis 9:19. The whole earth was populated by these three sons of Noah.

Now, here are some questions I want you to think about as we go through this passage.

1. Why does righteous Noah sin? What did he do?

2. What did Ham do to Noah? The Bible doesn't tell us.

3. Why is Ham's son, Canaan, cursed for something he didn't do?

Read Genesis 9:20-21. Drunkenness is never excused in the Bible. It is always wrong. It is always condemned. Now for a footnote. I have never drunk alcohol. I made a choice not to drink a long time ago. I didn't want drinking to be a stumbling block for anybody. Look what happened to Noah. He got drunk and became naked, which is immoral behavior.

Read Genesis 9:22. There is no indication of sexual impropriety. But we really don't know what happened. There are two viewpoints about this. 1. Ham had homosexual relations with his father. 2. Ham gazed and then went out and made fun of his father.

Read Genesis 9:23. Shem and Japheth, in this verse, show respect to their father by not looking at his nakedness and by covering him up.

Read Genesis 9:24. Noah knew what Ham, his younger son, had done to him. Maybe his other sons told him. We don't know. But Noah's sin and Ham's sin affected everyone's descendants. In the next few verses, we are going to see a curse and a blessing.

Read Genesis 9:25. This is the cursing. Noah cursed Canaan. (Canaanites - people whom God gave over to Joshua and the Hebrews). Not Ham. Not Ham's other sons, who were Cush (Ethiopia), Mizraim (Egypt), and Put (Libia). Noah gives a prophetic statement about the future Canaanite nation. When Joshua and the Hebrews entered the Promised Land, they destroyed the Canaanites. Which was the ultimate fulfilment of Noah's curse. The prophecy against Canaan was possibly because the future people, called the Canaanites, wouldn't follow the true God and also had sexual perversion lifestyles.

Read Genesis 9:26-27. This is a blessing. The Lord is blessed or praised because of Shem's blessing. He is also the God of Shem. Eber will be the descendant of Shem. Abraham will be a descendant of Shem. So that means that Isaac, Jacob, Joseph, David and eventually Jesus would be descendants of Shem.

Read Genesis 9:28-29. Noah died at the age of 950.

CHAPTER NINE

The Tower of Babel
Genesis 10 - 11

We are going to study chapters 10-11. Now, don't worry. I will get us out on time. We are going to go through the passage pretty quickly because chapter 10 and most of chapter 11 is just a listing of the descendants of Noah's sons. Also, we are going to see once again the wickedness of man as man continues to rebel against God's commands.

Do you wish you could speak other languages? Have you ever wondered why there are so many different languages? There are over 3000 different languages and dialects. Some are more difficult than others. Chinese is one of the most difficult languages. People who come to America say that English is tough because there is no egg in eggplant, no pine in pineapple, no ham in hamburger, and why do we park on a driveway and drive on a parkway? We ship by truck and send cargo by ship. How can a slim chance and a fat chance be the same thing? A house burns up as it burns down. We fill in a form as we fill it out. And finally, do you know anybody you would touch with a ten-foot pole? Languages are barriers sometimes.

Now, we are going to see the beginning of the languages. Remember, the book of Genesis, which is the book of beginnings, can be divided into two big sections. The first 11 chapters deal with four big events in the human race (creation, Fall, Flood, division of the nations), and then beginning in chapter 12, which is our study, the next lesson through chapter 50 is about four people (Abraham, Isaac, Jacob, Joseph).

From the three sons of Noah, Shem, Ham, and Japheth, the people spread across the world. The nations that descended from Shem include the Hebrews, Chaldeans, Assyrians, Persians, and Syrians. Abraham, David, and Jesus descended from Shem. They basically settled in Western Mesopotamia, Assyria, Arabia, and other lands of the Middle East. The nations that descended from Ham include Canaanites, Egyptians, the Philistines, the Hittites, and the Amorites. They basically settled in Canaan, Egypt, Ethiopia, Arabia, Asia Minor and the rest of Africa. The nations that descended from Japheth include the Greeks, the Thracians, and the Scythians. They basically settled in Europe and the northern areas of Asia.

Read Genesis 10:1. The purpose of these generational listings here is to identify the geographical distributions of the people and the nations that came from the sons of Noah after the flood.

Read verse 2. Japheth had seven sons.

Read verse 6. Ham had four sons.

Read verse 22. Shem had six sons.

Look at verses 9-10. Nimrod wasn't really a mighty hunter. In Hebrew, it literally meant that he was a man or had become a renowned person. Notice he founded Babel or Babylon (which is only 20 miles south of Baghdad, Iraq)

Notice in verse 11 that he also built the capital city of Assyria, which is called Nineveh. This was the wicked city that the prophet Jonah was sent to later.

Read verse 25. What does it mean that the earth was divided? A couple of theories. Some believe that it just means that the people were spread out across the world. But God already told them to do that. But I don't know if that is the best theory. Some believe that up to that time, many of the continents were still close together, and then God moved the continents apart. We don't know. But how did people get on all these different continents?

Read verse 32. This is a summary statement about the families separating around the world after the flood.

Now, turn to chapter 11. The first nine verses of this chapter talk about the tower of Babel. Realize this: the reason they were supposed to spread out across the world was because God commanded it. They actually spread out because of God's action. The people decided not to spread out. They came to the plain of Shinar, and the people decided to stay there and build this big tall tower, most likely a ziggurat, which looked like a pyramid. They were most often built as pagan temples. They would worship false gods on the top of the ziggurat. Some ziggurats were as high as 300 feet and were often just as wide. They were the focal point of the city. They wanted it to reach into heaven as a monument to their own greatness. But God told them to spread out. He told the people to scatter out. But they didn't obey, so God had to deal with them.

Read Chapter 11:1. It literally said: "that the whole world had one lip." Which means that everyone in the world spoke the same language. What language do you think they spoke? We don't know.

Read Chapter 11:2. Best that we can determine is that this is modern-day Iraq, which was located in ancient Babylonia (southern Mesopotamia). Probably between the Tigris (east side) and the Euphrates (west side) rivers. Notice in this verse that it says they settled there. Weren't they supposed to spread out like God told them to do?

Read Chapter 11:3-4. They wanted to build a tower and make a name for themselves because we didn't want to scatter abroad. Three problems here.

1. They wanted to make a tower to worship false gods or be like God.

2. They wanted to make a name for themselves, which is pride. Pride caused the fall of man, and pride caused the fall of Lucifer.

3. They disobey God's word. He told them to spread out. People have always wanted to do their own thing.

Read Chapter 11:5. God sees everything. Read verse 6. The Lord said that they were disobeying, not spreading out, worshipping false gods, and being prideful. So, how is God going to deal with this? Look at verse 7.

Read Chapter 11:7. We are going to find that when God goes down there, He is going to confuse their language. Can you imagine the scene when God changes up their language into thousands of different ones? Panic time, right? Read chapter 11:8. So the people then scatter out in order to find people who speak the same language as themselves. But there was a time in history that God reversed this temporarily. When? At Pentecost everyone could hear in their own language.

Read Genesis 11:9. Babel literally means confusion. The city of Babylon is a picture of false worship all through the Bible. Whenever you read about Babylon in the Bible, it has that connotation. False worship, rebellion and confusion. In the book of Isaiah 14, when Lucifer's fall is told about, do you remember what Lucifer is called in this chapter? He is called the king of Babylon.

Read Genesis 11:10. Shem's generation is detailed here. Why not Ham's or Japheth's generation? Because it will be Shem whom Abraham, Isaac, Jacob, Joseph, David, and Jesus will come.

Read Genesis 11:27. Here is where Abram is introduced.

CHAPTER TEN

Promise to Abram
Genesis 12:1-3

In this lesson, we will begin looking at the life of Abram. He is one of the descendants of Noah through Shem. God called Abram from the city of Ur in the Chaldeans to go to the land of Canaan, which we know as the Promised Land of Israel. Beginning with this lesson, we are going to see a change in the way that God deals with mankind. Because up to this point, God has dealt with the human race as a whole. But now God is going to choose one man. God is going to make a promise to that one man. And through this man will come a people we call the Jewish people. And the rest of the Bible, especially the OT, deals with this man and his descendants.

We are going to look at the promises God gave to Abram. Three questions.

1. What was the covenant?

2. Was the covenant conditional or unconditional?

3. How does this most important covenant affect the rest of the Bible?

Did you ever have to move? Go to another place where you didn't know anyone? I have had to do so many times in my life. Each time is stressful and difficult. Because you live in a place of security going to an unknown. Well, we are going to study about Abram leaving his home in Ur of the Chaldeans to a land that God says He will show you.

Beginning with chapter 12 and continuing through the end of the book, there are four people who stand out. Abraham, Isaac, Jacob, Joseph.

Ur of the Chaldeans is in southern Iraq, and Abram and his family, including his father Teerah, move to Haran, which is in southern Turkey. Then, finally, to Canaan.

In Ur, the people there worshipped a moon goddess called Nana, which means sin. This was false worship, of course.

Read Genesis 11:27-28. So Abram's brother (Haran) dies, and his boy, Lot, needs someone to look after him. Abram's wife was Sarai, which means naggar. Abram's name means high father. So you have big daddy and naggar. Read Genesis 11:29. Why do you think Moses wanted us to know that Sarai was barren? Well, because we are going to see that Abram's descendants are going to come through Sarai. And it is vital that she has the baby. When Abram leaves, Abram is 75 years old, and Sarai is 65 years old. (Genesis 12:4). Back then, people thought that if you didn't have babies, then God wasn't blessing you.

Read Genesis 11:31. Is it Terah's idea to go to Canaan? Look at Acts 7:2-4. Abram was supposed to leave his relatives in Ur. But his father, Teerah, went with him. Then died in the city of Haran. Then God had Abram move into the land that He would show him, which is Canaan.

Read Genesis 12:1-3. This is what we call the Abrahamic covenant, which God makes with him. This is an unconditional covenant. Abram didn't have to do anything. Except leave Ur of the Chaldeans. The Mosaic covenant was conditional upon obedience to God's commandments.

Why was Abram chosen and not somebody else? It wasn't because he was a great man. It was only because God chose him.

However, after he was chosen by God, what made him a special man? First of all, he was a man of faith. All of us who come to God by faith are children of Abraham in that sense. Because he is the father of all who believe. Second, he is a pattern of justification. He is a picture of when you believe, you become righteous and declared righteous. He is that picture. Thirdly, the promises to Abraham affect all the rest of the Bible. Who comes through Abraham? First of all, the Jewish people do. And ultimately, who comes through Abraham? Yeshua. Who is Jesus Christ.

And also the second thing that comes from this covenant is the nation. There is a people called the Jews or the offspring of Abraham. God is going to have a land for them. God is going to bless them. He says He will bless those who bless them. And God says that He will curse those who curse them. Also, notice in verse 3 that all the families on the earth will be blessed by this nation. This covenant that God made with Abram over 3000 years ago affects every one of us in this room. How are we blessed through Abraham? Well, because the Messiah came, died for us, conquered death, and was resurrected because God was satisfied. And if we put our faith in Jesus as our savior, we have eternal life. That's a blessing to us.

In this covenant, there are three parts. Land, seed, blessing.

First of all, the land promised to his descendants. It is called Canaan. We see the dimensions of the land in chapter 15. It was from the river of Egypt, which might be the modern-day river called Wadi el-Arish, to the Euphrates, which is in Iraq. This might have included modern-day Jordan and Syria. Now, they have never possessed it all yet. But they will when Jesus returns, and they accept him as the Messiah. God said that as long as they obeyed Him, they would get to live in the land. But if they didn't obey, God would move them out of the land for a while. Then bring them back. Happened over and over and over. In that chapter, we see God signing this agreement by giving Abram a sign, a smoking oven and a flaming torch passing between the pieces of cut heifer, female goat, and ram. Also, a turtledove and pigeon.

Second, the promise of seed. The offspring of Abram was Isaac, Jacob, who had 12 sons that became the 12 tribes. Then Judah and David. And the ultimate seed was Jesus Christ. God promises to make Abram a great nation. And they have been. How could there come a great nation from Abram since Sarai was barren? Well, he could adopt his nephew Lot and make him his heir. Nope. He could have come from his servant, Eliezer, but God said "no." Did God want him to take another woman? No. He did and messed up. God was going to do a miracle in his wife, Sarai. And that is what is going to happen.

The third aspect of the covenant is the blessing. The greatest blessing to mankind is in Jesus Christ. Matthew 1 begins by giving the generation of Jesus, who was the son of David and the son of Abraham. This is the promise. The blessing. Jesus was the Messiah.

We will see in chapter 17 that God changes his name to Abraham, which means father of many nations. And changed Sarai to Sarah, which means princess of God. Through them is going to be the people. And ultimately, the Messiah. Also, the Jewish people are the ones who wrote down God's revelation, the Bible. All 66 books were written by Jews. The only author who might be a gentile is Luke. Because of one of the statements that Paul makes. But he probably was Jewish also.

Abram's Failure in Egypt
Genesis 12:4-20

So far in Genesis, we have studied the story of Creation, the story of Adam, the story of Noah and have begun the story of Abraham. Last time, we studied what God said to Abram to leave his country and go to the land, which He would show him. Then, God made a covenant with Abram. In that covenant, there was a land which God would show him, the seed (great nation), and the blessing (ultimately the blessing of the coming Messiah). And we discovered that this covenant is the key to understanding the whole Bible. We are going to look at old Abram. We are going to see that he worships God. In fact, it seems to be the characteristic of his life, especially in the first part of chapter 12, that wherever he goes, he worships God. But then we are going to see failure. One of the things that we see in the Bible, over and over, is that it hides nothing. May we worship God and trust Him.

Have you ever heard of a white lie? People say, "That's just a little white lie." A white lie is sort of a lie, kind of a half-truth. Well, there isn't such a thing as a half-truth. Either it is true, or it is false. When you lie, it destroys how people look at you. And what people are going to believe about you. Question. Do you tell the truth? Do you sometimes tell white lies? Abram is going to tell a half-truth. A white lie. And when he lies, it causes a failure and causes a loss of his testimony with an unbelieving king. How did it happen? He failed to trust God. It was dealing with his circumstances. You can't control your circumstances. But you can control your response to things that happen.

Read Genesis 12:4. So Abram has now left Haran. Remember, his father went with him to Haran (Syria) from Ur (Iraq). But his father, Terah, died at the age of 205 in Haran. Abram is now 75 years old. He has 100 more years to live.

Read Genesis 12:5. They have made this long trip north to Haran via the route of the two rivers, and now they (Abram, Sarai, and Lot) are leaving and heading south to the land of Canaan. And there are people who have agreed to come with them too. We are going to find later on that there are 318 men in his household. This was when they rescued Lot in chapter 14:14.

Read Genesis 12:6. They went through Canaan all the way to Shechem, which is about 30 miles north of Jerusalem. Notice that the descendants of Ham's son, Canaan, are living on the land.

Read Genesis 12:7. God appeared to Abram to reaffirm the covenant. God says to Abram, "To your descendants, I will give this land." Over 4000 years ago, according to the Jewish calendar. Now, throughout history, the Assyrians, Babylonians, Medes & Persians, Macedonians, Romans, Turks, Ottoman Empire, and Arabs have controlled it. But this land doesn't belong to anybody but 1 group of people. The Jewish people because God gave it to them. Do you see what Abram did? He built an altar to the Lord. An altar is a place of sacrifice and a place of worship. Today, we don't sacrifice animals to cover sin anymore. Why? Because our sins have already been paid for by Christ on the cross, he sacrificed for us. We do, however, offer the sacrifice of our lives for Christ. We offer the sacrifice of our lips. We offer the sacrifice of praise, good works, giving, etc. The second aspect of an altar is worship. Worship is responding to God. Many people are confused about worship. They think worship is an emotion. The truth is Worship is singing, praying, giving, or applying the truths of God's Word. And you worship individually during your daily quiet time.

Read Genesis 12:8. Abram built another altar to the Lord near Bethel (south of Shechem) and worshipped Him. Abram calls upon the name of the Lord. This is an act of trust. Bethel means house of God. In a footnote, Romans 10:13 where says, "Whoever will call on the name of the Lord will be saved." This is not for eternal salvation. It actually is calling upon the name of the Lord for deliverance from some type of enemy or some type of fear that they may have. Because the next verse says, "How then will they call on Him in whom they have not believed?"

Now, we are going to see Abram's failure. The truth is that in our own lives, things are going great, and then something happens, and we fail. Read Genesis 12:9. The Negev is the southern part of Israel.

Read Genesis 12:10. Question? Do you think Abram should have left the land? Why? God didn't tell him to. We also don't see Abram asking God if he should leave the land. All we see is God telling him to go to that land that He was going to give him. But now Abram is going to leave that land because things aren't going that great right now. He didn't trust God there. Does the famine mean that he is out of the will of God? No. Abram decides to go south to Egypt, probably the leading nation in the world at that time.

So what happened? Read Genesis 12:11. How old is Sarai? At least 65. And Abram thinks that she is beautiful. Right.

Read Genesis 12:12. Abram feared that if the Pharaoh knew she was his wife, they would kill him so that she could be added to the Egyptian's harem. He has forgotten God's promise to make him a great nation. He isn't trusting God.

Read Genesis 12:13. Was Sarai, his sister? Well, kind of. She was his half-sister. (daughter of his father but not his mother) So, he pleads with Sarai to tell a white lie. A half-truth. He is depending on Sarai to protect him instead of God.

Read Genesis 12:14-16. It happened just as Abram had worried. The Egyptians found Sarai to be beautiful and took her into Pharaoh's house. And have Abram lots of presents. Do you see the problem? If Sarai now belongs to Pharaoh, how is the nation of Israel ever going to come through her? Abram has jeopardized the promise of the seed. The Messiah. Can you imagine the shame of Abram as he gave away his wife? He was fearing man instead of fearing God. But look what happens?

God is going to take care of His plan. Through whom is the seed going to come? Abram and his wife, Sarai. Does Abram believe that? No. What does Abram do later in chapter 16? He sleeps with one of those Egyptian maids named Hagar, whom he picked up down there in Egypt.

Read Genesis 12:17. The Lord struck Pharaoh and his house with plagues because of Sarai.

Read Genesis 12:18. Pharaoh asks Abram, "Why have you lied to me? I didn't lie to you. I didn't do anything wrong to you. You are a *real* man of God, Abram. Why didn't you tell me Sarai was your wife." The worshipper of the true God has lied.

Read Genesis 12:19. Pharaoh tells Abram to take his wife and go.

Read Genesis 12:20. Pharaoh has them escorted out. *"Don't let the door hit you as you leave."*

Abram failed to trust God. He lied. He lost his testimony. Folks, your actions will reflect what you believe. And when you are not trusting God, sometimes it pushes people away. Instead of bringing people to God.

CHAPTER ELEVEN

Abram Trusts God
Genesis 13

Open your Bibles to Genesis 13. We are going to see how God is always faithful and keeps His promises. By the way, God's promises to us are not based on our faithfulness but on God's faithfulness. He promised to us in this room, all of us who have put our faith in Jesus as Savior, eternal life. Is it based on our faithfulness or His faithfulness? His faithfulness. We are going to see that even the promises that God gave Abram are based on God's character, His promise, and His faithfulness. Not Abram's. He has already messed up. Remember, we saw Abram's failure as he went down to Egypt and lied. Well, we are going to see how Abram trusts God. Some great things happen. His actions and God's promises. Let's begin by going to the Lord in prayer. Let's pray.

Yo-Yos. Did anybody here grow up playing with a yo-yo? They have been around for a long time. Yo-Yos go up and down. Do you ever think that you are a yo-yo? Sometimes, you feel like you're up when things are going well, and sometimes, you feel like you're down when things aren't going well. We have started studying the life of Abram. And when you look at his life, he is like a yo-yo in this section. Because he is up, and he is down. Last time, we studied about a time when he was down. There was a famine in Canaan, so Abram went down to Egypt. He lies to the Pharaoh about his wife, Sarai. And Pharaoh catches him in the lie and exhorts them away. Well, we are going to see him come back up. And we are going to see that he trusts God.

We are going to see the story of Abram and Lot in chapter 13. Now, God is going to make one conditional covenant and four unconditional covenants with the nation of Israel. So far, we have seen one of those unconditional covenants. The Abrahamic covenant. The land, the seed, and the blessing. The other three un-conditional covenants all tie into the Abrahamic covenant. They are Genesis 15 and Deuteronomy 28, which is the Palestinian or the land covenant. The one in 2 Samuel is the Davidic covenant, which dealt with the seed or the Messiah. The covenant in Jeremiah 31:31-34 dealt with the new covenant, the blessing. The only conditional covenant that God made dealt with the law. The Mosaic Covenant. Now remember the Abrahamic covenant is going to come through Abram and Sarai. Not Sarai and Pharoah. Not Abram and Hagar.

Read Genesis 13:1. So here we see Abram, Sarai, and Lot are coming back from Egypt to the Negev.

Read Genesis 13:2. Why is Abram rich? Yes, Pharaoh gave him some things. But really, because God said, "I will bless you. I will make you a great nation." Abram is already getting blessed. Why? Because God is going to take care of him. But a conflict is fixing to start. Can you think of anyone he brought back from Egypt that he shouldn't have brought with him? Hagar, the Egyptian slave woman, becomes Sarai's servant. Because later in chapter 16, we are going to see Abram and Sarai make a big mistake, and they once again fail to trust God.

Read Genesis 13:3. Do you remember what Abram did the first time he stopped at Bethel? (Beit-el in Hebrew means house of God). He put an altar there and worshipped God. He is coming back there and probably saying, "I should have never left this place." Sometimes in our lives, we are doing really good, and then we blow it. And then we come back to God. We confess our sins.

Read 13:4. What does it mean to "call upon the name of the Lord?" He is saying, "God, take care of me." Asking for blessing and protection. It is the aspect of worship. Folks, remember that with God, you can also come back to Him and start over. When we fail, that 1 John 1:9 passage is there for us. "If we confess our sins, He is faithful and righteous to forgive us our sins and to cleanse us from all unrighteousness."

Abram is rich in livestock, silver, and gold. He has been given land, a blessing, and a promise to become a great nation. He has a place where he can worship the Lord. But with all of that, problems are going to arise. Folks, even if you are a Christian living for God, you will have problems because we live in a Fallen world. Abram is going to have a problem with his family and Lot. Is he going to trust God or fail again by trusting himself?

Read Genesis 13:5-6. They have so many possessions that they are crowded.

Read Genesis 13:7. Notice that it is the herdsmen of Lot and Abram that were conflicting. And notice that the Canaanites and the Perizzites were also dwelling in the land. So, I guess the famine didn't get them.

Now, look at who takes the initiative in settling the dispute. Read Genesis 13:8. Abram goes to deal with this situation because a family shouldn't argue. Abram probably told Lot, "Hey, we are family. We have got to stick together. There are foreign and hostile neighbors all around. We need to take care of one another." There is a truth there. Christians, we are brothers and sisters. We live in a hostile world. We need to take care of one another and not let arguments and disagreements damage our relationship and hamper our progress toward our goals of serving Christ and loving one another.

Look what Abram is going to do next. He could have said, "Lot, I am your elder. God gave this land to me. So you need to leave." But Abram didn't do that even though He had a right to. Let's see what he did.

Read Genesis 13:9. This is an incredible truth. Abram is offering Lot his choice. "Lot, if you want to go this direction, I will leave and go someplace else." For the sake of the family. He put family peace above personal freedom.

Question: Is Abram about to give away the land that God gave him?

No. Because Abram knew it was all his land anyway. Doesn't matter where he goes. He is trusting God. Watch what happens.

Read Genesis 13:10. Now, south of the Dead Sea, the area where Sodom and Gomorrah were, is completely barren. The land looks like it has been completely burned off. The whole place is just wiped out. That used to be a well-watered area where these two cities were. And God zonked it. And we are going to see in chapter 19 why. Now here, Lot looked at that piece of land and said, "Hmmm. There is a good piece of land. Well-watered. Like a garden. Lots of places for my animals. If I get to pick first, I am going to pick the very best place." And Abram didn't say a word. Abram had faith in the Lord. But Lot didn't look at the character of the people that lived there. We are going to see in verse 13 that they were very wicked. He knew that but didn't care. He was selfish.

Read Genesis 13:11-12. Life is a series of choices. We, too, can choose the best while ignoring the needs of others. When we stop making choices in God's direction, all that is left is to make choices in the wrong direction. Lot failed to recognize that wicked Sodom could provide temptations strong enough to destroy his family. Folks, do get caught up in the world.

Question: Are you living for God or living for yourself?

It is a choice.

Read Genesis 13:13. Do you think Lot knew the people of Sodom were wicked before he moved there? Yes, I think he did. And didn't care. He was caught in it. Folks, if you think you can go and mess around with worldly pleasures and not have it affect you, you are wrong. You are fooling yourself. It will warp you.

Now, watch what God is going to do with Abram.

Read Genesis 13:14-15. God is saying to Abram, look around, see all this land; I am going to give it to you and to your descendants forever." How long? Forever. When they are arguing now in Israel about whose land is it, Whose land is it? It is the Jewish people. And the idea of giving the Palestinians land for peace is absolutely the craziest thing I have ever heard. Lot chose for himself. God chose for Abram. Lot said, "I will take that." God said, "I will give that." Lot ended up losing his family in chapter 19. Abram ended up gaining a family because he trusted God.

Read Genesis 13:16. How many kids does Abram have at that time? None. He is probably 80 years old, and God says, "You are going to have a big family."

Read Genesis 13:17. Now, why did God tell Abram to do that? Because in that culture, if you walked on the land and marked it off, it was yours. To exercise authority over it.

Read Genesis 13:18. How did Abram respond to God? He worshipped Him. How do you and I respond to God? We worship Him.

CHAPTER TWELVE

Abram's Choices
Genesis 14

Open your Bibles to Genesis 14. Last time, we saw strife between the herdsmen of Abram and the herdsmen of Lot, so they separated. And we saw that Abram trusted God and allowed Lot to settle in any part of the land he desired. And we read that Lot, Abram's nephew, chose the beautiful, well-watered valley *near* Sodom. (70 miles south near the southern tip of the Dead Sea). But then the Lord came to Abram on the mountain near Bethel (10 miles north of Jerusalem) and told him to look in all directions because God would give him and his descendants all the land he could see forever. And then Abram again (third altar) built an altar to the Lord. This time in Hebron (20 miles south of Jerusalem).

Now, the passage is going to deal with choices. Lot chose to live in Sodom. We will read about a war in chapter 14, and Lot gets taken off in captivity. We are going to see Abram make the choice to try to save Lot from these raiding kings. Then, when

Abram comes back from the battle, two kings come out to meet him. One is the king of Sodom, and the other is a man named Melchizedek, who is the king of Salem (Jerusalem). And Abram has a choice to make when these kings come out to meet him. Choices. May we realize that we are responsible for the choices that we make.

Choices. We make them every day. We are accountable for the choices that we make. Are we living our lives based on the Word of God? Or are we living our lives based on the pulls of this world? The Word or the world? We are going to see several choices that Abram makes.

Well, let me break down the passage for you. Genesis 14. Verses 1-12 – the land gets invaded. Verses 13-16 is Abram going to rescue Lot, and we are going to see what happens there. Then, verses 17-24, we will look at Melchizedek. He is mentioned here in Genesis 14:17-20, Psalm 110:4, and Hebrews 5-7.

Well, let's begin. Read Genesis 14:1-3. So we see that four kings of the north made a Suzerain treaty with five kings of the south. This was kind of like paying protection to the bully on the street so he wouldn't beat you up or let anyone else do so, either. Now, these places were actually city-states. There was a wall around each city, and there was a leader of the city called a king.

Read Genesis 14:4. So for 12 years, the five southern cities paid tribute to the Chedorlaomer, the king of Elam, who whooped them. But in the 13th year, they rebelled and stopped paying.

Read Genesis 14:5. So that made King Chedorlaomer mad, so he and his other cronies decided to go get them. They put the whoop on lots of cities as they headed south to rough up the five kings who stopped paying tribute. Read Genesis 14:6-9. They actually go past Abram and make a loop back towards Sodom.

Read Genesis 14:10-11. So we see that the four kings of the north really defeated the five rebellious kings of the south.

Read Genesis 14:12. Notice that Lot is now living *in* Sodom. Lot made the choice to live among the exceedingly wicked and sinners against the Lord. Now, he and his possessions have been captured by the powerful Chedorlaomer. Now, Abram may have had a Suzerain treaty with Lot to protect and look after him. So Abram now has a choice. Is he going to fulfill his responsibility and attempt to rescue his nephew Lot? Or is Abram going to say, "Well, he shouldn't have been down with the Sodomites anyway." What will he do? Look at Genesis 14:13.

So they came and told Abram what had happened. Notice Abram is known as the Hebrew. Remember what Hebrew meant? One who crosses over. Remember Abram crossed over the Tigris and the Euphrates rivers to come into Canaan when he left the homeland of the Ur of the Chaldeans.

Read Genesis 14:14. So Abram made the choice to rescue Lot. He led his trained (prepared to fight) men; how many men? 318 men and went in pursuit as far as Dan. Do you know where Dan is? It's way up north of the Sea of Galilee. (about 225 miles). By the way, how many fighting men did the four northern kings, including the powerful Chedorlaomer, have in their army? Probably a whole lot more than just 318. So Abram had the courage that came from God! He trusted the Lord! God is the mightiest warrior! What is impossible with men is always possible with God!

Read Genesis 14:15. God defeated the bad guys. God removed them from the land. Damascus is even further north than Dan. God gets the victory.

Read Genesis 14:16. Abram brought back Lot, the possessions, the women, the people, everybody! We need to trust God. You never know when you will be called upon to complete difficult tasks. Also, we need to be willing to act immediately when others need our help. Be prepared.

Read Genesis 14:17-18. Now, when Abram comes back down south, two kings go out to meet him. The first one is the King of Sodom. And the second one is the king of Salem (Jerusalem). He was the king of peace. That is what Salem means. Jerusalem means Jehovah's peace. His name is Melchizedek. His name means "king of righteousness".

Notice he is also a priest of God Most High. The first priest in Scripture. He wasn't from the Aaronic lineage of the tribe of Levi. Because they came later in history. He brings Abram bread and wine. It sounds like the Lord's Supper, doesn't it? Melchizedek is a foreshadowing of Christ. He was a picture of Christ. Just the Passover lamb is a picture of Christ. He wasn't Christ, as some have theorized.

Read Hebrews 7:1-3. In fact, Jesus became a priest after the order of Melchizedek. (Psalm 110:4) He is a foreshadowing of Christ. Christ was from the tribe of Judah. Not the tribe of Levi. But Christ was a priest because of the order of Melchizedek. (Psalm 110:4)

Melchizedek was a king-priest, just like Jesus was to be. Melchizedek was a foreshadow of Christ. Read Hebrews 9:11-12. Jesus was the high priest who, after the resurrection, went into a 'tabernacle' in heaven into the holy place with his own blood offered up to God. Read Hebrews 10:4. Blood of animals can't take away sins. But look at Hebrews 10:12. Jesus offered one sacrifice for sins for all time, then sat down at the right hand of God. It is finished, so He sits down.

Read Genesis 14:19-20. Melchizedek recognized God as the Creator of heaven and earth. God owns it all. He blesses Abram and praises God. "Blessed be God Most High" (el el elyown). And look what Abram did? Abram gave a tenth of everything he had to Melchizedek. Abram recognizes that Melchizedek worshipped the same God as he did.

Read Genesis 14:21. The king of Sodom says to Abram, "Give me the people of my city, and you can keep the spoil." "I am rich because God gave it to me. Not you. "

Read Genesis 14:22-23. Abram replies to the king of Sodom, "I'm not taking anything from you." Why? These Sodomites were wicked. And he didn't want anything to do with them. They weren't friends of God. In fact, Abram promises the Lord

God that he won't take the money. And Abram keeps his promise.

Read Genesis 14:24. Abram only wants his own fighting men that he took with him. Trust God.

The choices you make will be the consequences of tomorrow. We are responsible for our choices.

Question: Where are you seeking blessing? From the world or from God? Are you seeking the things temporal or seeking the things eternal? Lot wanted the temporal stuff. And Abram rested in the unseen God and trusted Him.

Question: Who are you identifying with? The world or the Word? The unrighteous or the righteous? Lot's choice was with the unrighteous of Sodom. Abram's choice was with the righteous. Melchizedek.

CHAPTER THIRTEEN

Abrahamic Covenant Confirmed
Genesis 15:1-21

Open your Bibles to Genesis 15. In this chapter, we are going to see a number of things. What we are first going to see here is that Abram and God are dialoging. Because Abram, in a sense, is questioning, "Is God really going to take care of him?" Apparently, Abram has got himself in trouble. Then God is going to remind him of his promises. He talks about the offspring, the seed and the land. Then Abram asks God again about the future, and God comes back and answers Abram. And before the end of this chapter, God is going to tell Abram about the land and how big it is. The key to the passage is the trustworthiness of God. Whatever God says comes to pass. Whatever God promises comes to pass. God will always do what He says.

Question for us: Do we trust the promises of God? And do you even know the promises that He has given to us?

Two things we are going to study.

1. How can a person be righteous with God? God is a righteous God, and if anyone is going to have a relationship with God, they are going to have to be righteous.

2. We are going to see God ratify His covenant. Now, He made the covenant, but He didn't cut the covenant or sign the document, so to speak.

People will ask me, How did people in the OT get saved? And the question that they are asking is: Is it different from the NT? I mean, we see all these OT people coming to God with these sacrifices; they had the laws, first of the ten commandments, then the 613 commandments that God gave the nation of Israel. Well, first of all, how are people saved in the NT? By faith in the Messiah. Jesus died on the cross, paying for our sins, was buried and rose again. He offers us eternal life when we believe in Him. Well, the people in the OT are saved exactly the same way as the people in the NT. We are saved by faith. Now, the OT people didn't know Him as Jesus Christ, but they knew him by the seed of woman, the seed of Abraham, and the seed of David. By faith, they believed in the coming of the Messiah. And not only does God give them and us eternal life, but righteousness.

That's what we are going to look at in Genesis 15. You see, none of us are righteous. None of us can measure up. So what does God do? He says, "The righteousness you demand, I give it to you." And we are going to see that in this passage. Genesis 15 is one of the great chapters in the Bible. We will see the trustworthiness of God. He does exactly what He says He will do. And God assures Abram of His promises. Remember, in Genesis 12, God made a covenant with Abram. God said, leave your home and go to the land He would show Him. He was going to give Abram a seed, a land and a blessing. Now, we will see God stamp the covenant, so to speak. And they did it a little differently back then.

Now, put yourself in Abram's place for a moment. You have 318 men and a big victory over four powerful kings. Now you are back at your house. What if those four kings come back? What if they get more armies than they had? What if they decide to come after just Abram? What if they kill me? What if they take all my possessions? What if they take the land that God has given to me? I think Abram begins to worry in chapter 15, and so God assures him. God says, "I am your strength. I am your shield. I am your provision."

Here's the breakdown of this chapter. Verses 1-6 are the promises given to Abram of an offspring. Verses 7-21 are the promises of the land. God cuts the covenant.

Read Genesis 15:1. Why is Abram afraid? Maybe he was afraid that the kings might regroup and come after him. But God is going to remind him not to be afraid.

God is going to protect him. God is going to be a shield to him. And God provided for him. God says your reward shall be very great. What more do we want? Provision and protection. You want what you need, and you want to be taken care of and protected. In the Psalms, it says, the Lord is our strength and our shield. What does He do for us? He says He will never leave us nor forsake us. He provides for us. He supplies all our needs according to His riches in Christ Jesus. Philippians 4:19. We don't have to be afraid.

So I think Abram has settled down a little now, but he still has 1 question. This is my land, I think, I guess, and how am I really going to have any kids? He is older than 75 years. That is how old he was when he left Harran. We don't know how many years have passed. God made the promise, "Through you, you are going to have an offspring, a nation."

So look what he says.

Read Genesis 15:2. What is the world? What does that mean? Well, first of all, he isn't trusting God. He is saying to God, "How am I going to have any offspring since I don't have any kids? The only person who is going to get anything is my servant, Eliezer of Damascus. I treat him like a son because I don't have any kids myself. So what am I supposed to do?" Abram is thinking, "Is this the plan?" How many times does he second-guess this thing? I mean, later on, when they have Hagar, don't they second-guess it again?

Read Genesis 15:3. So after addressing the Lord God (Adonai YHWH), which is the first time it appears in the Bible, he thinks he should adopt his eldest servant as a son, which was a common practice of couples without an heir.

By the way, is this day or night? It's got to be what? Night. What's God going to show him? Stars.

Read Genesis 15:4. God tells him that his heir wouldn't be Eliezer, but one who will come forth from his own body would be his heir.

Read Genesis 15:5. Incredible statement. God promised Abram descendants like the stars in the sky, too numerous to count. Beyond comprehension. When God makes a promise, He keeps it. God has promised us, those of us who have put our faith in Christ, God promises us eternal life. Is it ever going to end? No. If we die, where are we? With Jesus Christ. If we live until He comes, where are we going to be? With Jesus Christ. Are we ever going to be separated from Him? No. Are we going to live with Him? Yes. That's a promise. I see so many people say, "I hope I am going." Hope you're going? He gave His promise.

Now, from this point, how long will it be until Abram has that son? At least 20 years. In God's timing, it will happen. He promised.

Now, there is going to be a little pause in the narrative. You can't see it in your English Bibles. But in Hebrew, it is called a Veuve disjunctive. It's like it sets it apart. It is actually past tense.

Read Genesis 15:6. NASB says, "then", and NIV says, "makes the statement." And NKJV says, "And Abram." But it really could almost translate as "*Now* Abram had believed in the Lord, and it was counted to him as righteousness." When do you think Abram believed God for the first time? When he left Ur in the Chaldeans. The writer of Genesis reminds us that Abram believed in God. The word believes in Hebrew is "Aman" Transliterated into Greek, it is "Amen", which we say verily, verily or truly, truly amen, amen. Transliterated into English, it is Amen. Which means the prayer is over. Which actually means it is true.

Abram believed it was true. And it was counted to him for righteousness. It is faith. He believed in the Lord.

Faith is incredible. But faith isn't the key. What's the key? What you put your faith in. The object of your faith. People say, "Did you really believe?" People really believe in Budda, but that doesn't get them anywhere. It is the object of your faith that counts. Abram believed what the Lord had told him.

Faith has no value unless it links us with God. We don't need a wonderful faith in God; I need faith in a wonderful God. That's the key. Abram believed in the Lord, and God gave him righteousness. And just like Abram, what do we get when we believe in the Lord? We get righteousness. Romans 4:5 Imputation. God gives you His righteousness if you believe by faith in Jesus Christ. This sets us apart from all man-made religions.

Read Genesis 15:7. This is the next day. Now, God is talking to Abram about the land.

Read Genesis 15:8. Abram is looking for confirmation and assurance that the land was his.

Read Genesis 15:9. So God says, "Bring me a heifer, goat, ram, turtledove, and a pigeon."

Read Genesis 15:10. So Abram got the animals and brought them to God and cut them in two, laying each half opposite the other. But not the birds. Now, what would happen back then was when two people were making an agreement, they would get some animals, cut them in two, and then you would grab arms and walk in between the animals that were cut in two. Symbolically saying, "If you don't hold up your half, we are cutting you in two." Now, since both had a part in the agreement, both would walk through. But we are going to find that when God makes a covenant with Abram, does Abram walk through the animals? No. Who walks through the animals? Only God. Because this is an unconditional covenant. Abram doesn't have a part he has to do to make it work. God is going to do it all.

Read Genesis 15:11. Why did the writer even mention that? Probably because God is going to sign the covenant immediately but is going to wait until the sun goes down.

Read Genesis 15:12. There is a reason for this. This deep sleep is called tardemah in Hebrew, the same word which was used for Adam when God took a part of his side to make the woman. I think Abram is seeing the future, a foreshadowing of the terror and the darkness of slavery in Egypt which is to come.

Read Genesis 15:13. If I were Abram, I would probably ask God, "What are my people doing in a land that isn't theirs if you are given this land?" God tells Abram the future. The enslavement of Abram's descendants in Egypt for 400 years.

Read Genesis 15:14. This is the prophecy of Exodus 12:35. The Hebrews plundered their captors before they left Egypt. Did it happen as God said it would? Yes.

Read Genesis 15:15. Abram died at the ripe old age of 175. Genesis 25:8.

Read Genesis 15:16. Who are the four generations? Isaac, Jacob, Joseph, Moses. That doesn't mean that Moses was a descendant of Joseph, but that was the fourth generation from Abram. Everything matches just perfectly. Why does God wait to bring them back to the land? Because the people who were living in the land, the Amorites, the descendants of Canaan, because their iniquity or wickedness is to the point that God is going to judge them, how does God judge the Amorites? God used Abram's descendants, the Hebrews, coming back from 400 years of enslavement, to punish the Amorites by giving their land away.

Question: Are we in America as bad as God is going to let us get before He judges us? Do you think He is going to overlook us? What is God going to do to our country?

Read Genesis 15:17. There is a pot with this flaming torch passing through the cut pieces of animals. That is a manifestation of God. It is called a theophany. It is an unconditional covenant. God didn't get Abram up and make him walk through there with Him. God is going to give Abram an offspring, the land, and a blessing. And He signed the deal.

How big is the land?

Read Genesis 15:18-21. The land is between the Great River in Egypt all the way to the Euphrates. When will Israel possess the land totally? They haven't ever totally possessed it yet. But they will in the future when the king of kings and the Lord of Lords sets on the throne in Jerusalem.

CHAPTER FOURTEEN

Failure to Wait upon the Lord
Genesis 16

We have begun studying the life of Abram, beginning with chapter 12. We have seen him trusting in the Lord, and we have seen him in his failure. Well, in chapter 16, we will see his failure once again. We are glad that the Bible shows people as they are. Sometimes, when we read about Abraham, Isaac, Jacob, Joseph, David, and Saul, we think, "Wow, they are perfect, and we aren't." But the truth is they are just like us. They failed at times, also. Abram fails to wait on God. He fails to trust God to fulfil His plan.

If you remember, God told Abram that in the covenant, He would give him the land, the seed, and the blessing. And God told him to go and look at the stars, and that is how many descendants Abram was going to have. How many offspring through him.

Now Abram and Sarai are talking, and the issue is: I don't know if God is going to do this. And maybe God isn't going to do it through Abram and Sarai. Maybe we have to do something else. We are going to see that Abram fathers a child, but it's not the one that God promised. As we study, may we be reminded that God sees and hears and knows all that goes on. We will always fail if we seek to do things our own way instead of God's way. And the goal, of course, is to wait and trust the Lord. He always does what He promises to do.

When you think about patience, there really are two ways to think about it.

1. God's patience. God is patient with us in His love and mercy; in His grace, He holds back His judgment.

2. Second, when we think about our own patience. We are to wait upon the Lord and trust in Him.

Well, we see Abram not resting in God. And in a sense, Abram loses his patience, and he moves ahead with his own plan for bringing about God's promises. He tried to do it in his own way. He is thinking, "God told me that He would bless me and give me offspring, and now I am 85 years old (10 years have passed since that promise). Where are these kids that God has promised me?" And Sarai is about 75 years old now. No, we see Abram's failure.

Sometimes, in our lives or in the life of the local church, things don't look right. And we look at our life or the problems in it and don't see how it is going to work together for the good. We say, "God, I don't know how this is possibly going to work out." Well, there is never a problem with God's promises. We must trust Him and wait upon Him.

Let me break down this chapter. Chapter 16.

Verses 1-6 – Sarai comes up with a plan so that they can have a child.

Verses 7-14 – We meet Hagar, what happens to her, and how God has to take care of her.

Verses 15-16 – We see the birth of a son.

Read Genesis 16:1. This is a little background verse. Where did Sarai get an Egyptian maid?

Genesis 12, where they journeyed down to Egypt because of the famine in the land. Didn't trust God.

Read Genesis 16:2. Sarai said, "The LORD has prevented her from having children." Well, she is right about that in one sense. It's not time. When it is the right time, she will have the child because God made the promise. So she says, "Why don't we just have the children through Hagar." Now, this is another test. It is a test for Abram. Remember what happened when the famine came into the land? What did Abram do? He failed because he left the land and went to Egypt. Now, there is a famine in the womb.

And Abram is going to fail in the same way he failed earlier. It is always a mistake when we take God's matter into our own hands. It is always a mistake to do our own plans instead of God's.

Now, a common practice of that time was that a married woman who could not have children was shamed by her peers and was often required to give a female servant to her husband for sex in order to produce heirs. The children born to the servant woman were considered the children of the wife.

But polygamy violates God's basic ordinance for marriage, which dates back to creation itself. (Genesis 2:24). Now, think about Jacob (Genesis 30).

Jacob fathered how many sons – 12.

How many women produced those sons – 4.

Two were his wives (Rachel birthed JOSEPH and BENJAMIN) and (Leah birthed REUBEN, SIMEON, LEVI, JUDAH, ISSACHAR, and ZEBULUN), and two were their maids (Bilhah – Rachel's maid birthed DAN, NAPHTALI) and (Zilpah – Leah's maid birthed GAD, ASHER)

By the way, anger, resentment, fighting, rivalry, and jealousy was fierce between their children and descendants.

David had how many wives? 8.

Did that work? No.

Soloman had how many wives? 700. And 300 concubines.

Was it right? No.

What happened? They turned his heart from God. Just because the culture said it was okay for Abram to go into Hagar and produce a child didn't make it right. Sometimes, we follow the flow of the culture. We let it catch us. Everybody does that. They had moved from the Word to the world. And it never works. Why? Because he isn't going to fulfil His promises through sinful methods.

Abram listened to the voice of whom in verse 2. God or Sarai? Sarai. He didn't wait upon the Lord. He abandoned his responsibility of leadership. Whenever there is sin, there are consequences. There is going to be a conflict between Abram and Sarai. Conflict between Sarai and Hagar. Conflict between the offspring of Hagar's child (Ishmael) and descendants (Arabs) and Sarai's child (Isaac) and descendants. (Jews). Have they ever fought? Yes. Do they get along today? No.

Read Genesis 16:3. They took matters into their own hands. They didn't wait upon the Lord. They didn't believe God's promises.

Read Genesis 16:4. Hagar got pregnant and immediately thought, "I'm better than Sarai" Hagar actually looks down upon her mistress. Now, do you think anybody named Naggar (Sarai) is going to put up with that attitude? "Abram get over her right now. Houston, I think we have a problem." You see, the conflict has already started. The result of the disobedience will be the conflict and the consequences.

Read Genesis 16:5. Sarai tells Abram, "It's your fault that this has happened." And in a way, she's right. Abram is the head of the household and he should have said "honey, I'm not going to sleep with Hagar. Bad idea. We need to trust in God." Of course, she is also at fault for coming up with this crazy plan. She didn't trust God either.

Now, sometimes, we do things that put us in a tough situation. Sometimes, we openly violate God's Word, and then we have the consequences for it. Whatever you sow, you shall reap.

Read Genesis 16:6. Abram says "She's your maid, you can do anything you want to do." So Sarai treats Hagar badly, and so Hagar runs away. There is nothing right about this situation.

Sin, Consequences, and Conflict. Now, watch what happens because God is such a gracious God.

Read Genesis 16:7. Now, who is 'The angel of the Lord?' Not just an angel but The angel. Now, here in this passage and several others in the OT, when it reads The angel of the Lord, it appears that The angel of the Lord is the pre-incarnate Christ. It is called a Christophany. What we also find is – after Jesus became a person, The angel of the Lord isn't mentioned again from that point on. So many would say that The angel of the Lord must be the pre-incarnate Christ. Now we find out that The angel of the Lord has to be God. For example, in Judges 6:11-24 (story of Gideon), he is called YHWH. In Exodus 3:1-8 (story of Moses), he is called the God of Abraham, Isaac, Jacob, and Joseph. In Joshua 5:13-15 (story of Joshua), Joshua actually worships The angel of the Lord. So, The angel of the Lord must be God. And there are other examples in the OT.

Also, here in Genesis 16:7-10 (story of Hagar), The angel of the Lord could be the pre-incarnate Christ.

Read Genesis 16:8. Hagar, where are you going?

Question: Do you think He knows? What does He want her to say? I blew it. I didn't come under the authority of my mistress. I should not have been prideful.

Read Genesis 16:9. In the Bible and in relationships, there are levels of authority. God is over the whole creation. Christ is over the church, and the whole church submits to Christ as the head. The husband is over the wife and the family in the Bible. Parents are over the children. Children are to obey their parents. The employers are over the employees. Leaders in government. We have elders in the local church body. We are to submit to the authorities over us if they don't conflict with the Word of God.

The Angel of the Lord tells Hagar to go back to her mistress, Sarai and submit to her authority. Now, watch the next verse.

Read Genesis 16:10. The Angel of the Lord says, "I will greatly multiply your descendants so that they will be too many to count." Sounds like what God would say, huh? Question: who fathered this child? Abraham. What does Abraham mean? - Father of many nations. Not just the Jews came out of Abraham. These Arabs, as well. We will see that's who they will be.

Read Genesis 16:11-12. The Angel of the Lord told Hagar to call the son Ishmael, which means 'God hears.' God knows everything. The Angel continued telling Hagar that Ishmael would be against everybody, and everybody would be against him. And he will live to the east literally means that he will be 'in the face of everybody.' Not literally to the east, but that Ishmael will be in conflict with everybody. He won't win any contest for Mr. Congeniality.

Read Genesis 16:13. Hagar calls the name of the Lord "the God who sees." God sees and hears all things. He knows our situations. He knows our circumstances. He knows we are here worshipping Him.

Read Genesis 16:14-15. Hagar apparently tells Abram to name the boy Ishmael, and he does.

Read Genesis 16:16. Abram is now 86 years old. He has been waiting for the promise for 11 years. He had the son, but it was the wrong son. It doesn't count. He wasn't the one that God promised. Even though God is going to make a large nation from Ishmael, he isn't the one. Abram didn't wait on the Lord.

Questions:

1. Do you believe in the promises of God?

2. Are you resting in God and trusting that He will fulfil the promises?

3. Are you patient, or are you trying to fulfil what you think God's plan might be?

4. Are you living by the Word or by the pulls of the world?

5. Do you realize the consequences and the conflict that comes because of sin?

6. Do you realize that God sees, hears, and knows our circumstances?

CHAPTER FIFTEEN

The Sign of the Abrahamic Covenant
Genesis 17:1-14

Remember, the covenant with Abram included the land, the seed, and the blessing. God said He would give Abram land. The land we know as Canaan. God said he would give Abram a seed, which would be an offspring, and a great nation would come from him. And then there would be a blessing. A dual aspect of cursing and blessing. God said that He would bless those who bless you and curse those who curse you. And in you, Abram, all the nations of the world would be blessed. So we realize that the Messiah would come through Abram and salvation come through the Messiah. It was an unconditional promise. God would do it all. Over and over, God continues to remind Abram of these promises. In fact, in this passage, something special happens. God will do something that Abram will not forget. God changes both Abram's name to Abraham (5) and Sarai's name to Sarah (15). Go also reminds Abram of the promises once again and then gives him the sign of the covenant. There are a lot of things here.

May we, as we study God's Word in this lesson, be reminded of God's promises to us. Realizing that they are always true.

How do people know that we are Christians? We come in contact with people every day. How can they know that we have trusted Christ as our savior? Well, there are several ways.

1. The message. As we take the time to tell them about Christ. To tell them that Jesus died on the cross paying for sin and that if they would trust in Him, they would have eternal life.

2. Our actions, lifestyle, and our work. How we live from day to day. Baptism shows people that we have trusted in Jesus Christ as our savior.

In this lesson in Genesis 17, God gives Abraham a sign to show that he is connected with the covenant. And it was circumcision. God tells him that this will be the sign of the covenant that I have made with you and your offspring.

Well, let's begin. We have seen a time of failure and a time of change tied together by the grace of God. So even though Abram isn't faithful, God is faithful. That is something you need to remember. When you put your faith in Jesus Christ as Savior, God says He gives you eternal life. You are saved and saved forever. Whether you are faithful or not, God is faithful. We share, not perish. God comes to Abram this lesson and reminds him of the promises. Now, there is a gap of 13 years between the end of chapter 16 and the start of chapter 17. Look at Genesis 16:16. When that son was born that he wasn't supposed to have, Abram was 86 years old. This is 11 years since the original promise. Sometimes, we say, "God, I really want this to happen," and a week goes by, and we are upset. After 11 years, Abram took matters into his own hands and got the wrong son. Now, another 13 years have passed. (24 years since the original promise.)

Read Genesis 17:1. Abram is now 99 years old. Why do you think God is making Abram wait? Maybe God is getting Abram to a point in his life where the only way he would have this child would be by a miracle. God's timing is always perfect. Realize that God is Sovereign and knows what He is doing. Notice he comes to Abram and says, "I am God Almighty." That's the famous name El Shaddai. He is the one who provides. And God says, "Walk before Me and be blameless." Live for me as a righteous man. Obey my word. This is how one is to live who is saved. Abram has already believed in God. We are to live righteously and blameless because we are saved.

Read Genesis 17:2. God reminds Abram once again about his covenant.

Read Genesis 17:3. He fell on his face and worshipped God.

Read Genesis 17:4. God tells Abram that he would be the father of a multitude of nations. You see, not just the Jews come from Abraham. Really, all the Jews and all the Abrams come from Abraham.

Read Genesis 17:5. Abram means "exalted father". Big daddy. Abraham means "the father of the multitudes." God changed his name.

Read Genesis 17:6. God says, "I am going to make you really special."

Read Genesis 17:7. God tells him over and over and does so to remind him. Just like God's Word has truths in there that continuing reminds us. That God says what He says.

From this unconditional Covenant come three other unconditional covenants.

1. The Palestinian Covenant that dealt with the land.

2. The Davidic Covenant dealt basically with the seed and the Messiah.

3. The Jeremiah or new Covenant that dealt with the blessings.

Read Genesis 17:8. Notice how he ends this verse. 'I will be their God." God gave the Jews the Holy Land. It is an everlasting possession. God never breaks his promise.

Read Genesis 17:9. Now the Covenant is unconditional. But God tells them that Abram and his descendants are to do these things that we are going to see in just a minute to show that they are part of this Covenant. That they agreed with God. It is not to be a part of the Covenant. But because they are under the Covenant. In the same way, that we are saved by faith. But we obey God not to be saved or stay saved but because we are saved.

Read Genesis 17:10. This is going to be the sign. Circumcision.

Read Genesis 17:11. God made the promise. They are to live righteous. Circumcision was to set Abraham and his descendants apart. We (Abraham's descendants) are part of the Covenant of the true God.

Read Genesis 17:12-13 God says, "Whoever is connected with you, Abraham, whoever is connected with my Covenant" This is the sign for the men. If a foreigner comes in and wants to connect, they are going to have to be circumcised."

Read Genesis 17:14. God says, "When a person refuses to be circumcised, then you aren't identifying with the people of God." That is what he is saying there in the OT. What does it mean "to be cut off?" Some people think this means to be removed from the land. Others think it means that you would be put to death. Or they expect the Divine judgment of God, whatever it might be. Whichever one is correct, that person is saying, "I am not connecting with God's people."

Nothing Is Impossible With God

Genesis 17:15 - 18:15

Go ahead and turn in your Bibles to Genesis 17. We are continuing in our study of the book of Genesis, which is the book of beginnings. As you remember, we are now in the section dealing with four people. Abraham, Isaac, Jacob and Joseph. And we are looking at Abraham. The covenant was made with him. Then the covenant will pass onto Isaac; then it passes on to Jacob. Now, it doesn't pass on to Joseph because it goes down to Judah, but Joseph is the main person from about chapter 37 until the end of the book.

God made an unconditional covenant with Abraham. God said He would give him a land (Canaan), a seed (offspring including an offspring that all the nations would be blessed who the Messiah is), and a blessing (a dual aspect of blessing those that bless him and curse those that curse him).

Remember the last lesson, we studied that God changed Abram's name to Abraham. Also, God required circumcision as a sign of obedience, dedication to God, and belonging to his covenant people.

Read Genesis 17:15. God changed Sarai's (naggar) name to Sarah (princess). She is to be connected to Abraham, who is the father of the multitude. Sometimes, I think we forget that God is in the business of changing people. Look at your own life. When you trust Christ as Savior, you aren't the same person you used to be like. First of all, you were changed on the inside.

You were dead, and now you are alive. You are now a child of God. God's plan is that we will be changed day by day, moment by moment, to be conformed in the image of Jesus Christ. God is in the change business.

Read Genesis 17:16. Now remember she has had it pretty rough. She was 65 years old when they left the Ur of the Caldees, and she didn't know where they were moving to. Then, the Pharaoh in Egypt tried to take her as his wife but found out that she really was married, so he kicked them out. Then, 25 years passed, so she gave up her husband to a handmaiden named Hagar and watched her have a child. 13 years passed, and Ishmael wasn't her son. So here, in verse 16, God says that He "will bless her and give her a son." And "she shall be a mother of nations; kings of people will come from her." Kings? David, Soloman, the Messiah, who is the greatest king of all. Is a man 100 years old and a woman 90 years old going to have a baby? It is already impossible for man, but it is always possible with God. The nation of Israel is going to come through Abraham and Sarah.

Think of your own life. Most of us say, "I don't know what God is going to do with me. Probably not much." But what we need to realize is God will do what He chooses to do with you. And the things you might think are impossible, He can do. He can use any one of us. And He can use every one of us in this room. And He can use us to do things beyond what we can even imagine. And sometimes, in our lives, we sit around as if we aren't a servant of the almighty God. Folks, we work for the greatest one that has ever existed. Ask God to use you for His glory, and I guarantee you He will. And by the way, it doesn't matter whether you are young or whether you are old. Be faithful to be used by God.

Read Genesis 17:17. Abraham laughed. It just seemed too good to be true. Now, I don't think he is laughing because he doesn't believe it is true. I think he is laughing, saying, "This is wonderful. Too good to be true." "Are you sure it is going to happen?" Isn't that what we say? "God, I know that you will provide all my needs. Will you?" We know it, but sometimes we just hope He does. Sometimes, the promises of God seem too good to be true. Salvation for some people is too good to be true. Some people say, "It can't be that easy. Just put my faith in Christ as savior and I will be saved? Impossible. Surely, I have to do something. Maybe live a clean and honest life. Or go to church or something."

Read Genesis 17:18. Remember, Abraham had a 13-year-old son by the wrong woman. But he loves the boy. What's going to happen to Ishmael? So Abraham asks again, "Is the promise going to come through Ishmael?" What's the answer? No. Look at verse 19.

Read Genesis 17:19. God could not have been more clear. "It is going to be you, Abraham, your wife Sarah, who will bear you a son whom you will name Isaac. And I am making the everlasting covenant with him." Isaac means laughter. Because they are laughing, it's going to be so good; they are going to laugh about this for years to come what God has done. Now, sometimes people make his name, laughing in a negative sense. Abraham and Sarah didn't believe, so they had to name him Laughter and remember that for the rest of their lives. I don't think that's what's happening. I think it is because the joy of God's grace brings laughter. This is too wonderful. Just name him laughter. And every time you call him, you will remember how great I am, says God.

Read Genesis 17:20. God says, "I heard your plea about Ishmael. I will bless him and multiply him exceedingly." What people came from Ishmael? The Arabs.

Read Genesis 17:21. BUT, my covenant I will establish with Isaac. Who will be born next year? Folks, if God says it, He will do it. Every time.

Read Genesis 17:22-27. Abraham immediately obeyed God. "Sarai, could you come in here for a moment, please? God says your name is now Sarah. And you are to call me Abraham. Call all the men together; I have a little news for them. It might not go over too good, but it is part of the deal. And by the way, you are going to have a baby next year, and when he is born, we will name him Isaac."

Read Genesis 18:1-2a. Abraham is sitting in front of his tent. He looks up, and three men are standing right in front of him. Now, they didn't walk up to his tent. They just appeared there. And notice it says "the LORD or YHWH in Hebrew" appeared to him. Theologians call this a theophany, which is an appearance of God in a human-like form or sometimes called a Christophany, which is an appearance of Christ in the OT. So these three men could be two angels and Christ standing in front of Abraham.

Read 18:2b. Look what he did. Abraham bowed down in front of these men. I believe he understood this was God standing before him.

Read Genesis 18:3-5. In the culture of that day, visitors were respected in this way. With rest, water, food etc. May we, too, treat people with respect, hospitality and courtesy. Abraham calls himself a servant.

Question: Do you call yourself a servant of God?

Read Genesis 18:6. Abraham runs into the tent and tells Sarah to make three pieces of bread with *good* flour and make it fast. Notice he isn't going to eat with them.

Read Genesis 18:7. Abraham then runs and gets a *choice* calf for the visitors to eat.

Read Genesis 18:8. Curds and milk. Mmmm.

Now God, for the 4th or 5th time, is going to tell Abraham about the son, Isaac, who is to be born.

Read Genesis 18:9. First of all, how does this person know Abraham's wife's name? Also, if this wasn't God but just a man in that culture, he wouldn't have addressed her. But this is God speaking and giving some details about the birth of Isaac.

Read Genesis 18:10. God tells him again about having a son next year. (chapter 21). But notice Sarah is listening at the tent door.

Read Genesis 18:11. Sarah is 89 years old. Abraham is 99 years old. For them to have a child would be a miracle from God.

Read Genesis 18:12. Notice Sarah laughed to herself, not out loud. If this is going to happen, it is too good to be true. Salvation is too good to be true. But it is. 41 times in the NT, the Word of God promises us eternal life.

Read Genesis 18:13. You can almost see Sarah thinking to herself, "How did He know I laughed? I didn't laugh out loud." God knows everything. God is asking, "Does she not believe that I am able to give her a child?"

Read Genesis 18:14. God is asking if anything is too wonderful (difficult) for the LORD. No. He can do anything that fits His character.

Ask yourself, Is this day in my life too hard for the Lord? No. Is this habit I'm trying to break too hard for the Lord? No. Is the communication problem I'm having too hard for the Lord? No. Are the problems in my marriage or family too hard for the Lord? No. Is anything too difficult for the Lord? No.

Whatever He has promised, He will do. He promised that He would provide for us, protect us, and empower us. God's character says He will do it. God's power enables Him to do it. He will do everything that He promises.

What would you do if God caught you in a lie? God caught you doing something wrong. You see, a lot of times, when we get caught doing something wrong, we lie about it.

Read Genesis 18:15. Fear of being discovered is the most common motive for lying. We are afraid that our inner thoughts and emotions will be exposed. But God knows everything. And God says to Sarah, "No. You laughed." Lying causes greater complications than telling the truth and brings even more problems. Trust God with your innermost thoughts and fears.

CHAPTER SIXTEEN

Abraham Intercedes for the Righteous
Genesis 18:16-33

Well, go ahead and turn in your Bibles to Genesis 18. We are continuing in our study of the book of Beginnings. Genesis is a book that not only gives us the truth about the creation of all things but actually, we are beginning to see the setting of a people for His name, which we call the Jews. We have been focusing on Abraham since chapter 12. Remember, God made a covenant, a promise to Abraham to give him land, a seed, and a blessing. Now God is going to reveal to Abraham His coming judgment on what cities? Sodom, Gomorrah. And in chapter 19, we see that there were actually five cities that God had planned to destroy. God said that these cities were in total rebellion against Him. They were known for their wickedness.

Question: Why is it important for the LORD (YHWH) to tell Abraham what He is planning to do?

As we look at this passage, we see several truths.

1. Sin brings consequences. God deals with sin.

2. Lot was living in the city of Sodom. What was going to happen to him?

Question: Would God destroy the righteous with the wicked?

3. Abraham's intercession makes a difference. May we realize that our intercession can make a difference.

The Word of God tells us in Romans 3:10, "that there are none righteous, no not one". Romans 3:23 says "that we all have sinned and come short of the glory of God." But the Bible gives us a great truth. And that is this: when a person puts their faith in Jesus Christ as their savior, they trust in Him, and He gives them His righteousness. Romans 4:5 says, "To him, that doesn't work but believes in Him that justifies the ungodly, his faith is counted as righteousness." That is a great truth. If anyone puts their faith in Jesus and believes in God's provision through the Messiah, He gives them His righteousness.

Let me break down the passage. In verses 16-18, God makes a decision to tell Abraham. In verses 19-22, God actually tells Abraham about the judgment against Sodom and Gomorrah. Then, in verses 23-33, Abraham makes intercession for others.

Read Genesis 18:16. Abraham is walking with the men (Lord and possibly two angels) towards Sodom. Remember, the oaks of Mamre are near Hebron, which is north of Sodom.

Read Genesis 18:17. Notice that the LORD doesn't go to Sodom, only the other two men (angels). It says that the LORD is asking, "Shall I hide from Abraham what I am about to do?" This shows the relationship that Abraham had with the LORD. He was a friend of God. Does Abraham need to know this? One of the great truths that we find in the Bible is God tells us what we need to know. And there are some things that we don't need to know.

Judgment is coming. It is not an accident. When the destruction of these cities comes, God wants Abraham to know that this was no accident. This was judgment. Two things here what He tells him.

1. Abraham is going to be a blessing. A blessing to the nations.

2. Abraham has a responsibility to teach his own family and his own nation about God, about judgement, and about righteousness.

Read Genesis 18:18. All the nations will be blessed because the Messiah will come from him.

Read Genesis 18:19. Abraham is going to have the responsibility to teach his family about God. Abraham must teach his future descendants to keep the way of the Lord. He must do this by living righteously. Abraham must teach them to obey God is the plan; to disobey God brings judgment. Righteousness exalts. Unrighteousness brings down. That is a truth for us today. Obey God and be blessed. Disobey God, and there will be judgment.

So here it is:

Read Genesis 18:20 YHWH tells him, "The wickedness of Sodom and Gomorrah cries out to God, and their sin is exceedingly grave (horrible)." Folks, if you think that you can live in the world and buy into the world, and it does not affect us, just look at Lot's life, how he treated these angels when they came, how he treated his family, how his family laughed at him, and the result how his family (2 daughters) acted after they were delivered out. Horrible things are coming up in chapter 19.

Question: Do you think America is any worse or better than Sodom and Gomorrah? Why hasn't He judged us yet?

I think we are going to see something in this passage in just a moment.

Read Genesis 18:21. Do you think the LORD knows what is going on in Sodom? Yes. This is called an andromorphic statement. He is using things that a human being would do in order to explain what He is doing. The LORD is saying, "I'm going to go check it out. I already know it. But I am going to show you that I am a just Judge and a just God. I don't judge unless I know the facts. But of course, I know everything." God is not mocked. What you sow, you reap.

Question: What were these people doing?

Sodomy (homosexual acts) is named after the city of Sodom. We have an idea, especially when we get into chapter 19 that there was much homosexuality, illicit sex, and wickedness.

Now Abraham is figuring out that something is about to happen to these cities that isn't going to be good. And I am sure he is thinking, "Hey, my nephew and his family live down there."

Read Genesis 18:22. These two men (angels) head toward Sodom. The LORD doesn't go with them.

Read Genesis 18:23. Look at the question. When Abraham says "righteous", does he mean that in that town, Lot is a man who is living righteously and godly? No. Or does he mean that Lot was a believer connected in the midst of those unbelievers? So Abraham is asking the LORD, "Are You going to destroy the believers along with the unbelievers?

Now, when Jesus Christ died on the cross 2000 years ago, He paid for everybody's sins. 1 John 2:2. The thing that separates us from God is not the payment for sin because it has already been made. Even the unbelieving person who might be your next-door neighbor their sins have already been paid for. But what do they need? They need three things, and they all come by faith:

1. When you believe by faith in Christ's death and resurrection, you get eternal life. John 3:16.

2. You also get righteousness. Romans 4:5.

3. You also get forgiveness of sins. Acts. 13:38.

And before God can answer Abraham's question. Notice what Abraham says.

Read Genesis 18:24. Abraham asks the LORD, "What if there are 50 believers in that city? Would you destroy them?" And before God can answer, Abraham answers it for God. Watch.

Read Genesis 18:25. "I know you wouldn't do that. You wouldn't sweep away the righteous with the wicked as if they are equal."

Read Genesis 18:26. And the LORD answers, "If there are 50 righteous within the city, I will spare the whole place on their account." Why? Because those 50 were the believers. Maybe that is why America hasn't been wiped clean, because there are believers in this nation. He lets us go and keep going.

Read Genesis 18:27-28 Now that I have started to talk to You, and I am nothing, just dust, I supposed there were only 45. And the Lord says, " OK, I won't destroy it if I find 45 there."

Read Genesis 18:29. Abraham keeps throwing out the number 40, and the LORD says OK.

Read Genesis 18:30 Down to 30. OK.

Read Genesis 18:31. Down to 20. OK

Read Genesis 18:32. Down to 10. OK. This was the number of his family. (two sons, two married daughters, two unmarried daughters, Lot and his wife) Did the LORD destroy the city? Yes. So there couldn't have been ten. It almost appears there may have been only 4. But Lot's wife really didn't make it. And the two daughters, well, not sure they were righteous. So maybe only one was righteous. Lot. The LORD was going to hold off his judgment against the wicked because of a small group of believers.

Question: Do you realize that a small group of believers can make a difference?

Folks, we can make an impact in our communities. With God's help, this group can turn this whole town upside down. Eleven men (disciples) turned the world upside down after Christ returned to heaven.

Read Genesis 18:33. I think God is sparing America because there are Christians living in this land. Do you realize that 70% of all missionaries come from the USA? Do you realize that 85% of all mission money comes from the USA? Folks, we must continue praying, serving, and evangelizing in this country. We must continue to teach our children to obey God. Obedience brings blessing. But sin brings judgment. May God continue to hold back his wrath against our nation.

CHAPTER SEVENTEEN

God Delivers the Righteous From the Judgment
Genesis 19

In this lesson, our focus really goes from Abraham to his nephew, Lot. A man who was influenced by the world. He was a believer in God. But loved the world. This passage, the doom of Sodom. Certain truths come from Genesis 19.

1. God judges sin.

2. God delivers the righteous from the judgment.

The world has a great influence on us. And the Bible tells us not to love the world. We are going to see what happens when you do. In this lesson, we are going to see the world's influence on Lot. And God's warning of the coming judgement on Sodom and the surrounding cities.

One day, a man sat down and took out a sheet of paper and wrote across the top, "goals that I have for my life."

1. To lose all sense of moral values.

2. To forfeit all spiritual authority in my home.

3. To have no influence for good in my community.

4. To lose everything that is dear to me.

5. And to be conformed to the values of this world.

Who was that man?

That was Lot. Of course, we know that he really didn't sit down and write out those terrible goals for his life. But in reality, his unwritten goals became the natural consequences of his worldly choices. Lot loved the world, became conformed to the world, and suffered the consequences of being identified with the world.

Well, this lesson is the sad story of Lot. It is one of the saddest, grossest events in the Bible.

Read Genesis 19:1. Notice in this verse that the two men are now called two angels. They have now traveled from Hebron down to the city of Sodom. And Lot is sitting in the gate. The gateway of the city was the meeting place for city officials and other men to discuss current events and transact business. It was a place of authority and status where a person could be seen. So evidently, Lot held an important position in the city government or associated with those who did. Remember, he had been in Sodom for 20 years now. First, Lot moved towards Sodom; then he lived in Sodom, and now we find him at the gate of the city. Notice that when Lot saw the two angels, he rose to meet them and bowed down with his face to the ground. Question: Did Lot know they were angels? Probably did. The powerful presence of God's angels almost always causes this reaction.

People will sacrifice their spiritual growth for a number of reasons. For position. People will do whatever it takes to have authority. They will compromise everything for it. Sometimes it is just for pleasure. They think the whole purpose of life is just to enjoy yourself and do whatever you want to do. Some people would sacrifice their spiritual growth for possessions. I mean, their whole life is tied up in material things, stuff that they have or want. Then, some people just want to be left alone. I want to build my house, put my fence around it, and not have to deal with people when I get off my job. Well, folks, if you are going to touch lives for Christ, you are going to have to be with people. Well, look what happens next.

Read Genesis 19:2. Lot asks the two angels to spend the night at his house. But they said, "No, we will just spend the night in the square." But let's read on.

Read Genesis 19:3. Lot urged them strongly, so they went with him and entered his house. And he prepared some bread, a feast for them. Question: Did Lot know what would happen to the two angels if they stayed in the square for the night? Probably.

Read Genesis 19:4. Notice that men are from every quarter of the city, not just the bad side of town? Why? Because the whole town was bad. Also, notice that both young and old came over to Lot's house and surrounded it. It wasn't just the ruffing gangs, the young hoodlums, but wicked men of all different ages.

Read Genesis 19:5. These men that have surrounded Lot's house are demanding that Lot bring them out so that they can have relations with them. The Hebrew word is yada, which means to know. They wanted to have homosexual relations with them. The Bible doesn't beat around the bush. What perversion. What wickedness. Homosexuality isn't an alternative lifestyle; it is a sin. And it is wrong. It is clearly condemned by God in His Word.

What is Lot going to do?

Read Genesis 19:6-7. My brothers? Lot went out of his house and said, "Hey guys, let's not do this. Don't act wickedly."

Then, look at what Lot does.

Just picture yourself as Lot in this scene. You have taken two strangers into your house; the homosexual men in the city have surrounded your house, demanding that you bring these two strangers out so they can have sex with them. So you step out and say, "No. No. No. Don't act wickedly. I have something else I will do for you."

Read Genesis 19:8. Understand that one? Lot says to this mob of perverts, "Here, take my two daughters and do whatever you like to them; just don't do anything to these two strangers that I have invited into my house." Wow. How could any father give his daughters away like that? This terrible suggestion reveals how deeply sin had been absorbed into Lot's life. Was he so afraid that he was willing to sacrifice his daughters so they wouldn't kill him? Is that what he thought?

Read Genesis 19:9. Do you see what the wicked men of Sodom are saying? "Who do you think you are? You're not one of us. Stand aside. You are a stranger here, and now you are acting like our judge. Here's what we are going to do. We are going to treat you worse than we are going to treat them." And they pressed against Lot to break down the door. And you can just imagine Lot going, "Oh, oh. What am I going to do?" People today say, "I don't know why I get into trouble." Well, a lot of the decisions we make get ourselves in trouble. The things that happen to us are usually based on the choices that we made earlier.

Read Genesis 19:10. The two angels reached out and pulled Lot into the house and shut the door.

Then, notice what happens next.

Read Genesis 19:11. The word blindness in Hebrew doesn't mean that the wicked men of the city couldn't see. The word actually means "bewilderment." The idea is that the angels struck them, and all of a sudden, they don't know where the house is; what are we doing here? What are we looking for? They couldn't figure out anything.

Next, the angels will give their message to Lot. And there are two reasons for the angels coming.

1. Get Lot and his family out.

2. Destroy this city and the area around it.

Read Genesis 19:12-13. They tell Lot to get his family out because they are about to destroy the place because their outcry is so great before the Lord that the Lord has sent them to destroy it. Now, in a sense, this is a picture of God delivering the righteous before the judgment. Because He is about to bring the fire and brimstone to destroy the wicked. But the Lord comes to get the righteous ones out. All of us who have believed by faith in Jesus as savior before God bring the judgement on this earth called the Tribulation, which will be the worst time in the history of the earth. And He will deliver the righteous ones out of here. It is called the Rapture.

Question: Who do you want Jesus to take out of here? Do you have a member of your family that is lost?

Well, go teach them immediately about Jesus. Because folks, judgment is coming. Maybe sooner than you think.

Question: If Lot goes and tells his family to get out because God is going to destroy the city, do you think they will believe him? Has Lot been a spiritual man for 20 years?

No. He has lost his testimony. He has allowed the world to affect him.

Read Genesis 19:14. Well, he did go and tell his family about the coming judgment, but they thought he was just kidding. Just jesting. Lot was no longer a believable witness to God. He had allowed his environment to corrupt him.

Question: Do those whom you work with, live next to, or go to school with, do they see you as a witness for God, or are you just one of the crowd, blending in unnoticed? Have you, too, become almost useless to God because you are too much like the world?

To make a difference, you must first decide to be different in your faith and in your conduct.

Read Genesis 19:15. The two angels urged Lot to get up, get out, and take your family lest you be destroyed in the punishment of the city.

Read Genesis 19:16. What did he do? He hesitated. He failed to obey. Can you believe this? The angels literally had to take them by the hand and pull them out of the city. God has compassion. Lot didn't want to abandon the wealth, position, and comfort he enjoyed. False attractions of our culture's pleasures.

Read Genesis 19:17. One of the angels tells them, "Escape for your life. Don't look behind you, don't stay anywhere in the valley, escape to the mountains, or you will be swept away."

Read Genesis 19:18-23. Lot didn't want to go to the mountains, so he pleaded to just take his family to another town called Zoar, which was a small town.

Read Genesis 19:24-25. God rained brimstone and fire on Sodom and Gomorrah. Even today, south of the Dead Sea, there is this valley just filled with little volcano rocks. And people think this might have been the place where the cities were.

Read Genesis 19:26. Lot's wife didn't just look back to see what was happening; she looked longingly. She was unwilling to turn completely away from sin. You can't make progress with God as long as you are holding on to pieces of your old life.

Read Genesis 19:27-29. Abraham looked down toward Sodom and Gomorrah, and it wasn't there. It was on fire. Smoke everywhere.

Read Genesis 19:30-31. Lot's two daughters think that there aren't any other men in the world. And they wanted to marry and have children.

Read Genesis 19:32-36. So they got their father, Lot, drunk and slept with him. They stooped to incest. Influence of the sin in Sodom. And became pregnant by the father while he was sleeping off a drunken stupor.

Read Genesis 19:37-38. The oldest bore a son named Moab. The youngest bore a son named Ben-Ammi, the father of the Ammon. These two became the Moabites and the Ammonites. Two people groups became the greatest enemies of the Israelites when they entered the Promised Land when they left Egypt. Israel never conquered them.

CHAPTER EIGHTEEN

Abraham and Abimelech
Genesis 20

We are continuing our study of the book of Genesis. And this part of the book is about Abraham. The man set apart, called by God, head of the chosen people of the nation of Israel. God promised him the land, the seed, and the blessing. Last time, we saw the judgement on the wicked people in Sodom. Now, in this chapter, chapter 20, we see Abraham's failure for the third time. And he fails in basically the same way. And unfortunately, we repeat mistakes over and over again, too. But it will help us because we see God's faithfulness and God's protection. God always does what He says. He always keeps his promises. He takes care of us even when we fail. We are going to see Abraham lie. The man of God: lies. Again. Note, however, that we all have sinned and come short of the glory of God. Take heed lest we think we stand. That we fall. Well, we are going to see something that contributes to Abraham's failure and how to deal with this. May we see how good God is and how faithful God is, even when we are not faithful.

Man should learn from history, but most of the time, we don't. We make the same mistakes over and over again. Not only that but when we make mistakes, we tend to want to blame someone else for our mistakes. We see Abraham, and he makes the same mistake, the same sin as before: he lies about Sarah. He told another king that she was his sister. Remember the story back in Genesis 12. He found himself in a situation, was afraid, and thought that the king of that area (Egypt) would kill him to get to his wife. Maybe they would take care of me if they thought Sarah was my sister. So he lied, got found out, got in trouble and was embarrassed.

In Genesis 20, he does exactly the same thing. You are probably thinking, "Wouldn't he have learned by now." Well, do we do some of the same things over and over? Yes. But God is faithful even when we aren't. That is a great truth.

Here's the outline.

In verses 1-8, we see Abraham's treachery.

In verses 9-15, we see the pagan king of Gerar, Abimelech, confronting the man of God, Abraham.

Then, in verses 16-18, we discuss the restoration.

But we follow the same pattern today in our behavior. We say, "I'm not going to gossip anymore – but we do." "I'm not going to lie anymore – but we do." "I'm not going to lust anymore – then we do." "I am going to be sensitive to my wife/husband – and we are not." "I'm going to have my quiet times – and we don't" "I am going to exercise on a regular basis – and we don't" "I will show kindness to these people – but we don't" "I will witness to my lost family members or lost friends – and we don't."

Read Genesis 20:1. So Abraham left Hebron and journeyed south to the Negev (which is the pork chop-shaped looking land, settled between Kadesh and Shur and then sojourned in Gerar, which is southwest of Hebron. Now remember Sarah has been promised a son, and they are to name him what? Isaac. Which means laughter.

Read Genesis 20:2. Abraham tells the king of Gerar, named Abimelech, the same lie that he told the king of Egypt. Not only that, but his future son, Isaac, will lie about his wife, Rebekkah. Wonder where he learned to play that trick to protect himself? Well, Abimelech takes Sarah. Now, Gerar was a city-state of the Philistines. Now, how old is Sarah at this time? 90 years old. This guy, Abimelech, wants her as one of his wives. She was a good-looking 90. Let's just face it, right?

He gave up his wife again because of fear and foolishness. Because he failed to trust God, you can't get away with actions that are wrong. What you sow, you shall reap. This foolish act has caused Sarah to possibly commit adultery. And what about the child who is to be born? What if Abimelech has sexual relations with Sarah? Whose baby is it going to be? Is the baby going to be the promised seed? How would you know? Don't you just want to go up to Abraham and say, "You idiot. How could you be so dumb?" But of course, sometimes we look at ourselves in the mirror and say, "How could I be so dumb?" You put any of us in the wrong situation, and we are capable of any sin. So, the best thing to do isn't get yourself in those situations.

Read Genesis 20:3. I like that. God says to Abimelech, "You are a dead man." God is serious about people fooling around. People will say, "It's no big deal. Everybody does it." Do you think God cares? You better believe it. God will judge adulterers and fornicators (Heb. 13)

Read Genesis 20:4. This man is the opposite of who Abraham thought he was going to be. He acknowledges the Lord and asks Him, "You aren't going to slay the innocent, are you? I didn't know.

Read Genesis 20:5. Abimelech says to God, "Did he not say to me 'she is my sister?" And not only that, Sarah also said to me, "he is my brother?" She was guilty of deceitfulness also. I didn't know. I wouldn't do this on purpose. I didn't come near her. He didn't know he was doing something wrong. What do we do if we are doing something wrong that we didn't know was wrong? - Stop doing it if we find out it is wrong.

What about your integrity? Do you do what you promise? Do people trust you? Are you an honest person? Folks, we must do what is right in the right way. To live by the Word of God.

Do you do an honest day's work for a day's pay? Employers all the time say, "It is hard to find someone that wants to work. They want to get paid, and they show up, but they don't like to work" Will you do what you say? We must be people of integrity in the midst of a fallen world.

Read Genesis 20:6. Is God Sovereign or what? God prevented him from touching Sarah and held him back from sinning. What a merciful God. God often works in ways we can't even see.

Read Genesis 20:7. God takes seriously the relationship between Abraham and Sarah.

Question: What would happen if Sarah never returned back to Abraham? Where would the Messiah be?

Because the Messiah has to come through Issac, Jacob, Judah, David, etc.

That is why Abimelech and all who are his are dead.

Now, we are going to see a pagan king confront dishonest Abe.

Read Genesis 20:8. Abimelech first went to his servants and told them about this problem. And they were greatly frightened. Which means having respect for God's sovereign will. God will do what he chooses to do. It is realizing that God is the Almighty, Holy One.

Read Genesis 20:9-10. Abimelech asks Abraham 3 directed questions.

1. What have you done? He lied.

2. What did I do? The answer is nothing.

3. What could have caused this? And the answer is: Fear.

Did Abraham think he could get away with this?

Sometimes, we think that maybe God will not know or that God might let us get away with it.

Read Genesis 20:11-13. Because Abraham mistakenly assumed that Abimelech was a wicked man. He was afraid. So he made a quick decision to tell a half-truth. But there is no such thing as a half-truth. It is all a lie. We rationalize why we do wrong. "You just don't understand my background." "You don't live with my wife/husband." "This is the society that we live in. Everybody does it." "This is just the way I am. There is nothing I can do about it." We all want to blame somebody else for our actions and our choices. Abraham thought it would be more effective to deceive Abimelech than to trust God. Not only that, but Abraham and Sarah planned from the beginning to do wrong. To tell lies. Folks, never, ever do presumptuous sins. Knowing something is wrong, and you do it anyway.

Read Genesis 20:14. Abimelech gives back Sarah and a bunch of presents. "I don't want to get in trouble with God."

Read Genesis 20:15. Basically, in a nice way, Abimelech tells Abraham to leave town. "You can go anywhere; just go away from here."

Read Genesis 20:16. Abimelech tells Sarah that he gave Abraham 1000 pieces of silver. "I want it known to everyone: 'I didn't touch you.'"

Read Genesis 20:17-18. Abraham prayed to God to open up the wombs of the household of Abimelech. Because as long as Abimelech was in danger of sleeping with Sarah, there were no babies in his household. Sin is a poison that damages us and those around us.

CHAPTER NINETEEN

God's Provision and Protection
Genesis 21

Well, go ahead and turn in your Bibles to Genesis 21 as we continue in our study of Genesis and the life of Abraham. This passage shows us the provision and the protection of the birth of Isaac (Yiz'chak). In this lesson, we will see the fulfilment of the promise that was made 25 years back in Abraham's life. Also, we will discuss how God provided and protected Ishmael (Yishma'el). And Ishmael will be removed from the family. So we will see what happens there. These two boys, Isaac and Ishmael, can be compared in a sense, one of the promise and the other in the flesh. Ishmael came into being through works and the flesh. And Isaac is the one who came by faith in the promise. And we will see that also. This lesson's focus will be the provision and protection of our great God and Savior.

One of the great verses in the Bible is Philippians 4:19: "And my God will supply all your needs according to His riches in glory in Christ Jesus." He didn't say He would provide all our wants, but He did say He would provide all our needs." Have there ever been a time in your life in which God intervened? You could say, "Hey, that's God doing something." Probably most of us could tell a story, "Well, one time this happened..."

There is a true story about Dallas Theological Seminary back in 1940; Dr. Luis Shaffer was the president. And the seminary back then was having some financial problems. In fact, the seminary needed $50,000 to keep going. So Dr. Shaffer and the board of directors had a prayer time and asked God for help. While they were praying, Dr. Shaffer's secretary knocked on the office door and gave him an envelope. The mail had arrived. In that envelope, there was a check for $50,000. And it was from a man who hadn't had any connection to the seminary up until then. But God had impressed on his heart to sell some of his cattle and give the money to the seminary. So he did. God provides and intervenes.

Now, Abraham was 75 years old, and Sarah was 65 years old when they moved from the Ur of the Chaldeans to the land that God was going to show him. Then give him. Then they failed to trust God, so Abraham, at age 86, had a son through Hagar, Sarah's maidservant. But that wasn't what God wanted. Now, over 25 years have passed. Abraham is now 100 years old, and as we look at verse 7 of Genesis 21, the promised child comes. It is a glorious time.

Read Genesis 21:1. The LORD (YHWH) decided to do something. He intervened. Do you understand that for this couple to have a child, God must intervene? It's not going to be natural. Why? Because Sarah is 90 years old. She is past the age of having children. In fact, I think God waited on purpose. In order to say, "This is the child of promise." It is a supernatural event. God's promises are not dependent on our faithfulness. But on God's faithfulness. Do you understand that God must intervene in order for you and I to have salvation? It is God who loved the world that He gave his only beloved Son. It is Jesus who was willing to die on the cross to pay for our sins. It is God who draws us to Himself. It isn't something that you can do.

Well, look what happens.

Read Genesis 21:2. Sarah conceived and bore a son at God's appointed time. Just like He said back in chapter 18. God is able to do what He promises.

Read Genesis 21:3. Abraham names the boy Isaac (Yitz'chak), just like God told him to do. Remember, Isaac means 'laughter'. It is laughing time. This is so great. This is fantastic. They have a son! The baby brought so much joy into their lives. The blessing of God.

Read Genesis 21:4. Remember, circumcision was the sign of the Covenant. It was for everyone in Abraham's household. It showed God that they believed in God and obeyed Him. It has nothing to do with salvation.

Read Genesis 21:5. Abraham was 100 years old. He has waited 25 years. By the way, God didn't tell him 25 years ago when the child was to come. Abraham just needed to believe and trust in God. Normally, God doesn't tell us what is going to happen tomorrow. Aren't you glad? I don't want to know. The good or the bad. "Well, it is about time I fall down those stairs in my house." I just want to live moment by moment, running the race with endurance, looking unto Jesus. God is gracious by giving one day at a time.

Read Genesis 21:6-7. Sarah now has the joy and the laughter. It is a great day in the Lord! What is impossible with people is possible with God. Rest in God's promises. They always come true. Well, that was the provision. Now we are going to see the protection.

Now, put yourself in Ishamel's shoes. He is about 12-13 years old now, and all of a sudden, there is talk about the promised son that Abraham is looking for is coming next year. And he probably says, "What about me?" I am your son, too. And then the baby comes, and everybody dances around, sings, and is joyful.

Read Genesis 21:8. Now Isaac is about two years old and is weaned. And Abraham throws a party for him. Jewish families would throw a party when babies are born, when they are weaned, and when they are about 12 years old. It is called a bar-mitzvah for boys and a bat-mitzvah for girls.

Read Genesis 21:9. Oh, oh. Ishmael, who is 15 years old, is mocking Isaac, who is two years old. He is making fun of him. And Sarah sees it. And she is partial to her boy.

Read Genesis 21:10. She tells Abraham to kick Hagar and Ishmael out of the house. "I'm not going to put up with this." Remember, her name used to be Sarai, called "Naggar." Do you think if she starts on this, she is going to let up?" No way. "Abraham, I want them gone. I want them out of here right now." And remember, this conflict has been going on for a long time, hasn't it? The descendants of Ishmael are the Arabs, and the descendants of Isaac are the Jews. And they still don't get along.

Hagar and Ishmael are symbolic of works and flesh. While Sarah and Isaac are symbolic of grace, faith and the promise. And we see a contrast between the two ways that people try to come to God. We come to God by faith, not by doing good works.

Read Genesis 21:11. Abraham loved both of his sons. But the promised son, Isaac, must be protected. Who knows? Maybe Ishmael hurt Isaac because of jealousy. Don't know.

Read Genesis 21:12. God reminds Abraham that Isaac is the one whom the promise of the Messiah comes. So whatever Sarah says to do, do it. Ishmael must be removed. It looks bad. Romans 8:28: "And we know that in all things God works for the good of those who love him, who have been called according to his purpose."

Read Genesis 21:13. Remember the promise to Abraham that through him he would be the father of what? Many nations. Not just the Jews. Please think about this situation in this way. It is not the abandonment of Ishmael, but it is the protection of Isaac. That is what we are seeing.

Read Genesis 21:14. Beersheba is south of Gerar. About 50 miles south-southwest of Jerusalem. This situation looks bad for Hagar, the Egyptian servant, and her son, Ishmael. Where are they going to go? But God will intervene once again.

Read Genesis 21:15-16. She has run out of water. Maybe they are lost. They are just wandering around. It looks hopeless. She thinks Ishmael is about to die from dehydration.

Read Genesis 21:17. God heard Ishmael, age 15-16, crying. And an angel asks Hagar, "What's the matter with you?" "Don't be afraid; God has heard the lad." Folks, no matter where you are, you can lift up your voice, and God will hear you. Just keep praying. God will answer in the perfect way. And sometimes, it isn't what we are asking for. God is gracious.

Read Genesis 21:18. God says again to Hagar to make Ishmael a great nation. He didn't promise a land, and He didn't promise a blessing. The Messiah would come from Isaac, not Ishmael. But God did say he would have lots of descendants. He had 12 sons.

Read Genesis 21:19. God provided water for them. God provides and protects.

Read Genesis 21:20-21. Hagar gets a wife from her home country of Egypt.

Read Genesis 21:22-34. People knew that God was blessing this man, Abraham. So King Abimelech wants Abraham to swear to be nice. To promise not to lie anymore to him. But before he promises, he says to Abimelech, "Keep your men out of my water well. And I want it back."

So Abraham and Abimelech cut sheep and oxen into two, locked arms, and walked through the cut animals, which was a covenant to 'be nice to one another. No more lying and no more stealing water wells."

Then Abraham gives Abimelech 7 lambs in order to show everyone that this well was his. No doubts. Abraham called the place Beersheba (Be'er-Sheva), which means "the well of the 7". Beersheba was the southernmost city of Israel.

Then, in verse 33, Abraham planted a tree like a memorial to remember how God provided for him. And he once again calls on the name of the Lord. He worshipped God. And calls him another name. El Olan, everlasting God.

CHAPTER TWENTY

Abraham's Greatest Test
Genesis 22

Go ahead and turn in your Bibles to Genesis 22 as we continue in our study of the life of Abraham. Abraham's greatest test. Abraham is told by God to offer his son, Isaac, as a burnt offering. This is the son that he has waited for 25 years. This is the son through whom the seed would come, the promised Messiah. Here are a few questions to think about as we go through the passage, and we will answer them at the conclusion.

1. Does God want a human sacrifice?

2. How could Abraham offer Him, Isaac? How could the seed come if his son died?

3. How is Isaac a picture of Jesus Christ?

4. What can we learn about God in His provision?

How do we understand this passage? It is so powerful. How do we respond to God's Word when it doesn't always seem to make sense? May we realize that when God directs us, He also provides. He provides all the needs that we have. Whatever He needs for us to do to carry out His will.

Now, some tests like your driving test or a test at school are written. But some tests are choices. We are tested whether we choose to obey or not. Some come as events and circumstances. Are we going to trust God in sickness or failure? How do we respond to the tests that come? Well, our goal is to trust God. Now, we will see that Abraham faces the biggest test of his life. Will he trust God? We are going to look at one of the most famous passages in the OT. It is also probably the greatest scene in the OT.

Here's the outline.

Verses 1-2 are God's instructions.

Verses 3-8 are the preparation for the trip to Mt. Moriah.

Verses 9-19 are the offering.

Verses 20-24 provide some information about Abraham's relatives.

Read Genesis 22:1. It says, "After these things..." What things? Remember that Abraham trusted God enough to remove Ishmael. God has been preparing Abraham for the biggest test of his life. God is trying to get Abraham to get his act together, so to speak. It says, "God tested Abraham...". The Hebrew word for test is almost the same as the Greek word, which means "testing for approval." God never tests a person to cause them to fail. God never tests a person to cause them to sin. Tests are really for us to trust God. Whenever tests come, remember God is Sovereign; these are for our good. To deepen our capacity to obey Him. To stretch us to develop our character. Abraham responded to God, "Here I am." He is saying, I am available. God is looking for people who are faithful, people who are available, people who are teachable.

Read Genesis 22:2. Now, the best that we can tell because they have been moving around is that, most likely, they are pretty south near Beersheba and leave there and go 50 miles or so north to Jerusalem. Mt. Moriah (Mt. Zion) is where Jerusalem is. It is about a three-day trip to get there. God says, "Take now your son, your only son, whom you love, Isaac." The Muslims believe that this wasn't Isaac but Ishmael. But God is very clear that it is Isaac. Now, with burnt offerings, you would take either a bull, ram or a male bird with no defect, and you would kill it, and the blood would run out, and you would put it on this altar and set fire to it. You burn that animal completely up. A burnt offering is a picture of total dedication to God.

Abraham isn't only going to go up to the mountain and kill their son, but he is also going to burn him up. Notice God says, "Your only son". This literally means the son who is unique. The son of promise. This was the only son from whom the promise came. Isaac. Laughter. No one is laughing right now. This is not going to be happy. His son, Isaac, may be 14-15 years old by now. Will Abraham obey this command from God? Question: Do we obey clear commands from God?

First Question: Does God want a human sacrifice? I mean, isn't this a pagan practice? Does God want a human sacrifice? And the answer is yes. Realize in the OT that whenever there was sin, they would kill an animal without blemish, and the sacrifice would cover their sins but not pay for their sins. All the way through the OT, animals could never take care of a human being's sin. The only blood that can pay for a human being's sin has to be that of a perfect, sinless, without-blemish human being. And so far, up to this point, there never has been one. "All have sinned and come short of the glory of God" until exactly the right time, God brought forth His Son, born of a woman, born under the law. Jesus Christ lived a perfect, sinless life as the lamb of God, who can take away the sin of the world. Not cover it up.

Let me ask you a question: What would you do? For those of us who have children, "There is no way. I am not going to kill my own child." Try and put yourself in Abraham's shoes for a moment. He has waited 25 years for this son to be born. And now, some 15 years later, God wants Abraham to put Isaac to death. And didn't God say, "Through Isaac shall the seed come?" There is a dilemma. Do you obey God and eliminate the seed and the savior of the world? Or do we disobey God? Genesis 22 doesn't tell us anything that Abraham said back to God. There is nothing recorded here. If you were Abraham, what would you say to God?

What we have in verse 3 (read verse 3): What does Abraham do? He obeys. Wow. And Isaac doesn't know what the father-son trip is about.

Read verse 4. What is built on the top of Mt. Moriah? Jerusalem. Where was Jesus crucified? In Jerusalem. This story in Genesis is a foreshadowing of the Messiah. This is a foreshadowing as Abraham is going to sacrifice his son, and God, many years later, sacrifices His Son.

Read verse 5. Notice Abraham tells his servants that he and Isaac will go and worship, literally in Hebrew, and we will return to you. Now, what is his plan once he gets up there? He has got to kill his son, cut his throat, he has got to put him up on that altar, then burn him up. So how in the world can they both come back? Turn to Hebrews 11:17-19. Abraham believed that God somehow would raise Isaac back from the dead. "We will go up. We will worship. We will return."

Read verse 6. How old is Abraham now? Probably at least 115 years old. So, he lets Isaac carry the wood.

Read verse 7. Isaac says to Abraham, "Dad, I am thinking through this thing. We have the fire and the wood, but where is the lamb for the burnt offering?"

Can you imagine being in Abraham's shoes and hearing that question?

But look how Abraham responds.

Read verse 8. Abraham says, "God will provide or see for Himself the lamb for the burnt offering." God will do that. What do we need? Every one of us has sinned and come short of the glory of God. The wages of sin is death. We all owe God a death. So what do we need? We need a Savior. And we need a substitute. We need someone to die in our place. We need someone to save us. You can't save yourself. "God will provide for Himself the lamb for the offering" God provided for us. The lamb of God who takes away the sin of the world.

Read verse 9. Could you imagine the hugs, kisses and tears during all of this? We see the faith of Abraham. We also see Isaac's faith as well. He had to believe also.

Read verse 10. He was actually going to do it. He was going to cut his throat.

Read verse 11. The angel of the LORD (again possibly a Christophany – appearance of Christ in the OT) calls to Abraham. And he replies, "Here I am." Don't you know he was glad to hear the voice from heaven?

Read verse 12. God stopped it. "I know that you have respect and awe for God. This is not a perfect sacrifice. About 2 thousand years from now, I will sacrifice a Son on top of this hill. And He will be the savior of the world. Abraham to Isaac to Jacob to Judah to David, Jesus.

Well, look what happened. Read verse 13. There is a substitute. I betcha Isaac was going "whew." Did God provide? Isaac asked where the animal for the sacrifice was. The Lord will provide. And Abraham looks up, and there it is.

Read verse 14. Abraham calls the place YHWH Jireh. Some people say Jehovah Jireh, but really, there isn't a word, Jehovah. YHWH will provide. Each one of us has a substitute. Jesus died in our place. God always provides. Jesus provides for us every day, but the greatest provision was made by Christ so that we wouldn't be separated from God.

Read verses 15-17. The angel of the LORD is reminding him of the covenant and all the blessings.

Read verse 18. The ultimate seed, Jesus Christ, has blessed all the nations of the earth.

Read verse 19. And that basically ends the greatest event in the OT.

Now, at the end of this chapter, there is a listing of Abraham's relatives. Why?

Read verses 20-24. Notice verse 23 again. "Betheul became the father of Rebekah." Who is Rebekah? That is going to be Isaac's wife.

1. Does God want a human sacrifice? *YES. But it had to be a perfect one. Jesus Christ.*

2. How could Abraham offer Him, Isaac? How could the seed come if his son died? *Because he believed that God could raise him from the dead.*

3. How is Isaac a picture of Jesus Christ? *A foreshadow of offering up the only begotten son.*

4. What can we learn about God in His provision? *God provides. YHWH Jireh.*

CHAPTER TWENTY-ONE

Death of Sarah
Genesis 23

Open your Bibles to the book of Genesis chapter 23. Remember, we studied probably the greatest chapters in the OT in which Abraham was willing to offer up his son, Isaac, because God told him to do that. Trusting and believing that God would raise Isaac from the dead because the promise was to come through him. We have seen some incredible events already in this book. Now this lesson is really a sad time because Sarah has died. This event takes place some 37 years after the birth of Isaac because this passage tells us that she was 127 years old at the time of her passing. And the baby was born when she was 90 years old. She dies, and Abraham's companion is gone.

As we look at this passage, I want us to think about three big things.

1. Facing death. How Abraham deals with the death of Sarah. And how do we think about death.

2. Facing life. How Abraham viewed his life, and how he viewed his life at this time. And how do we look at our lives.

3. To see how Abraham believed God's promises dealing with the land and the future.

Let me break down the passage for us.

Verses 1-2 - death of Sarah and the mourning for her

Verse 3-16 - Abraham goes to buy the plot

Verses 17-20 – Abraham buries Sarah

Read Genesis 23:1. She lived 127 years. It has been 37 years since Isaac was born.

Read Genesis 23:2. This is the only time we see Abraham weeping in the book. Notice that Sarah died in Hebron, not Beersheba, which is where they were living in the last chapter, which was about 22 years in the past. Remember, Hebron was where they were living to begin with. Where they were living when they first got into the land that God promised them. Sarah was a special woman. Just like Abraham is called the Father of all who believe. Sarah is called the Mother of all who believe. By faith, she trusted God to have a child when she was 90 years old.

From Adam and Eve all the way through, people die. How do we view death? And how did Abraham look at death? Well, remember, in Adam, all die, but in Christ, all shall be made alive. Jesus Christ, the promised Messiah, came to this earth to die on the cross to pay for our sins. He is the satisfactory payment for the sins of the entire world. When He died on the cross and then rose again, He conquered death. One of the great truths is that death is not the end. I have been asked to do several funerals this year. And the wonderful hope is that when a person puts their faith in Jesus Christ. His death, burial and resurrection mean that when they die, they are with Jesus Christ. To be absent from the body is to be present with the Lord. And death is conquered for all human beings. And someday in the future, Jesus will raise all people from the dead. Some will live forever with Jesus, which we call eternal life because they put their faith in Christ. But some will live forever separated from Jesus, which the Bible calls the lake of fire because they didn't put their faith in Christ.

Sarah has died. But the truth is that isn't the end of Sarah. Because death is not the end. By the way, I think Christians should be sad when they have lost someone that they love and will not be with them. But 1 Thess. says, "We grieve not as those who have no hope." We grieve as those who have the hope of eternal life and that we will see our Christian family again. Jesus Christ has conquered death, and every human being will be raised from the dead.

Well, what happens?

Read verses 3-4. After the mourning period (possibly eight days), he went to the Hittites, who lived in the land near Hebron at that time. And what Abraham needs is a place to bury Sarah. He doesn't own any land.

Question: Who does the land belong to? Abraham. God already said, "This is your land." Does he possess it? No. But one day, he will have the promises that God promised him.

Second question: How does Abraham view his life?

Notice how he describes himself in verse 4. Abraham describes himself as a stranger and a sojourner. Now, what he means is that I am just passing through. And that is how we should look at our lives. Our citizenship is in heaven. Phil. 3:20-21.

Abraham is looking to the future. He is a stranger and a pilgrim. He is looking at life from the eternal perspective. Question: Do you look at your life from the eternal perspective or the temporal?

Sometimes we look at life and say, "This is all there is." We think we need to grab for all that we can because we are only going around one time. Well, folks, you are not just going to live here for a while, but you all who have trusted Christ will live forever. So, we need to be about seeking things eternally.

There are only two things that are eternal (not counting God). People <u>and</u> the Word of God.

Read Genesis 23:5-6. So, these strangers offered to help him because they respected him.

Read Genesis 23:7-9. Abraham just wants to buy the cave, not the field, at this initial request.

Read Genesis 23:10. If you want to buy this property, you have to go to the gate of the city (sort of like the courthouse), and you sit down with the elders so that everybody can witness the transaction, and then you make your deal which becomes a legal transaction.

Read Genesis 23:11. Ephron offers to give his land to Abraham, but Abraham insists on paying for it. In the Hittite culture, if a person had part of a person's property, such as the cave, then the owner of the entire property would be responsible for the upkeep of the cave and also for the protection of Abraham. So, Ephron doesn't want this responsibility. So he is telling Abraham he has to buy the whole thing. The cave and the field.

So watch what Abraham does. Read Genesis 23:12-13. Abraham says, "Let's just cut to the chase. I will buy the whole field with the cave, whatever it costs."

Normally, they would barter back and forth over a fair price.

But look what Abraham does. Read Genesis 23:14-15. This Ephron quotes him a price of 400 shekels of silver. Was that a small price? Do you know what a normal field would sell for on that day? Only 40 shekels of silver. He is cheating Abraham.

Read Genesis 23:16. He gives this Ephron guy the 400 shekels of silver. Wow. This is the first land that Abraham owns, and it is an overpriced burial plot.

Read Genesis 23:17-18. Do you know what Abraham believed? He took God at His Word. "Doesn't matter the price of the land. It is all my land. God promised it to me."

Sometimes, in our lives, things go wrong. Maybe you aren't sure you will have enough money to last until payday. But remember, God has promised to provide all your needs. Trust Him.

Read Genesis 23:19-20. Not only will Sarah be buried here, but Abraham will also. Isaac will be buried there with Rebecah. Jacob will be buried there. And Leah. I guess at the resurrection, they all want to be together in the Promised Land.

CHAPTER TWENTY-TWO

A Bride for Isaac
Genesis 24:1-32

Go ahead and turn in your Bibles to Genesis 24 as we continue with our study of the life of Abraham. This is a very special event. God gives a bride to Isaac. Isaac is now 40 years old. We are going to see God's sovereign providence. In this passage, we are going to see the sovereignty and providence of God as He directs events and circumstances in the life of Abraham's servant. We will also see man's side, which is prayer, obedience and choices. And they go together.

One of the deeper subjects of the Bible is the Sovereignty of God. We say things like 'God is Sovereign. He is in control. He works all events according to the council of His will.' - Eph. 1. He controls everything. There is nothing outside of His control. In our lives, there are incidences but never coincidences.

Question: If God is sovereign, and He is in complete control, where does our part fit in?

Realize that we have decision-making capacity. We are free to choose to obey God or disobey God. You have heard some people say that man has free will. But I don't see in the Scripture that we have "free will." I see that before we trust Christ as Savior, we are slaves to sin. And after we trust Christ as Savior, we are slaves to Christ. But I see that we have decision-making capacity. So we are going to see how incredible it is that we are allowed to make decisions, and we make decisions, and yet this fits in the Sovereign plan of God.

We are going to see Abraham sending his servant to get a bride for Isaac. As we see this passage, we are going to see the Sovereignty and providence of God, but it is a dual aspect. We see how God works in the events, how He works it all out, and at the same time, how the servant trusts God, prays, and obeys. Do you ever realize that God is working in all of the events of your life, even right now? He directs it. Nothing happens by chance. You are not here by chance. You made choices. You choose to come and be here right now, and yet it is not by chance. It is in the Sovereign plan of God.

We are going to study only about half of the story because it is a long one. About 67 verses, so we are only going to study the first 32 verses.

In our culture, we date. Then, after spending a lot of time with that other person, we ask them to be our spouse. But in the culture of Abraham's day, they did things a little differently. Abraham didn't want his son to marry a local Canaanite woman, so he sent his servant all the way back to his relatives in Mesopotamia (southern Turkey) to come up with a wife. She will be brought back, and Isaac will have never seen her until they arrive. And she will be his wife.

So, let's look at this. Here's the commission.

Read Genesis 24:1. The Best that we can tell from the Scriptures is that Abraham is now 140 years old. It says here that "the Lord had blessed Abraham in every way." Remember the covenant: 'I will bless those that bless you and curse those that curse you. And in you, all the nations will be blessed.' So Abraham has had a great life. Look what happens.

Read Genesis 24:2-3. We don't know who his oldest servant is because he doesn't give a list of names here. However, many believe it could be Eliezer mentioned in Genesis 15:2, but we really don't know. And Abraham tells him to place his hand under his thigh. This was a way of making an oath and swearing by the LORD (YHWH in Hebrew) that he wouldn't find a wife for Isaac from the Canaanite woman because God said not to. Because they were pagan. Remember, they were living near Hebron in the land of Canaan.

Read Genesis 24:4. So the servant is instructed to leave and go all the way back north to Mesopotamia, where Haran was located. This was going to be a long trip. Possibly around 500 miles. He was to go and take a wife from Abraham's relatives living up there. We discovered back in Genesis 22:23 that one of Abraham's brothers was named Nahor. And Nahor had a son who had a daughter named Rebekah. And we will see that she is going to be Isaac's future bride.

So watch what happens. Read Genesis 24:5. Abraham's servant asks, "What if I find a woman, but she won't come back here? Shall I come back here and take Isaac and take him with me?" What do you think Abraham is going to say?

Read Genesis 24:6. No. This is the Promised Land. He has got to stay here. God promised me this land.

Read Genesis 24:7. Abraham says that 'God is going to provide a way. Abraham tells his servant to go because the Lord will send His angel before you. The LORD will direct you. The LORD will get you there and get you the right one." God is Sovereign.

But what if...

Read Genesis 24:8. Abraham says, "But if no woman isn't agreeing to come back with you, then you are free from the oath, and that isn't what God wants to do."

Read Genesis 24:9. The servant swears the oath. The servant is going to have to make choices. But he knows that God is going to direct him.

Question: How do you know what God's will is for your life? How do you know what to do? How do you know whether to take this job or not? Well, I think you can divide the whole idea of the Will of God into three big areas.

1. The Sovereign Will of God – which is God working in all the events and circumstances. He is working all things according to the council of His will. Everything is going to come to pass as He decrees. It is going to happen as He plans. But He doesn't tell us what is going to happen. He doesn't tell us what the next two weeks are going to be like in your life. He has told us some of the things that He is going to do. For example, He told us that His Son is going to come back in the clouds and take the church out, and then He is going to come back to the earth and set up His Kingdom. Etc.

2. The specific will of God – where God does make his will known to us in His Word. In the Bible. There are areas, principles, and commands that we are to know and apply. Certain rights and wrongs. Remember, you can never get out of the Sovereign will of God. But you can get out of the specific will of God because you can disobey His commands to you. If God says, "Don't lie." And you lie. Then you have disobeyed the specific will of God. Now, what the incredible thing is: in the Sovereign plan of God, you disobeyed the specific will of God. That's your choice, yet that fits in His Sovereign plan.

3. The General Will of God – in areas not covered by direct revelation, areas that we don't have Scripture to tell us, we are free to make wise choices. If you have a job opportunity to take this job or another one, you won't find direct revelation in the Bible on which job to take. You can know that in the Sovereign plan of God, you are going to take one of those jobs and one of those will be the sovereign plan. You have the freedom to make a wise choice. It's not a right or wrong decision. You can't take the wrong job.

Read Genesis 24:10-11. Now, this servant isn't a dummy. If you want to find women, you have got to go where women are. And where do women go in the cool of the evening? The water well. He is hoping to find the woman who is to be his master's son's bride.

So he lifts up a prayer.

Read Genesis 24:12. The word lovingkindness in Hebrew is "hesed." Which is probably the most important word in the OT. This means a loyal love. And unchanging love. The servant is asking God to show his unchanging love to his master, Abraham.

Now, watch what he does. Read Genesis 24:13-14. The servant is asking God for a sign. When he asks for a drink, and if she says, "Drink, and I will water your camels also," then I will know that she is the one you have chosen. You see, offering to give water to somebody's animals was not the normal hospitality of that day. That would be unusual for a woman to do that. Abraham's servant knows that God's sovereign will be accomplished. He knows he is to obey his master and find that wife in Mesopotamia. He is praying for wisdom and asks God for help.

Read Genesis 24:15. It just so happens that she comes out. In the Bible, nothing just so happens.

Read Genesis 24:16. She was very beautiful. Don't you know that Isaac was glad that the servant looked for a pretty one?

Read Genesis 24:17. That's the first question. The servant asks for a drink of spring water.

Read Genesis 24:18. OK. First test down. Remember what the second test is? Is she going to ask him, "How about I water your camels?"

Read Genesis 24:19 Wow. Passed that test. She offers to water the servant's ten camels. It was her choice.

Read Genesis 24:20. That is a lot of work. And time. Not normal.

Especially for a stranger. Did you know that each camel could drink up to 25 gallons of water after a week's travel?

Read Genesis 24:21. The servant knows this action of serving, going way beyond the bare minimum, was a special lady.

Now, remember what the third test is? The bride for Isaac had to be a relative of Abraham.

Read Genesis 24:22. Remember Abraham was a rich man. And this servant is putting gold jewelry on her.

Read Genesis 24:23. The servant is needing to know what family she belongs to. Also, he asks for another favor. He asks if he can stay the night. Now, remember, he doesn't even know her name yet. He is a traveling stranger. Plus, he has ten camels that need to be cared for.

Read Genesis 24:24-25. She tells the servant she is Nahor's granddaughter. And remember, Nahor is Abraham's brother. Can you just imagine the servant saying to himself, "This is it. I went on this whole trip. I prayed. I got there. A beautiful woman came out, gave me a drink of water, then watered my animals, and not only that, but she is a relative from my master's household."

Read Genesis 24:26-27. Abraham's servant responded by worshipping the LORD. He thanked God for his goodness, guidance, and faithfulness. It wasn't chance that this woman was at the well. This was the woman that God had picked for Isaac. God is Sovereign.

Read Genesis 24:28. So she ran home and told her family what had happened.

Read Genesis 24:29-32. Laban, her brother, likes the gold stuff that Rebekah received. We will read about Laban later. He takes advantage of Jacob in the future.

This passage is a picture of God sending a bride for His Son, Jesus Christ. Isaac is that picture.

Isaac Marries Rebekah
Genesis 24:33-67

If you remember, Abraham is now 140 years old. Isaac is 40 years old when Abraham sends his servant back to Mesopotamia to find a bride for his son. And we saw the first half of the story last time. The servant travels probably over 500 miles north to the land in and around Haran to the city of Nahor. He meets a girl, Rebekah, and she seems to fit.

Read Genesis 24:33. But when supper is set before Abraham's servant, he says, "I will not eat until I state my business." So they responded with "go ahead." In verses 34-48, he tells Rebekah's family the whole story. To see if the daughter, Rebekah, will go back with him so that she can marry Isaac. As we have seen in this passage over and over again, it is the Sovereignty of God. That fact that He is in control and works all things according to His counsel and Will.

Read Genesis 24:49. The servant says, "Now you have heard the story, do you think this is God's plan or not." "Tell me right now, can I take Rebekah back to my master, Isaac?" "Because if not, I need to look for another girl or return home." Tell me yes or no.

Read Genesis 24:50. And Rebekah's family said, "Obviously, this is from God. There is no such thing as fate or chance. We have to rest in God."

Read Genesis 24:51. Incredible. Question: Where is Rebekah during all of this? She's not there. You think they said, "Rebekah, come on in honey. This man, who you don't know, is from a far country. Would you like to go with him and marry some man you have never seen before?" Did they ask her? No. What did they say? "Take her and go." Why? Because in the culture of that day, the girl didn't have any input in the deal. And maybe she wanted to go. I mean, she did get a bunch of gold jewelry.

Read Genesis 24:52. This is it. The LORD has provided. So, he once again worshipped God and thanked Him.

Read Genesis 24:53. This was a down payment for the bride. And I am sure it was a lot of stuff. Remember, he came in with ten camels.

Read Genesis 24:54. So the head servant and his men who came with him ate and drank and spent the night, and the next morning, they were ready to take Rebekah back home to Isaac.

Read Genesis 24:55. But Rebekah's family wants Rebekah to wait a few days, ten days.

Read Genesis 24:56. But Abraham's servant responds with, "We ain't waiting ten days. The LORD has worked everything out. Let's not throw a kink into this thing by adding ten days to it. Send me on my way back to my master."

Read Genesis 24:57. So Rebekah's family said, "Let's call Rebekah to see if she wants to go or not."

Read Genesis 24:58. You may have heard of your great uncle, Abraham. But he has been gone for over 70 years. You have never met him. Now somebody, who is a servant of this Abraham, has come and wants to basically purchase you to be the bride of his son, whom you have never seen. You don't know what he looks like. You don't know what he is like. Her family asked her, "Will you go with this man?" and she said, "I will go."

Read Genesis 24:59. Have you ever wondered what she asks Abraham's servant about Isaac on their long journey south? What the place is going to be like where they were going? Where would she live? What type of house? What is the weather like? Did Isaac have any other wives? Did he have any children? What does Isaac look like? What is his occupation?

Read Genesis 24:60. Rebekah's family blessed her and wished her to have lots of children. May you overcome all your enemies.

Read Genesis 24:61. So Rebekah and her maids went back to Canaan with Abraham's servants.

The choice of the bride is God's choice. The sign is confirmed. Laban recognizes this. Rebekah complies. In God's sovereignty, each person's choices fit together. And every day of your life, you make choices based on information that you have, desires that you have, and things that you want to do and yet because we have such a great God, He works all things, including your choices, all fit in His Sovereign plan.

Read Genesis 24:62. The Negev is way down south near Kadesh Barnea. So Abraham's servants with Rebekah have to find Isaac. And they probably didn't have a satellite locator system.

Read Genesis 24:63. How many evenings do you think he went out looking for the camels to come? Probably every night. And he may be thinking, "I don't know what this woman looks like." "I don't even know there is a woman coming." "But one thing I do know, whichever way it does happen. It is God working. And it could be one day soon; I could have a bride." And that night, he looked up and saw camels coming.

Read Genesis 24:64. When Rebekah sees Isaac (she doesn't know who he is yet), she dismounts the camel she is riding. This is a way to show respect.

Read Genesis 24:65. So she asks who the man walking in the field is to meet them. And the servant tells her, "He is my master. It is Isaac coming." And so Rebekah covers her face with her veil. Why? This was a sign that she was unmarried. At their wedding, the bride would take the veil off and drape it over her husband's shoulder, which is symbolic of saying, "I belong to you. And you are to protect me."

Read Genesis 24:66. Can you imagine Isaac hearing the story for the first time? What happened then? So what did she say when you asked for some water? Did she give water to the camels? What about her family? What are they like? What did she say when they asked her if she would go with you?

Read Genesis 24:67. He loved her. He didn't know her. Is love a feeling? Yes and no. You choose to love. You choose to say, "I love you. I commit to you. I will be there for you as long as I live." Please don't buy into the world's view of love. Believe the Bible's view of love, which is a commitment.

CHAPTER TWENTY-THREE

God Chooses Jacob
Genesis 25:1-26

Open your Bibles to Genesis 25 as we continue in our study of the first book of the Bible, Genesis, the book of beginnings.

Let me remind you of our outline.

Remember, we take the book of Genesis and divide it into two parts.

Chapters 1-11 have four big events – creation, the Fall, the Flood, and the division of the nations.

Then, Chapters 12-50 have four big people highlighted: Abraham, Isaac, Jacob, and Joseph.

In this lesson, we move into the second section of this second part. Because Abraham dies, we are going to move into a study of Isaac. And Isaac's story is really in two chapters – 25 and 26. And even in this chapter, even though it is Isaac's story, the emphasis will be on the birth of his son. So, in a sense, we are kind of moving into the third section pretty quickly. There isn't a whole lot about Isaac. And some people even call him – the forgotten man.

We are going to see the death of Abraham and the death of Ishmael; the focus will switch to Isaac and then to the birth of his twin sons, Jacob and Esau. In this chapter, there is an incredible thing – even before the birth of these twin boys, God chooses Jacob over Esau. And when we look at their actions, we see that these two boys are really different. One saw things from a temporal view, and one saw things from an eternal view. God, in His sovereignty, chooses Jacob to be the one whom the seed will come – the promise. Remember, it began with Abraham, then Isaac, and now Jacob. The covenant will be carried on through him.

Sometimes, when we see God choosing or election, we want to ask the question: Why would God choose Abraham, or why would God choose Isaac over Ishmael, or why would God choose Jacob over Esau? Well, the only answer that God gives us is that God decided to choose these. When you look in the Bible, God doesn't say, " I chose this person because he is better than anyone else." He says, "I chose them because I chose them." The election of God. The Bible tells us that every believer has been chosen in Christ before the foundation of the world. You and I, who have trusted Jesus as Savior, were chosen by God; we are elected because salvation is all of God. He has brought us to Himself.

Read Genesis 25:1-4. Apparently, Keturah is probably one of his slave women. Remember, Abraham was wealthy and had lots of servants. So through her, he has 6-7 other sons. So what about the promise to Isaac? Notice verse 5.

Read Genesis 25:5. What he is doing is making sure that everyone understands that the inheritance and the seed, the promise, and the blessing go through Isaac. Now, we are going to see this all the way through the OT. Abraham was chosen. And through him will come the Messiah, the seed. It is then promised that it would come through the son, Isaac. Then promised that it would come through the son, Jacob. It is then promised that it would come through the son, Judah, and it goes on and on. Then, it is promised that it will come through the son, David.

The truth and principle here is that we have the privilege and responsibility of making sure that we pass on the blessings and the truths of God's Word to the next generation.

Read Genesis 25:6. Concubines didn't have the same privileges as wives, nor did the children of concubines have the same privileges. Notice that Abraham gave them some possessions and then sent them away. He didn't give them the inheritance. He wanted to show that Isaac was the chosen one. He is the promised son. Abraham didn't want any conflict between these boys and Isaac.

Read Genesis 25:7. He died at 175 years old.

Question: How many years have we known Abraham? (100 years).

How old was he when he heard God's call? 75 years old.

Read Genesis 25:8. Remember what Genesis 15:15 said? God said that Abraham would die having a good life and being satisfied.

Question: What people was he gathered to? He has only had Sarah go before him. Possibly "gathered to his people" were those who came before him with the idea that there is life after death. When we think of Abraham, we think about a man of faith. The apostle Paul tells us that 'all who are believers are children of Abraham.' And when we trust in Jesus Christ, we believe in God; we are children of Abraham in that sense because we are people of faith. - Gal. 3:7.

May we be people of faith. Be people who take God at His Word. Believe the promises, the truths that God gives to us. We want to know and apply God's Word. Faith comes by hearing and hearing the Word of God.

This is a sad time. The man of faith, the Father of the Jewish people, the man whom God established the covenant – is dead. Now watch what happens.

Read Genesis 25:9-10. The only piece of property that he actually owned was this burial plot where Sarah was laid to rest. Notice that both Ishmael and Isaac buried their father. Have you ever noticed that sometimes it takes a big event to bring people closer together? It causes you to stop and say, "Wait a minute. What's really important in life? What am I here for? What should I be seeking to do with the time that I have?"

Read Genesis 25:11. God blessed his son, Isaac. I think that is said there for a reason, to remind us that the promise of the covenant is that there would be blessings. And here is the blessing coming to Isaac.

Now, let's see what happened to Ishmael.

Read Genesis 25:12-16. Ishmael had 12 sons, just like God promised in Genesis 17:19-20. God's Word is always true.

Read Genesis 25:17. Ishmael died at 137 years old.

Read Genesis 25:18. Remember, God said that he would be a wild donkey of a man. He was going to be a man always in trouble. Always angry. Always defiant and argumentative.

Read Genesis 25:19-20. Isaac inherited everything from his father, including God's promise to make his descendants into a great nation. As a boy, Isaac did not resist as his father prepared to sacrifice him, and as a man, he accepted the wife that others chose for him. Through Isaac, we learn how to let God guide our lives.

Read Genesis 25:21. Rebekah was barren 20 years after she married Isaac. They had to wait a long time to have kids, just like Abraham and Sarah. But Isaac prayed to the LORD, and He answered him, and Rebekah conceived. God wants to grant our requests, but he wants us to ask Him. And then He answers according to His perfect Will.

Read Genesis 25:22. I don't think she thought there were twins inside her womb. I don't think she knew what was going on. In fact, the way it is written in Hebrew, "Why then am I this way?" She is saying, "If God has promised the child is going to come through me, why am I having all these problems? Something must be wrong. In Hebrew, "the children struggled within her" means *extreme pain.* She thought something was wrong. When things are looking a little dim, trust God.

Read Genesis 25:23. Essau's descendants will be the Edomites. Jacob's descendants will be the Jews. Two nations are within your womb. The younger will be stronger. And the older will serve the younger, which is unusual. Because in the family, the older one gets the birthright. What were the privileges of the birthright?

1. Priesthood of the family.

2. Double portion.

3. Got the blessing.

So, the firstborn son is a big deal.

These two babies are struggling inside Rebekah's womb, which is a foreshadowing of the struggle that will go on from this time forward. The younger will rule over the older. The older normally had the privileges, but in this case, the younger is going to get the privileges. And that means that the younger son will be the one in which the seed shall come.

Read Genesis 25:24-25. The name Edom is a pun that means red (adom in Hebrew). Esau is almost like the Hebrew word for hairy. He probably had red hair.

Read Genesis 25:26. The younger son is holding on to Esau's heel, so they name him Jacob, which means the tripper, the deceiver. The one who causes others to stumble. So we have two great names here. Hairy and Tripper.

Read Romans 9:10. Paul writes about this event. God chose Jacob over Esau. It's just the way it is. God chose before their birth. According to His purpose, his choice might stand. It is not of works but of the One who calls. God's choices have nothing to do with human merit. God didn't choose Jacob because he is better than Esau. God chose Abraham, Isaac, Jacob, Judah, David, etc.

You and I who know Jesus Christ as savior have been chosen in Christ before the foundation of the world. That is what the Bible tells us. Not based on anything that we have ever done or will do. That's why it is by grace we have been saved through faith. It isn't through what we do. It is God in His grace to us, bringing us to Himself.

Live For the Eternal Not the Temporal
Genesis 25:27-34

Open your Bibles to Genesis 25. If you remember, in this passage, Abraham died, and his sons, Isaac and Ishmael, buried him in verse 9. Then Ishmael died. And we read the names of his twelve sons in verses 13-15. And remember that Isaac marries Rebekah at age 40 in Genesis 24:67. Now look with me again at Genesis 2:19-20. And remember, sometimes Isaac is called the forgotten man. Abraham is a man of faith. Jacob would be the powerful, dominating man who had a nation named after him; Joseph would be the ruler of Egypt. But Isaac is sometimes called Abraham's son and Jacob's father. And he is just left out. It seems that his greatest event in life is when he is offered as a sacrifice by his father. But he is a faithful man.

But when I look at his life, I come to realize that most of us are not going to be famous. It doesn't mean we aren't important. It doesn't mean that God doesn't use us. We may not be famous. But we can be faithful. In fact, it is so much better to be faithful than famous. Isaac was a faithful man. And that is what we want to hear Jesus Christ say: "Well done, good and faithful servant."

In this chapter, we are going to see the birth of Isaac's sons. Let's see what happens. Read verse 21. Remember, they got married 20 years before they had children. So now Isaac is 60 years old when Rebekah gives birth to these two boys. Now remember the promise to Abraham that through him, the Messiah would come. The land, the seed, the blessing. The seed that has come so far is Isaac. Guess what? God is going to tell Isaac the same thing. God is going to say to Isaac that he is going to have a seed. But instead of one son, he is going to have twin boys. Which one is going to be the chosen one? And we saw that God tells him actually before the babies are even born.

Read verse 22. Rebekah is in extreme pain and is wondering why. Because the promise of the seed is going to come through the child in her womb. Why is she having complications during her pregnancy? So she went and inquired to the Lord.

And God answered her in verse 23. God tells Rebekah that there are two nations inside of her, two boys that will come great nations, and as they struggle in her womb, it is a foreshadowing of the struggle that goes on even today. The Jews and the Edomites (Arabs). Because Esau's descendants are Edom. The Edomites lived just east of the Jordan River and became enemies that had conflicts with the nation of Israel. And if you remember, God says that the older son will serve the younger.

You see, the older ones are supposed to have the privileges. But God doesn't always do it that way. The first Adam and the second Adam. The blessings came through the second Adam. Ishmael and Isaac. Blessings came through Isaac. Jacob and Esau. Blessings are going to come through Jacob. Reuben was the oldest son of the twelve. But the blessings are going to come through Judah (fourth son down). In the family of Jesse (David's father), the oldest son was the handsome, tall one. But God said, "Not him. I have chosen the youngest, David."

Now remember the privileges of being the firstborn son were:

1. double portion. Which means the oldest got twice as much of the inheritance.

2. Blessing.

3. Priesthood of the family.

This was before we had the Levitical priesthood being set aside in the nation of Israel. The father, or the head of the family, had the priesthood. And the oldest son inherited that.

So, being the oldest son is a big deal. And yet, even before the twins are born, God tells Rebekah that the oldest will serve the younger. And that is God's way of saying that the younger one, Jacob, will be the leader and get those privileges.

Watch what happens. It's pretty powerful. I want you to see something because it deals with a choice. Let me ask you this question: Why is it that God chooses Jacob over Esau? The answer is Because God did it. Romans 9:10-13. God chose Jacob according to his purpose and plan. The statement of hating Esau is just a Hebrew way of saying he chose the Jews.

And from God's standpoint, by His grace in your life, He chose you and brought you to Himself. That is why you put your faith in Christ as Savior. That is what the Bible tells us. He chooses us in Christ before the foundation of the world. Jesus said, "No one comes to me unless they are drawn by the Father."

And from our side, every one of us must put our faith in Jesus Christ as savior, believing in his death and resurrection in order to be saved.

Now, look at what happened in Genesis 25:24. Just like God had said, they're twins.

Read Genesis 25:25. This is a play on words because the Hebrew word for hairy is "adom." Apparently, he had red hair, so they named the first son Esau (hairy).

Then, the next son is going to be born. Genesis 25:26. He seized his brother's foot, so they named him Jacob. Which became known as a supplanter, a trickster, a cunning person who sort of trips you up. And we know he lived up to that name. He tricked his brother two different times. But it came back to him. What you sow, you shall reap. He got tricked himself, especially when he got married. He thought he was marrying Rachel, and he married Leah.

Who has the birthright right now? Esau. Because he is the oldest. If you come to Isaac and ask him, "Which son do you want to have the promise?" He would probably say, "Esau." Esau is his hunter-man. Jacob is a cooking man. That is the way he would look at it. Now watch it. Isaac is going to almost disobey God's plan. But he can't get away with it. Watch.

Read Genesis 25:27. By the way, the word 'peaceful' literally means 'a blameless and under control man.' That means he was wise, he lived righteously, he was a godly man, and he knew what was good and what was best. Esau was a skillful hunter, a man of the field. One cared about the things of this life. One cared about the things of God.

Read Genesis 25:28. Are you supposed to love one child more than another? No. You love both the same. You love them differently because they are different people. But you love them exactly the same. But Jacob is loved by Rebekah. Esau is loved by Isaac. There is favoritism going on. And when Isaac looks at Esau. He says, "Now that's my man, my son." But Rebekah looks at Jacob and says, "That's my son." Anytime you have favoritism in a family, you are going to have some problems. These boys didn't get along in the womb, and they aren't getting along now. But Rebekah remembers who is supposed to get the best stuff. The one she loves. Watch what happens.

Read Genesis 25:29-30. Esau is a man of the what? Flesh. "Man, am I hungry. When I am hungry, I'm hungry. And I am hungry right now." Apparently, he didn't catch anything today. "So what are you doing?" "I am making some soup. Want to smell it? Smells pretty good, doesn't it?" "I famished." "Let me have a shallow of that that red stuff there." It was red soup. The word "shallow" literally means to gulp. He didn't say, "Let me just a little taste of that." The idea is, "I want to cram all this into my mouth." I want one of those 44-ounce things. I am famished. I got to have it right now."

Read Genesis 25:31. Are you that hungry? The supper will be in a couple of hours. But I will swap you right now. You sell me your birthright, and I will give this red soup." Could you sell your birthright? Yes. The birthright could be forfeited. A sinful act could forfeit it. Reuben forfeited his birthright. He didn't get the double portion, the blessing, or the priesthood. Because he had sexual relations with one of his father's women, and his father said, "You don't get your birthright." You could also sell or barter off your birthright if you choose to.

I think Jacob had been trying to get this birthright for some time now. You know his mother told him that he was supposed to have it. "That is what God said before you were even born."

Read Genesis 25:32. Do you see how you rationalize it? "I'm starving to death. And if I starve to death, what's the good of the birthright anyway? I just got to have some soup right now."

Now watch; Jacob is pretty smart. Read Genesis 25:33. Esau swore and sold his birthright right then. People of the flesh are controlled by the flesh. Have you ever been with your children when they just had to have something in the store right then? Right at that second. I want these cookies. No. We have cookies at home. No. I want these cookies here. Please. And they can't wait. They can't see that there are better cookies at home. And Esau just can't wait a few minutes until the dinner hour. He had to have the soup right there and then.

There are people who sacrifice their marriages and their families for a minute of what they think is pleasure because they can't see beyond the moment. I have known pastors who have lost their ministries in a matter of a minute of sin and pleasure.

Read Genesis 25:34. Esau sold the privilege of being the firstborn son for a bowl of soup. Hebrews 12:16. "that there be no immoral or godless person like Esau, who sold his own birthright for a single meal." He lived for the temporal. Esau despised his birthright. Which means he counted it as nothing. You can almost hear him burp as he walks out of the tent. "Burp. I don't care." A man of the flesh. Sometimes, our character is shown in the little things of life. What we want, how we want it, what controls us. Jacob saw the future. Esau only saw the next 5 minutes. And he acted on impulse, satisfying his immediate desires without thinking about the long-range consequences of what he was about to do. Don't fall into the same trap.

Now Jacob has the birthright now. And he also is supposed to get the blessing. And we will see the continuation of this story next. But Isaac says, "I am giving it to Esau." But Rebekah says, "Didn't God say Jacob gets it above Esau?" And Isaac says, "I do what I want to do." And Rebekah says, "If I have to trick my husband in order for Jacob to get the blessing, I will." You know, whenever you show favoritism, and whenever you don't trust God, you get yourself into all kinds of problems. And that is what we are going to see in the next couple of lessons.

CHAPTER TWENTY-FOUR

Renewal of the Covenant With Isaac
Genesis 26:1-35

Go ahead and turn in your Bibles to Genesis 26 as we continue with our study of the Book of Beginnings. In this lesson, our focus will be on the life of Isaac. Remember Abraham has died, and Isaac, the promised son, is left to carry on. God made the covenant with Abraham, which is to be passed down through Isaac. Question: Will Isaac have the same promises and blessings that Abraham had? Well, it will continue through Isaac. God will promise to continue the covenant and all that is connected with it. Also, we see this faithful man in his failure. The Bible never hides anything. But one of the great truths is even in the midst of failure, God's promise areas hold true. God is faithful to do what He says, even if we aren't faithful. God's promises aren't based on faithfulness. But His faithfulness.

Ever hear the expression – 'a chip off the old block?' The idea is that the child is like the parent. And it is true. It is amazing how much our children are really like us. A lot of times, they look like us. A lot of times, they act like us. We don't always realize the influence that we have on our children or what we pass on to our children. Like father - like son. That is why what we say and how we live are so important; they are based on God's Word. Well, we are going to see Isaac's failure. And he does exactly the same thing that his father Abraham did. He lies about his wife and says, "She is my sister."

Here is a breakdown of the chapter.

Verses 1-11 - God comes to Isaac and reminds him of the covenant. Also, Isaac settles in Gerar.

Verses 12-35 - We will see the blessings and the failure.

Verses 18-25 - the quarrel over the wells.

Verses 26-35 - the covenant with Abimelech.

Now remember that the Abrahamic Covenant, Palestinian Covenant, the Davidic Covenant, and the New Covenant are ultimately fulfilled in Jesus Christ. He is the one when He sits on the throne of Israel as the king of kings and the Lord of Lords; they will live in the land, there will be the seed which is the Messiah, and there will be the blessings on the whole world. And that all will eventually come through Jesus Christ the Messiah.

Read Genesis 26:1. Now, this event is so much like Abraham's in chapter 20. If you remember, Abraham went to Gerar during that famine and spoke to the king of the Philistines, whose name was what? Abimelech. And where does Isaac go during this famine? Gerar. And who does Isaac go to? Abimelech, king of the Philistines. How could that be? It has been 100 years since that event with Abraham. So this Abimelech isn't the same Abimelech. Maybe it is Abimelech's son or something. The word Abimelech is a title such as Pharaoh. So Isaac moved from Beer-lanai-roi when his sons, Jacob and Esau, were born, north 50 miles to Gerar, which is west of the Dead Sea. The Philistines, who migrated from the Aegean Sea and settled in Palestine, are called the Sea People. The Philistine tribe would become one of Israel's fiercest enemies. They plagued Israel during the time of Joshua, the judges, and David. Goliath was a Philistine.

Read Genesis 26:2. The LORD says, "Don't make the same mistake your father, Abraham, did by going to Egypt." The word Lord is a theophany and an appearance of God in some way. Realize that in the land is the blessing. And the promise to Abraham is the land, the seed, and the blessing. The place for us to bless is in the Word. Go back to the word to see what God has for us. The truth is: if we stay with the Bible if we stay with the promises of God's Word – the truths and principles and live our lives based on that, there are always going to be blessings. That doesn't mean that there won't be sad things and bad things because there will be valleys at times, but the place of blessing is God's Word and God's truth.

Read Genesis 26:3-4. What does that sound like? Genesis 12:1-3. God is repeating the Abrahamic covenant with Isaac. The land, the seed, and the blessing. Just as the Messiah would be the seed of Abraham, the Messiah would be the seed of Isaac. Then Jacob, Judah, David.

Wouldn't you like God to give you a promise like that? Well, He did. God sent us a Messiah, and through the blood of this Messiah, He has made a covenant with us called the New Covenant, and the blood of the everlasting covenant is the blood that brings you redemption. And God promises to give us eternal life, and we shall never perish. God has promised to prepare a place for us, and when it is ready, the Messiah will come back and get us. God has promised to provide every need that we have. God has promised to empower us as we serve Him and live on this earth.

Read Genesis 26:5. Abraham was a man of faith. He took God at His Word. He obeyed God. May we be men and women who obey God's Word. May we be found faithful servants.

Read Genesis 26:6. So Isaac didn't leave the land as God instructed. He obeyed. He believes the promises that the covenant is coming through him. Now, what we are going to see in verses 7-11 is Isaac's failure. Sometimes, we do really good. We believe in God. We trust Him. Then, we turn right around and openly disobey and fail. So be careful.

Read Genesis 26:7. Isaac committed the exact same sin as his father Abraham did 100 years earlier. He lied about his wife to protect his own skin. Remember that little saying, "What a tangled web we weave when we first practice deceiving.

Read Genesis 26:8. Abimelech said, "I don't think she's his sister."

Read Genesis 26:9. Why would you lie to me? You Hebrews are the most untruthful people I have ever seen. You know, sometimes believers don't live as good as non-believers. Shouldn't we be the light in the midst of a crooked and perverse generation?

Read Genesis 26:10. What is this you have done to us? Listen, we aren't that ungodly. We are the ones that are lying. You put us in a bad position. A pagan king rebukes the promised son. Anytime we sin in public, we lose our testimony.

Read Genesis 26:11. Abimelech tells his people to stay away from Isaac and Rebekah. He isn't going to be the cause of anything to go wrong here. Sin can cause us to lose our testimony. We should be bringing people to Christ, not turning them away. But Isaac's failure doesn't cancel God's promises. God is faithful to do what He says even when we aren't faithful. Now, get this truth into your heads. Because there are people who put their faith in Christ, and then they fail, they don't live right, then they think God isn't going to let them go to heaven. Even though He said, "I give you eternal life." God is going to be faithful whether we are or not.

Read Genesis 26:12. The LORD blessed him. That is the promise. Have you ever been doing pretty good for God, then you blew it big time? And then you thought to yourself, "Well, no sense in me doing much. I mean all that God has done for me, and I go and do that. I might as well forget serving Him, really making a difference for Him." But we need to go on and live for Christ. Confess it, forsake it, and then go on.

Read Genesis 26:13-14. Isaac became rich. Things are going great for him. Why? How could God bless this guy after he blew it? Because God is a God of grace, He doesn't go back on His Word. He is going to give Isaac the same promise that He gave to Abraham, and it's not dependent on Isaac's faithfulness. But the Philistines are envious because he has become wealthy. Don't do that. Just thank God that He is blessing others, too.

Genesis 26:15. Why did the Philistines do that? Because they want Isaac to move away.

Genesis 26:16-17. Abimelech says to Isaac, "Go away."

Read Genesis 26:18-22a. When trouble came, Isaac basically said, "You want the well. Ok. I will just dig another well so they won't quarrel. Three different times.

Read Genesis 26:22b. Whenever you obey God, He gives you rest.

Read Genesis 26:23. So from Gerar, Isaac moves southeast 25 miles to Beersheba. Now remember that back in Genesis 21:22-24, Abraham makes a pact with Abimelech not to harm one another. Then Abraham bought a well for seven lambs.

Read Genesis 26:24. God reminds Isaac of His promises. The patriarchs are Abraham, Isaac, and Jacob. All the way through, God declares that He is the of Abraham, Isaac, and Jacob. God tells Isaac 'not to be afraid.' We don't have to be afraid. God is with us. He will never leave us nor forsake us. Then God tells Isaac the covenant again. But notice that God is going to bless him and multiply his descendants. Why? "For the sake of My servant Abraham." It is because God chose Abraham from the Ur of the Chaldeans, and brought him over to Palestine, gave him the covenant, not because of what Abraham did, but only because He wanted to. Notice – how is Abraham described in this verse? God describes Abraham as His servant. This is the key: if you ever want to be called something by God, you want to be called a faithful servant. We should use our spiritual gifts and talents for God's glory. Also, we need to invest our lives in the service of our Savior.

Read Genesis 26:25. This is Isaac's response to the appearance of the LORD. He built an altar in order to worship God. Worship is responding to God. Some people will ask, "What does your church have to offer me, or what can I get out of it?" Folks, when we gather together with other believers, you aren't coming to get out of it; you are coming to give. You are coming to worship our God and Savior. Worship is our response to Him. It is through the singing, giving, praying, and application of the truth of God's Word. If you walk out of church and say, "I didn't get anything out of it, you weren't there to get out, you are here to give. Give praise, honor, glory, and worship to your God and Savior.

1. We worship God who He is: He is God, the creator, redeemer, the Sovereign One who rules all things. He is all-inspiring.

2. We also need to recognize what He has done. He has saved us by His Son, Jesus Christ. That's the key.

Read Genesis 26:26-27. Abimelech comes to Isaac, and Isaac asks, "Why are you here?

I thought you hated me. You ran me off, remember?'

Read Genesis 26:28-29. Here is a pagan king saying to Isaac, "We see that the personal God, YHWH, has been with you. You are blessed by God. Let's make a pact not to harm one another. If God is with you, who can be against you? When we live for Jesus Christ, nothing can stop us. God will carry out His plan and His purpose for your life. And He will work all things together for good, and you don't have to be afraid, and you aren't going to die until it is time for Him to take you home. You don't have to be afraid of any circumstances or situations that come into your life, and you can walk out of this room and not be afraid of anything that comes into your life because God is with you.

Read Genesis 26:30-31. They recognize that Isaac is now the blessed of the Lord. First, it was Abraham, and now it is Isaac. When you live for Jesus Christ in a fallen world, people will look at you. You will be lights in a crooked and perverse generation. And whether they like you or not, they will recognize that God is blessing you. Now, I am not talking about materially, physically or anything. People will just know because you have a relationship with the living God. And the fact that you go through life trusting in the true God. People will see that it is something different. You are a light, the salt in a fallen world.

Read Genesis 26:32. They found water. God is still blessing him.

Read Genesis 26:33. He called the well Shibah, which means 7. Remember, Abraham bought the well for seven lambs. And the city is called Beersheba, which means the well of the 7. Remember, that is what Abraham called it also.

Now, right at the end of this chapter, look at what Esau does.

Read Genesis 26:34-35. Esau married pagan women and local girls, and it brought grief to his parents, Isaac and Rebekah. Not only that, he married two women. He should have known better.

CHAPTER TWENTY-FIVE

Isaac Blesses Jacob
Genesis 27:1-29

Go ahead and turn in your Bibles to Genesis 27. We are going to see three great people in the Bible at their worst. Isaac knows what is right and does what is wrong. Both Jacob and his mother, Rebekah, try to do what is right but do it in the wrong way. In this lesson, we are going to see deceit, secrecy, and lying. But even in the midst of all this, God carries out His plan and His Will.

We are going to see Isaac bless Jacob.

Well, Isaac is going to give the blessing out. Now remember that God said, even before these boys, Jacob and Esau, were born, that Jacob would be the one in whom the seed would carry on. He would be the one to have the blessing. But Isaac loves Esau more than he loves Jacob. When it comes time for the blessing, Isaac is going to bypass what God tells him to do and tries to bless Esau. When Jacob and his mother, Rebekah, find out that Isaac is going to do that. They, in their own way, are going to trick Isaac and get the blessing. They are going to go about it in the wrong way. Jacob is going to live up to his name, the deceiver.

Remember, Jacob already got Esau's birthright (bekorah in Hebrew) for a bowl of red soup. Jacob cared about things eternal, but Esau only cared about things temporal.

Now Isaac is getting old and thinks he is going to die, but what he doesn't realize is that he will live another 43 years after this event. He will die at the age of 180 in Genesis 35:29. So he is wanting to pass on his blessing. And he wants to pass it on to Esau. Not to Jacob, which is what the promise was.

Here is the breakdown for this lesson.

Verses 1-4 - Isaac's desire to bless Esau.

Verses 5-17 - Rebekah finds out about Isaac's plan

Verses 18-29 - Jacob and his mother, Rebekah, are deceived.

As you think about this family, it is in disarray. They have a terrible family. There are so many problems going on. First of all, there is partiality and favoritism. Isaac loves Esau, and Rebekah loves Jacob. Second, there is no communication in this family. We are going to see that neither Isaac nor Rebekah talk to each other. Each one is doing their own thing. Thirdly, we find lying and deceit, not only from Rebekah but from Jacob as well.

Read Genesis 27:1-2. Isaac is 137 years old right now. He thinks he is living his last days, so he calls in his son Esau.

Read Genesis 27:3-4. Isaac wants to bless Esau, who is his older son. That is what normally is done. But God had already told them differently. But he doesn't care. He wants to bless his favorite. Even though Esau isn't a godly man. He has already sold his birthright because he despised it, and he has already married two pagan Hittite women who grieved his parents. Many times, people know what is right, but they go ahead and do wrong anyway. Open rebellion. Sometimes we say to ourselves, "I don't think I would ever do that." Be not deceived; we are capable of any sin, given the situation.

Notice Isaac is doing this secretly. He calls in his son, Esau, and tells him to go get some food, cook it up the way I like it, and bring it to me to eat, and I will bless you before I die." Now, normally, when there was a blessing to be passed on, it was a family affair. They would bring the whole family together and have a big party. It normally was a public demonstration. But Isaac isn't doing that. Because he wants to hide it. Deep down, he knows he is supposed to bless Jacob and not Esau. But he is going to go behind his wife's back.

Read Genesis 27:5. What was Rebekah doing? She was eavesdropping. She is listening to see what is going on. And she is probably saying to herself, "Does he think he is going to get away with this?" What she should have done was walk into the tent, approach Isaac, and say, "Honey, know you remember what God said to us? God has always protected us. God has always done what is right. Don't you remember that Jacob is the one that should get the blessing? I heard what you said to Esau; you know that is wrong. We cannot violate the Word of God." But that isn't what she does. She does the same thing that Isaac. She is going to go behind his back.

Read Genesis 27:6-7. She is taking matters into her own hands. Instead of dealing with it and talking it over with her husband, she thinks she has to stop him from making a mistake.

Read Genesis 27:8-10. She commands Jacob to go get the goats so that she can cook up a tasty dish for his father, Isaac, so that he will bless him instead. Jacob is supposed to be blessed. But the end doesn't justify the means. It's not right to do wrong. They should have trusted God. But they didn't.

Read Genesis 27:11-12. Now the twins are probably 77 years old now. Now, notice that Jacob isn't saying, "Mama, this is the wrong thing to do." He is saying, "I don't want to get caught." But folks, wrong is wrong, even if everybody does it.

Now, watch what his mother said to him.

Read Genesis 27:13. She says to Jacob, if anything bad happens, I will take all the blame for it. When we deceive, whenever we do things wrong, there always are consequences. Now, when we will finish this passage, Jacob and Rebekah are going to get what they want. Jacob will get the blessing. But the whole family will be torn to pieces. And before it is over, Esau is going to want to kill his brother, Jacob. So Rebekah has to send her son away to live with Uncle Laban, and best that we can tell, she never sees him again.

Read Genesis 27:14-15. I thought Esau was married. He had two wives, didn't he? What is his clothes doing at his parent's house? I wonder if Rebekah has been planning this little stunt for a while.

Now look what she does.

Read Genesis 27:16. She puts goat skins on his hands and neck to resemble hair, as Esau had.

Read Genesis 27:17. Then she cooks up the goat and some bread and gives it to her son, Jacob. You know, whenever you have to do something, and you can't tell the truth when you do it. You need to stop and think, 'Am I really doing the right thing if I can't tell the truth.' If I have to deceive to do something, is it really the right thing to do.'

Well, Jacob now is dressed like Esau, has hair like Esau, and has food like Esau. But the problem is he doesn't have a voice like Esau. But Isaac can't see anymore because he is old and blind. Both Jacob and Rebekah should have believed if God wanted Jacob to have the blessing, then God would get Jacob the blessing without them having to do wrong.

Read Genesis 27:18. Isaac asks, "Who are you?" Who is he expecting? Esau. But his voice sounds like Jacob.

Read Genesis 27:19. He out and out lies to his father. "I am Esau, your firstborn." Jacob's plan is to get in and out of there fast before his older brother gets home.

Read Genesis 27:20. Isaac asks, "How did you catch a game animal so fast?" And Jacob lies again. "God caused it to happen." It's one thing to lie but to bring God in on the lie. Bad. Real bad.

Now Isaac can't see, but he knows something isn't right. He is thinking, 'he sure came back awfully fast. And he sure doesn't sound like Esau.'

Read Genesis 27:21. Isaac is doubting who is in the tent with him.

Read Genesis 27:22-23. Jacob went close to his dad so that he could feel his goat costume.

Read Genesis 27:24. Isaac asks him again, "Are you really my son Esau?" And Jacob lies a third time. "I am."

Read Genesis 27:25. You can almost picture Jacob hurrying his dad up to eat really fast.

Read Genesis 27:26-27. Jacob, the father of Israel, betrayed with a kiss. Jesus, the Son of Israel, who ultimately obtained the blessing for Israel, was betrayed with a kiss. (Matt 26:48)

Read Genesis 27:28-29. Isaac is actually blessing the right son, Jacob, even though he is trying to be disobedient. The whole family is in disarray. They are doing the right thing in the wrong way.

The Stolen Blessing
Genesis 27:30-46

We saw last time the problems within the family of Isaac, Jacob, Rebekah, and Esau. They aren't communicating, there is favoritism by the parents, and there is lying and deceit going on. Isaac plans to bless his son, Esau. Rebekah knows that Jacob is the one to be blessed. And we saw how Jacob deceived his father, Isaac, in order to steal the blessing. Now, in this lesson, we will see Esau returning from the field to get his blessing, but it is too late. But one thing we know as we look at the whole event is that God is in control. He is Sovereign. He works all things according to the council of His Will. No matter what is happening, no matter what these people think they are doing, God is going to work His plan. So may we rest in our Sovereign God.

One of the great truths in the Bible is the Sovereignty of God. Eph. 1 says He works out all things according to the counsel of His Will. So, no matter what happens, God is in control. There is no such thing as chance, no such thing as fate. God takes our actions, whether they are right or wrong, whether bad or good, whether obedience or disobedience, and they all work into His Sovereign plan. So powerful is our God that can take our actions, and everything fits into His plan.

Well, this lesson, as we continue in the life of Isaac, we are seeing God's Sovereign plan being worked out, even when all the people involved are doing wrong. Incredible.

Let's see what happens when Esau comes back from the field. Now, picture yourself in Esau's shoes. You think you are going to get the blessing. You have hated your brother for a long time now for tricking you into giving up the birthright. You sold your birthright for a bowl of red soup. And you hold your brother, Jacob, responsible. Even though it was your fault. And now your daddy, Isaac, says, "We are going to get you your blessing." And you think you are going to get it. You are coming back from the field with some game to cook up for your father. Then he is going to give you his blessing. Imagine what your feelings are going to be when you realize that your brother got you one more time. Now, put yourself in Isaac's place. He has been a man of God; he has trusted God most of the time. And you want to bless your son, Esau, even though you know you should be blessing Jacob. Imagine what your feelings are going to be when you realize that God didn't let you get away with it. And you actually have given your blessing to Jacob. Let's see what happens.

Read Genesis 27:30. If you remember, Isaac questioned Jacob several times if he was really Esau. And Jacob lied over and over with the reply, "Yes. I am." And you just get out of the tent with the stolen blessing when Esau arrives from the field.

Question: Do you feel sorry for Esau? Don't have too much pity for him. Remember, he sold his birthright for a bowl of soup and married two Hittite women, which brought grief to his parents.

Read Genesis 27:31. Esau cooks up so supper for his father and wants the blessing.

Read Genesis 27:32. Who are you? It's me, dad. Esau. Who do you think it is?

Read Genesis 27:33. What happened as soon as Isaac realized that Esau was just now coming in? He trembled with a great trembling. He just realized that he was tricked by his son, Jacob. Or maybe he realizes that God intervened in his disobedience. There are always consequences to sin. Sin affects our relationship with God and with others. Notice he asks the question about who he really blessed? He knew the answer. He knew it was Jacob. "Yes, and he shall be blessed." If God wants Jacob blessed, he will be blessed. I have already done it. Esau will serve Jacob. The blessing has passed to Jacob. Just as God has decreed. His Will, will be accomplished. God is a sovereign God. Prov. 16:9. "The mind of man plans his way, but the Lord directs his steps."

What is going to happen to Jacob by stealing this blessing? What is going to happen to Rebekah? What is going to happen to Esau? What is going to happen to Isaac? God's will is done. But all four of these people are at fault. Esau was trying to take something he knew wasn't his. Isaac was trying to give away something he knew he was supposed to go to the other son. Jacob took it by deceit. And Rebekah lied and was deceitful. Yet, God brought about what He had planned before the twins were even born. Watch what happens. Look at Esau's response.

Read Genesis 27:34. Come on, Dad, don't you have just one blessing for me? Please. Please.

Read Genesis 27:35. Is that true? Yes. It is. Jacob stole the blessing. It was wrong. Doing wrong is never right.

Read Genesis 27:36. Esau commits how Jacob was correctly named. He was a trickster. He had tricked me out of my birthright and now has sealed and bound it by getting the blessing. Of course, Esau actually sold his birthright because he despised it. And the blessing wasn't his. God said it was to be Jacob's.

Read Genesis 27:37-38. Isaac explains to Esau that Jacob will now be the master. So Esau begs again for just one blessing. And he began to weep.

Read Genesis 27:39-40. Esau, you aren't going to be any good growing things. Esau, you are going to be a fighter. You are going to have to serve your brother. There is always going to be a conflict with your brother. And even the descendants of Jacob, the Israelites, and the descendants of Esau, Edomites, will fight from this time on. They will always be enemies.

Read Genesis 27:41. As soon as my dad dies, I am going to kill my brother Jacob for stealing the blessing. Esau was so angry at Jacob that he failed to see his own wrong mistake in giving away the birthright for a bowl of red soup in the first place. He just reacted in anger. He wanted to kill his brother. Commit murder.

Read Genesis 27:42. Rebekah tells Jacob that Esau is planning on killing him to make himself feel better. Esau thinks his dad is going to die soon. He actually is going to live another 33 years. Notice Rebekah doesn't go to her husband; everything is always behind the back, and everything is deceitful. There is no communication. Look what she does.

Read Genesis 27:43. Remember Laban? When Abraham sent his servant to get a bride for Isaac. And when Laban saw all that money and gold jewelry said, "Come on in, have supper with us." And we will see that Laban is the only one who is a match for Jacob in deceitfulness and trickery. So Rebekah is going to send Jacob to his uncle Laban to hide.

Read Genesis 27:44-45. Rebekah tells Jacob to stay at Uncle Laban's house for a few days. Do you realize that when he leaves, she will never see him again? He is going to be gone over 20 years. In her deceitfulness, she wanted all of this for her son, and she will never see him again. Isn't that sad? Let's face it. You reap what you sow. When you do things that are wrong, there are consequences. Notice what she says: "I don't want to bereave the both of you in one day." She is saying that if Esau were to kill Jacob, then they would have to kill Esau (law of the kinsman-redeemer).

Now, what is she going to say to her husband? Has she ever been truthful with him before? No. Has she gone behind his back on everything? Yes. Is she going to go to Isaac, her husband, and say, "Honey, I think we need to talk. I heard that Esau wants to kill Jacob. We need to do something about this." But that isn't what she is going to do. Watch what she does.

Read Genesis 27:46. She says, "I am just tired of the women living around here. If my son were to marry one of these local girls, I would just die. We need to send him away so he can find a wife from a good family." Lies. And notice that Isaac didn't go to his wife either when you know he probably knew about Esau's plan to kill Jacob. Deceitfulness.

In the next lesson, we will study Jacob's trip to Uncle Laban.

CHAPTER TWENTY-SIX

Jacob's Dream at Bethel
Genesis 28:1-22

Go ahead and turn in your Bibles to Genesis 28. We are continuing in our study of the Book of Beginnings. We are now focusing on the life of Jacob. And we see him fleeing from his brother Esau. He is running for his life. He will be going up north to leave with his mother's relatives. In fact, as we study this chapter, Jacob has an encounter with God. God appears to him in a dream, giving him some great promises. In fact, He ties in the promises that He had given to Abraham, down to Isaac, and now Jacob. And Jacob realizes that God is with him.

Question: does Jacob really deserve for God to be with him?

No. But none of us do. Let me raise a question. Question: How do we come to God? The Grace of God. What promises in this covenant are given to Jacob? How do we respond to the grace of God in our lives? Let's begin by going to the Lord in prayer. Let's pray.

The word religion. It can mean different things to different people. For some, the word is bad because they say something like: "Religion was crammed down my throat when I was a kid." For others, the world is good because they say something like: "Just give me that old-time religion." There are many religions in the world. Religion is really a system in which man tries to do something to please God. Such as going to Mecca. Praying seven times a day. Giving up certain things in life. Doing something. But we realize that true Christianity isn't a religion. It isn't man pleasing God, but God-pleasing God. "For God so loved the world, that He gave his only begotten son." In Biblical Christianity, God does it all. Salvation is all of God. Man accepts and takes the gift of eternal life that Christ has given.

How does a person come to God? How is all this grace shown? In this passage, even though Jacob, as best as we can tell, has been chosen by God. He has got the blessing. We see in Jacob's life the grace of God. God comes, and Jacob never deserves it. It is just the grace of God. Jacob gets the promises. Promised to Abraham, then to Isaac, and now through Jacob.

Let's break down the passage. Genesis 28.

Verses 1-9 - Jacob has to leave. Leaves to find a wife up north. But really, he is escaping for his life because Esau is threatening to kill him.

Verses 10-22 - Jacob's dream at Bethel. And he responds in worship.

Read Genesis 27:41. Esau wants to kill Jacob for stealing his blessing. So Rebekah has a plan to get Jacob out of there.

Read Genesis 27:46. If Jacob would marry one of these foreign women, I would just die! So they come up with a plan to send Jacob up north to find a wife from her brother's family. Back to Haran.

Read Genesis 28:1-2. This is a charge. Jacob, don't take a wife from the local Canaanites. Go north to your Uncle Laban's house to find a wife.

Read Genesis 28:3 May the God Almighty, El Shaddai, which means God the power, God the provision, bless you and give you lots of kids.

Question: Did Jacob have many children? How many offspring did he have?

Twelve sons and a daughter. From these twelve sons come the twelve tribes of Israel.

Read Genesis 28:4. There is the blessing, the seed, and the land, just like Genesis 12. Now, Isaac is doing what is right. Finally. Here is the truth. It is never too late to do what is right. It is never too late to start over. It is never too late to deal with sin. Confess your sin and forsake it. God is faithful and just to forgive us and cleanse us.

Read Genesis 28:5. Now remember when Rebekah tells Jacob to stay with her brother for a few days until your brother's fury subsides back in Genesis 27:44. But what happens is that Jacob will be gone for over 20 years, and his mother Rebekah will die while he is away. He never sees his mother again, at least on this earth. That is part of the consequences of them doing wrong.

Now, put yourself in Esau's place. Your brother has tricked your dad out of the blessing. And now he is sending Jacob away to find a wife. How is Esau going to react?

Read Genesis 28:6-7. Esau sees that Dad has blessed Jacob again and has sent him north to take a wife.

Read Genesis 28:8. Esau knows that his dad doesn't like the local Canaanite girls. Remember, he has already taken two Hittite wives, which brought grief to his parents. So what is Esau going to do now?

Read Genesis 28:9. Esau marries again out of spite. This poor family. Didn't communicate with one another. Tricked each other. Threatened to kill your brother. Every family has ups and downs. That is why we need each other. That is why the body of Christ is to build each other up and to be there for one another. Think about Jacob for a minute. On the one hand, we find that he is a man of prayer, a man of faith, he desires a relationship with God, he is an obedient man; then, on the other hand, he is a slick con man who will lie, deceive, strong-willed, unethical, who will do whatever it takes to get his way. Does that sound like us?

Read Genesis 29:10-11. He has started north on his trip to Haran. It is over 500 miles away. He has to cross the Jordan River and the Euphrates River. How old do you think Jacob is at this time? Probably 76 years old. Is anybody here that old? Who wants to walk 500 miles through the desert and wilderness just to look for a wife?

Well, he traveled about 60 miles, which is a long way. He is spending the night at a place called Luz, sleeping outside under the stars, no Motel 6 like I am staying in tomorrow night in Topeka. And lays down on this stone, goes to sleep, and has a dream.

Read Genesis 29:12. Remember that old song, "We are climbing Jacob's ladder." And there are God's angels going up and down a ladder that reaches heaven. It is symbolic of God's messengers going up and down. Communication with God is open.

Read Genesis 29:13-14. The LORD (YHWH) is standing above the ladder. Notice this promise to Jacob is exactly what He said to Abraham. The land, seed, the blessing. Right now, the LORD says He is the God of Abraham and Isaac. But in the future, He will be the God of Abraham, Isaac, and Jacob. Through these three, the Messiah will come.

Question: What has Jacob done in order to deserve the promise of the blessing here?

Nothing. In fact, he hasn't been a good boy at all. God deals with him and with us in grace. We have eternal life based on the fact that we are nice people and that we try our best? No. It is by the grace of God that we are saved.

We have done nothing to earn God's love.

We have done nothing to earn salvation.

We have done nothing in order for God to send His Son to die for us.

Everything that He does for us is by His grace. And you can never get over that fact. The sooner we can understand this, the better off we will be.

Watch what happens.

Read Genesis 29:15. God says, "You don't have to be afraid." How do you think Jacob felt? He is going to a place that is 500 miles north. He has never been there. He doesn't know these people. He is leaving his mother, whom he is close to. And he is going to find a wife at his uncle's house. He doesn't know what she will be like. She could be ugly with a moustache. Not only that, but he is walking around in a land where there are hostile people. But God says, "I will be with you."

Every day, when you wake up in the morning, you can say with confidence, "I don't have to be afraid when I walk out this door. The things that are unknown. I never have to be afraid. Because God is with me. " The grace of God.

Now, watch his response. Read Genesis 29:16. Whoa. God is really here. You see, a lot of times, we go throughout life like God isn't around. We think if we aren't thinking about God, then He isn't thinking about us. We forget that His Holy Spirit lives inside of us. Folks, God is in every place.

Read Genesis 29:17. Jacob says, "How awesome is this place! This is the house of God. And so Jacob renames the place "Bietel in Hebrew" or Bethel. Today, the word awesome is used a lot. That music video is awesome. That Mustang is awesome. Folks, God is awesome! He is God. He is beyond anything you can comprehend. He is awesome.

Now, Jacob's response to God.

Read Genesis 29:18. This was a memorial of worship between man and God.

Read Genesis 29:19. Bethel was about 10 miles north of Jerusalem. This was where Abraham made one of his first sacrifices to God when he entered the land.

Read Genesis 29:20-22. He may have been saying, "Because you have blessed me, I will follow you." Jacob now acknowledges God has his own. Jacob also vows to return a portion back to God. We should also. We should give back to God by tithing and giving a portion of our finances to the local church to support its ministries so we can cooperate with others in sharing the good news around the world.

CHAPTER TWENTY-SEVEN

The Deceitful Wedding – Jacob Marries
Genesis 29:1-30

Well, go ahead and open your Bibles to the book of Genesis 29. We are continuing our study of Jacob's life. He has left home and is on his way to Haran to live with his uncle Laban. The plan is to find one of his uncle's daughters and marry her. But in reality, he is on the run because his brother is out to kill him. We studied that God is with him. God confirmed his promises, his protection, and his power. Now, we are going to see a twist in the story. Jacob, who is the deceiver, gets deceived. The one who tricks others is finally tricked. We will see this biblical principle of what is often called sowing and reaping. We will see "The Deceitful Wedding."

When I was a boy, I spent some time each summer with my grandpa Cinnamon on his farm. Now, I grew up in the city, so it was pretty neat to learn about sowing wheat and then reaping it every June. There is a principle in the Bible of sowing and reaping. Whatever you put it, you get out. You always reap what you sow. And usually, a principle is that you reap more than you sow. Well, in this lesson, we are going to see this principle.

Jacob, the man who deceived, will be deceived. Jacob meets his match. Uncle Laban is a trickster. A deceitful man. Jacob, who has been known all his life as a trickster, will get the tricks pulled on him.

Now, as we saw last time, Jacob stops for the night at a place called Luz. And while he was there sleeping, he had a dream. In this dream, he saw this ladder between the earth and heaven. And heaven was open, and God was above the ladder; angels were ascending and descending on the ladder. In the dream, God told him that he was going to take care of him and protect him. And when he woke up, Jacob said, "God is in this place." So he called it Bethel. The house of God. So, as he continues on his 500-mile journey north, he knows he is going to be okay because God is with him and has given him basically the covenantal blessings.

Here is the outline for this lesson.

Genesis 29:1-12 - Jacob meets Rachel. This is the girl he wants to marry.

Genesis 29:13-20 - He serves Laban for seven years as a dowry to compensate the family for Rachel.

Genesis 29:21-30 - The deception at the wedding.

Read Genesis 29:1. He "went on his journey," literally means in Hebrew 'he lifted up his feet.' We might say today, 'he had a spring in his steps.' The idea is that once he heads the dream and God gives him the promises, he is on his way to Haran and is on cloud nine. Everything is going great.

Read Genesis 29:2. So when he gets there, he sees a water well. And three flocks of sheep were there. But the well was covered by a large stone. Now, the custom of that day was that the owner of the well gave the locals a certain amount of time to use his well. So when Jacob gets there, apparently, there are people who are just standing around with their animals, waiting for the rock to be removed from the opening of the well so they can get the water.

Read Genesis 29:3. So the owner would decide how often non-family members could drink from the well. Apparently, the owner of this well said that you could only drink from his well one time, so when all the flocks get there, then you can open it up and drink. And so Jacob is arriving. Let's see what happens.

Read Genesis 29:4. He asks where they are from. And they replied, "Haran." This is good news.

Read Genesis 29:5. He asks if they knew Laban. And they replied, "We know him." What a lucky day. I come all this way. I get to this well and meet these people, and they know his uncle Laban.

Read Genesis 29:6 Laban's daughter. Ching-Ching. That is why he went right. To meet one of Laban's daughters. And we see the providence of God. The Sovereignty of God. Folks, there is no such thing as chance. Anything that ever comes into our lives, we don't have to look around and go, "What a bad break. How could things happen to me?" Because God is in control. He knew He was going to allow anything to come into our lives except what He had allowed. What He plans. Nothing takes God by surprise. He takes all those things and works them together for good. Trust Him.

Read Genesis 29:7. Jacob asks them why they aren't out in the pasture with the sheep. Get, um, some water and get going.

Read Genesis 29:8. They gave Jacob the rules. Until all the sheep are gathered, we wait.

Read Genesis 29:9. So here comes Rachel with her father's sheep. She was a shepherdess.

Read Genesis 29:10. He took charge and watered Laban's sheep whom Rachel was herding. Why would he do that? She was pretty, and he was there to get a wife.

Read Genesis 29:11. Now, that was probably the custom in that part of the world. We greeted one another in Chile with a kiss on the cheek. It is similar to a handshake. Notice that he also wept. He may be thinking to himself. "I have found the family that I have been looking for." The providence of God. God's promises cannot fail.

Read Genesis 29:12. Now Jacob tells Rachel who he is. Maybe she had heard the story of how Isaac had come years before and chose Rebekah. So she is excited about her cousin who has arrived.

Read Genesis 29:13. Uncle Laban runs out, hugs his nephew Jacob, and asks him to come into the house. And then Jacob told Laban the whole story of why he had come, which was to find a wife from within the family instead of taking a local Canaanite girl.

Read Genesis 29:14. So Laban welcomed him as family. And it says that Jacob stayed for a month. What do you think he did during that time? Probably tried to make a good impression. So he worked for free during that time, just helping out on the farm.

Read Genesis 29:15. But his uncle Laban asks him, you have served me for nothing; what kind of pay would you like?

Read Genesis 29:16-17. Laban has two daughters. Leah, whose name means "wild cow." And Rachel means "the little sheep." Be careful what you call your children; they have to live with it. Now listen to what the description is for these two girls. Leah's eyes were weak. This doesn't mean that she wasn't pretty. It actually means that she had tender eyes. She probably had the look of a sweet person. But Rachel's was beautiful of form and face. She was just striking. So you can see that Jacob likes Rachel.

Read Genesis 29:18. Does that sound like a long time? To us, it probably does. Because we do everything so fast now in our lives. Notice that Jacob said, "I will serve you seven years for your younger daughter, Rachel." You see, he didn't have any money for a dowry to compensate the family for the loss of the girl. So Jacob offers to work it off instead.

Now watch Laban's statement.

Read Genesis 29:19. Notice that Laban didn't say he would give Rachel to him after seven years. He didn't say that on purpose. Jacob has now met his match. Behind that scheme of Laban is "I got a guy who is willing to work seven years. I didn't say I would give Rachel to him. He said seven years."

Read Genesis 29:20. Seemed to him like a few days. Wow. He was in love. When we serve our savior, do we serve with that same kind of joy that the years just go by really fast? Or do we go around complaining about this or that? You see, sometimes, we forget that we are serving the living God. So, we need to serve Him out of love. As unto the Lord. May we just love obeying Him. No matter what ministry you have, we should have the attitude of joy.

So Jacob works for seven years before he gets to marry Rachel. It was a commitment. That is what love is. It is the decision to commit to another person for as long as you live. And for those of us who are married, show your love to your spouse based on your commitment to each other. By the grace of God, the one you got is the one you got.

Read Genesis 29:21. So Jacob has completed his time of 7 years.

Read Genesis 29:22. So Laban gathered all the men and had them prepare a feast.

Read Genesis 29:23. Why didn't Jacob know that it was Leah instead of Rachel? Don't really know. Maybe she was veiled. Maybe Jacob was a little drunk because it was a party. Don't know.

Read Genesis 29:24. So now Jacob has a new wife and a maid.

Read Genesis 29:25. Do you think this was a shock? Seven years down the drain. Why have you deceived me? Or, more appropriately, "Why have you Jacobed me?"

Laban's actions really affected a lot of people. First of all, Leah was given to a man who didn't want her. And what about Rachel? She has waited for seven years for Jacob to fulfill his obligation. She knows what has happened. Jacob has worked for seven years, and he wakes up and finds it is the wrong girl. And now Laban is called a deceiver.

When we do good, it affects others. And when we do bad, it affects others. That is the principle of sowing and reaping.

So what do you think Laban is going to say?

Read Genesis 29:26. He never even batted an eye. He planned this the whole time.

Read Genesis 29:27. Go ahead and have your honeymoon week with Leah, and then I will give you Rachel, but only if you serve me another seven years.

Well, what is he going to do?

Read Genesis 29:28-29. So now he has two wives and two maids.

Question: Is it right to have two wives at the same time? Not biblically. How can you become one flesh with more than one wife at a time?

By the way, Jacob has children with all four girls. *He has Gad and Asher with Zilpah (Leah's servant girl). He has Reuben, Simeon, Levi, Judah, Issachar, Zebulun, and Dinah (only daughter) with Leah. He has Joseph and Benjamin with Rachel. He also has Dan, Naphtali, and Bilhah (Rachel's servant girl).*

Read Genesis 29:30. He loves Rachel more than Leah.

And we will see in the next few chapters that there will be a conflict between these two wives. Because Leah knows she isn't loved as much.

The Battle of the Brides
Genesis 29:31 - 30:24

Jacob has children with all four girls. *He has Gad and Asher with Zilpah (Leah's servant girl). He has Reuben, Simeon, Levi, Judah, Issachar, Zebulun, and Dinah (only daughter) with Leah. He has Joseph and Benjamin with Rachel. And he has Dan, Naphtali with Bilhah (Rachel's servant girl)*

We are continuing with our study of Jacob. We saw last time when he got to Haran that he didn't get one wife; he got two wives, Rachel and Leah. Psalm 127 says, "that children are a gift from the Lord. Happy is the man who has a quiver full." Well, Jacob ends up with 12 sons and a daughter. And, of course, these 12 sons become the 12 tribes of the nation of Israel. In this lesson, we are going to see the birth of the children. All but one. We will see 11 boys and one girl born. And this is a strange family situation. It is really unique. This message is called the Battle of the Brides.

Children are a miracle of birth. There has been so much conflict in our country, especially in these last few years, especially concerning unborn children. The world acts as if the baby in the womb is a non-person. The truth from God's word is clear. At conception, it is a person. Psalm 139 says, "that even before we are born, God is working, shaping our lives, weaving us in our mother's womb." He knows us. And is planning our lives.

In this passage, we are going to see the birth of a whole bunch of kids. The life of Jacob and his two wives, Rachel and Leah. And what we are going to see is a contest. Leah feels unloved. Because we know that Jacob doesn't want to marry her. But Jacob was tricked into it. So he has two wives, but he only loves Rachel. And we are going to see what happens. And I think we will see that Leah seeks to somehow get Jacob to love her by the children she produces. And we will see that Rachel, who doesn't have any children, feels left out; she feels angry. And we are going to see tremendous conflict.

There are some truths and principles in this lesson.

1. Each child is unique, special, and different. As we go through these children being born, every time. Their names mean something dealing with the situation. Is there anyone here who can name all twelve sons? And what does each name mean? Why did each mother call her children what they did? Well, we will see that as we go through the verses.

2. God is sovereign and works all things. We are going to see a bad situation. In fact, the things that they are doing are not exactly right. And yet God takes what they do and still turns it into something great.

3. Remember this. Whenever you break God's Word, there will be consequences.

Read Genesis 29:31. Remember, the wedding week is over. And Jacob is working another seven years to get Rachel. Isn't that incredible? The one that Jacob loves, Rachel, can't have any babies. But the one that isn't loved, Leah, God is going to give her lots of babies. And, of course, Leah is going to be happy about this. Rachel won't be happy about it at all. And I'm not sure that Jacob even cares because we are going to see that he is just having kids with four different women.

Children are a gift from God. They are on loan. We have to provide, protect, and train them in the name of the Lord. And trust God in whatever the situation. Now, in this passage, we have a situation. Leah can have babies, and Rachel can't. In our lives, we know people who are having babies, and we know people who try and try but can't. And then there are couples that just don't desire to have children. And that's fine. Whatever the situation, trust in the Lord and rest in Him.

Let's see the birth of Jacob's children. And we are going to see the names that were given. You may have never stopped and thought, why is it Reuben, Dan, Gad, Issachar, Zebulun, Dinah, Joseph, Asher, Simeon, Levi, Judah, Naphtali, and Benjamin?

Well, as we go through the passage, we can go through it fairly quickly because basically, we are going to see verse after verse some babies being born and their names. But I want you to see how it fits because we see that their names reflect the situation.

We are going to see that Leah thinks, "If I can have a child with Jacob, he will love me." There are people who think like that today. And it is sad.

Read Genesis 29:32. The name Reuben means "reu - see" and "ben - a son." So Leah names her firstborn Re'uven because she wants Jacob to love her. There are couples who think that if they just could have children, then their marriage problems will be over. What does it usually do? Complicate everything.

Read Genesis 29:33. I guess having the first son didn't work because she is still unloved. Leah names him Simeon. In Hebrew Shim'on which means to hear. God has heard that I am still unloved.

Read Genesis 29:34. She's not through. What do you think Rachel is feeling during all this? Jacob loves me; why is he sleeping around with her? Leah is thinking that now Jacob will become attached to me. I have borne him three sons! Levi means joined.

Read Genesis 29:35. So Leah conceived again. But this time, she just praises the LORD. Judah (Y'hudah) means praise.

Well, in chapter 30, the problems are going to escalate. Here's why. Any time you go contrary to God's Word, there will be problems. If you openly disobey, you are going to have some problems. Polygamy is wrong. Jacob shouldn't have two wives. You can't be one flesh with two people. There is going to be conflicts. There is always favoritism.

Well, Rachel is pretty upset about this. Because her sister keeps having sons with her husband. In those days, producing children was a sign of blessing. Not having children meant that something could be wrong.

Genesis 30:1 There is jealousy of her sister and conflicts. Rachel thinks she will just die if Jacob won't give her any children. What is Jacob going to say? I can't do that. I'm not in charge of this thing. Who decides who has children? God does. Not Jacob.

Genesis 30:2. Notice that everybody's upset, mad and bothered. Jacob basically says, "It's your fault. God has held it from you. I don't know why He won't let you have kids." That's what he is saying. Great family life, huh?

Genesis 30:3. Did you see what she did? In those days, if a wife couldn't have children and they had a handmaiden, then the husband could have sex with the maid, and if she got pregnant, then the children would count as the wives. That's why Sarah did with Hagar. Was it a good thing? No. But God, in His Sovereignty, is going to take the bad that Jacob and these four women are doing and turn it for good. All the sex, all the anger, all the jealousy, all the conflict, and God is going to build the nation of Israel through this. The twelve boys will be the heads of the twelve tribes of the nation of Israel.

Genesis 30:4-6. God has vindicated or judged me, and I came out okay because He has given me a son. Actually, Bilhah gave Jacob a son. Anyway, Rachel claimed the boy as her own and named him Dan, which means 'judged.'

Genesis 30:7-8. It's hilarious that Rachel thinks she has beaten her sister. When Leah had four boys, and she didn't have any herself, only two boys from her maid Bilhah. Anyhow, the second boy she names Naphtali, which means 'my wrestling.'

Genesis 30:9. Now, when Leah thought Rachel might be catching up to her, she had her maid, Zilpah, sleep with her husband Jacob. Honey, have I got a deal for you... Remember, I called this sermon The Battle of the Brides. Who is going to have the most kids?

Genesis 30:10-11. Leah saw that her maid, Zilpah, bore Jacob a son, so she exclaimed, "How fortunate!" and named him Gad, which means good fortune.

Genesis 30:12-13 Then Zilpah got pregnant again. And Leah names him Asher, which means happy because she was very happy.

Now, who still doesn't have a baby of her own? Rachel.

Now watch what happens.

Genesis 30:14. Reuben, who is a little boy now, finds some mandrakes in the field. What are mandrakes? It is a fruit that looks like an apple. They are sometimes nicknamed the love apple. It was believed that if a woman were to eat mandrakes, it would make them fertile so they could have babies. And both women probably want to eat them. So we see here that Rachel asks Leah for some of the mandrakes.

Genesis 30:15. Leah is saying to Rachel, "My husband loves you already; now you my mandrakes too?" So Rachel comes up with a plan. "If you will give some mandrakes, then you can sleep with Jacob tonight." So Leah says, "Ok with me." Where's Jacob? Out in the field. He doesn't know anything is going on.

Genesis 30:16. He doesn't even get to come into the house. Leah meets him and says, "I bought you for sex tonight." So he laid with her. But this isn't a one-time deal.

Genesis 30:17-18. Rachel gets the mandrakes, and Leah is the one who gets pregnant. Can you just imagine Rachel? This is happening to me. And so Leah names her fifth son Issachar (Yissakhar), which means a man for hire.

Genesis 30:20. Here we go again. Leah gets pregnant again. Her sixth son is named Zebulun, which means living together or dwelling. She thinks Jacob will dwell with her. Is Jacob going to dwell with her? No.

Genesis 30:21. Lastly, she has a daughter and names her Dinah. Of which doesn't have a special meaning.

Now, watch what happens as we close this section.

Leah has six boys and a daughter. Bilhah has two sons. Zilpah has two sons. Rachel, so far, has zero.

Genesis 30:22. "God remembered Rachel." He opened her womb.

Genesis 30:23. She finally conceives and bore a son. And say, "God has taken away my reproach."

Genesis 30:23 She names him Joseph (Yosef), which means 'may he add.' As soon as she gets a son, she names him Joseph because I want another son. Well, remember, in the midst of all this conflict, God is still on His throne. He is Sovereign.

CHAPTER TWENTY-EIGHT

Honesty Is Honorable
Genesis 30:25-43

Go ahead and turn in your Bibles to Genesis 30 as we continue in our study of the life of Jacob. Remember, he has been living in Haran with Uncle Laban. And the goal, of course, was to find a wife. He has lived there now for about 15 years. He has two wives. Leah and Rachel. He has 12 children so far. 11 boys and one girl, Dinah. And from this family situation, God is building the nation of Israel. We know that Jacob's name will be changed to Israel in chapter 35. We see that God is working in his life. He is blessing him, providing. Remember that God had already come to him and confirmed the Abrahamic covenant with him.

Well, as we look closely at this passage, we are going to see the same old thing that we have been seeing in Jacob's life and in Laban's life. They both deceive each other and continually deceive each other. And God continues to bless. This lesson, Jacob's plan is to leave, to go back to his homeland. And Laban says, "I don't want you to go back. What will it take to get you to stay?" Jacob comes up with a plan, and both of them are deceitful in the plan. And we will see how it all works out.

When I was living in Curicó, Chile and I put some pesos into a Coke machine and got two cokes instead of just one. So I went to the customer service desk inside the supermarket. And told the clerk what had happened and gave back one of the cokes. And the clerk just looked at me weirdly. She had never had anybody do that before. And the question is this for all of us: what if we got something extra that wasn't yours? What if you were at the grocery store, and the checkout clerk gave you too much money back? Do you tell the truth? Are you honest? In a recent study, 80% of people admit to lying on a daily basis and lying on purpose.

Do we deceive, or do we try to take advantage? How do we deal with others?

In this lesson, we are going to see that both Jacob and Laban are dishonest, and both are going to try to deal with each other in a deceitful way. And this is what we have seen all the way through. In chapter 27, Jacob deceives Isaac. In chapter 29, Laban deceives Jacob. In chapters 30-31, they get on deceiving each other. This is the pattern. And as we think about this, I want us to think about some things in this passage.

1. God is the one who provides. God is the one who gives the blessing. Jacob and Laban think they are going to profit by tricking one another. But the bottom line is that the blessings all come from God.

2. The whole idea of relating to one another in honesty. And the whole idea of vengeance. Sometimes, people do you wrong. A lot of people say, 'I don't get mad, I get even.' But folks, we don't have to get people back. Just trust God. Let it to Him.

3. Remember that God keeps His promises. What God says He will do, He will do.

As we look at this passage, we are going to begin with verse 25. I am going to divide the passage into two parts.

Verses 25-36, where Jacob wants to leave, and Laban comes up with a deal to get him to stay.

Then, in verses 37-43, we will see what Jacob tries to do and what Laban does as well.

Well, let's begin; Jacob has been here for over 14 years. He has worked all this time for Laban. And Jacob hasn't accumulated anything of his own. And he is thinking to himself, "Hey, I have been here all this time; nothing is mine. It is all Laban's." So look at verse 25.

Read Genesis 30:25. Jacob tells his uncle Laban that it is time he goes back home. He thinks it is time to get settled down with his own family. He wants to go back south 400 miles to Beersheba. Even though his brother, Esau, may still be mad at him. And may still want to kill him. Remember that God told him that He would bless him. Has God blessed him?

Yes. Look at verse 26.

Read Genesis 30:26. Jacob says to Laban, "You know that I have worked for you for 14 years; I have two wives and kids. It is time for me to leave."

Read Genesis 30:27a. Now, if we stopped right there, you might think that Uncle Laban loves his nephew Jacob and doesn't want him to leave. But Laban doesn't love him. He really doesn't care anything about him except one thing. As long as Jacob is there since God is blessing Jacob, He is blessing him.

Read Genesis 30:27b. Uncle Laban isn't saying, 'Please don't leave; we are family.' He doesn't want Jacob to leave because he is making him rich. God is blessing you; it blesses me. I have figured out that God blesses me because of you. That is part of the covenant. 'I will bless those that bless you. Curse those who curse you.' Now, that is a great truth for us. All of the blessings that we have come from God. Everything that we have is because of His grace and mercy He has given to us. Remember the hymn 'Praise God from whom all blessings flow.'

Read Genesis 30:28. So Laban tells Jacob that he will pay him if he just stays because it is to Laban's advantage to keep Jacob there in Haran.

Now watch what Jacob says back to Uncle Laban.

Read Genesis 30:29-30. Jacob tells his uncle, "Now you that when I first came here, you had nothing. And now you have a multitude. And the only reason you have the multitude is because God blesses me, and He has blessed you through me, so to speak. Now, when is it going to be when I can start providing for my own household?"

Read Genesis 30:31a. So Laban asks, "What can I give you." There is no telling what Jacob is going to ask.

And Jacob responds with...

Read Genesis 30:31b. You don't have to give me anything if you will do this one thing for me. Now, why do you think Jacob didn't want to take anything directly from Laban? Because he didn't want to be blessed by Laban but by God.

Jacob is still going to try to trick his uncle, though. Watch.

Read Genesis 30:32. Jacob says, "First of all, I don't have a flock, so here's what I would like to do. Give me the rare ones, which were the speckled and the spotted ones. Most of the time, the sheep were either white solids." Now Laban knows that if Jacob gets only the rare spotted ones, there won't be many. So Laban goes, "That's not a bad idea." So Jacob says, "From this point on, I am going to have these speckled, spotted ones, which will be my personal ones. Now, I will take care of all of the sheep, yours and mine; that's my job. That's what I have been doing for 14 years. I just want some sheep to start my own retirement plan, so to speak."

Read Genesis 30:33. Jacob says, "Once I get my flock started, and the only ones I am supposed to have, are the spotted ones.

If you come and find some regular white solid-colored sheep, you can take them back because they will be considered yours.

Read Genesis 30:34. So Laban thinks this is a good deal for himself. Because he is just as deceitful as Jacob is, his wheels are turning. Watch what he does.

Read Genesis 30:35. Laban takes all the spotted sheep and gives them to his own sons instead of Jacob. He turns to Jacob and says, "Sorry, there isn't any spotted sheep here. I guess you will just have to hope that some of these of mine produce spotted babies." How deceitful can this guy be?

Read Genesis 30:36. So Laban runs away for a while. But you can't trick a trickster. Jacob has a plan as well. By the way, solid white sheep don't normally produce spotted babies. It is going to have to be something special. If there is going to be spotted sheep, how is it going to happen? God.

But Jacob thinks he can do it by himself. Watch what he does. He has got this plan. He is going to do two things.

1. He is going to use deceit because he thinks he can trick Laban.

2. He is going to try and get Laban back.

Now, before we see what he does, I want to raise two points.

1. You don't have to deceive other people to get what you want. It is God who blesses. He is in control. Trust Him. Do what is right. And let God decide.

2. You don't have to get people back who mistreat you. As you go through life, there are going to be times when people hurt you, mistreat you, people do things wrong, people say things about you. It just is going to happen in life. But you don't have to get people back. Romans says, 'Repay evil with good.'

Read Genesis 30:37-38. He thinks that if you take these spotted-looking branches, you cut them and set them near the feed and water troughs. And when the sheep come over to drink and mate, if they mate in front of all these stripes, poplar, almond, and plane, then the sheep will produce spotted babies. What are the chances of that? Not very good. Jacob thinks he is tricking Laban with these branches. And Jacob is getting spotted by baby sheep. But it is God is the one that causes the sheep to produce spotted babies. Why? Because of the grace of God. Now, watch the next thing that Jacob does.

Read Genesis 30:39-42. Jacob is giving all the weak, feeble sheep to Laban.

Read Genesis 30:43. So Jacob is getting rich. And he thinks it is because he is tricking his uncle Laban. But it isn't by his deceit. It is by the grace of God based on His promise. He is blessing Jacob because of the covenant. And what Jacob should have done was to trust in the LORD. It is so easy to get caught up in dishonesty. But folks, we don't seek revenge. We need to allow God to deal with those who mistreat us. We need to trust God to provide.

CHAPTER TWENTY-NINE

Afraid? Trust in the Lord
Genesis 31:1-32

Open your Bibles to Genesis 31. God gives instructions to Jacob, basically telling him to return to the Promised Land. He talks about the land that He had promised to Abraham, Isaac, and now Jacob. So Jacob says, "He will go." And God says that "He will be with him." But as they were leaving, there were going to be some problems because they didn't tell Laban that they were leaving. They were afraid to tell. They thought that Laban would probably try to stop them. So Laban comes after them. He pursues them and catches them. And there is a confrontation and accusations. At the end of the chapter, we will see the covenant between Jacob and Laban. As we look at this passage, let me raise several things.

1. You can do the right thing in the wrong way. And that is what Jacob does tonight.

2. Second, we have to continually realize that God is our protector and our provider.

3. What can we learn from Jacob and Laban's character? Because their character isn't very good at this stage.

Fear is a great paralyzer. It stops us from doing a lot of things. It stops us from doing things we want to do. It stops us from doing things we are supposed to do. Things we should do. One of the great American presidents said, "We have nothing to fear but fear itself." When you start thinking about it, we fear a lot of things. We fear failure; we fear that if we don't go to college, then we won't get a good job; we fear that we might lose our present job; we fear that we might get sick, and we fear disappointments in our lives. We fear the future. We live in a wild society in which there is a great time of uncertainty. We fear because we don't control things. And because we don't know what is going to happen. The Word of God gives us some great promises and some comfort to those of us who have trusted in Christ. Hebrews 13 says, "I will never leave you or forsake you, what should ever fear." That is a great thing to think about as we go through life. Realize that God is our protector and our provider as well.

As we once again look at the life of Jacob, we see he hasn't been a man of God. He has been deceitful all of his life. But remember, God promised Jacob to be with him, providing for him and protecting him. And we will see that as Jacob gets ready to go back home. God is with Jacob.

Let's begin with a brief review. Jacob decided it was time to return home to provide for his own family. Laban had taken advantage of him for all these years. And he was ready to leave. But Laban didn't want him to leave because God had blessed Laban because of Jacob.

Now Jacob decides to leave again. It has been about six years since the spotted flock trick. So he has been in Haran for about 20 years in total. Jacob realizes it is time to leave because Laban doesn't like him anymore. And because he is getting rich and Laban isn't.

Read Genesis 31:1. Jacob hears Laban's sons talking about how he is getting richer and how their dad isn't. And if Laban gets poor, then they do because they would be their inheritance. "this guy is taking away our stuff." Remember, Laban wanted Jacob to stay in town because he thought God would continue to bless him, too. But it isn't working out this way. So see what happens...

Read Genesis 31:2. Now, up to this time, Laban had been friendly toward Jacob. But now his attitude is not friendly anymore. Laban now doesn't like Jacob. So look what happens...

Read Genesis 31:3. God says, "Go back to your homeland, <u>and</u> I will be with you." This is based on God's covenant and His promises. And that is something we have to remember about our own lives. God has said to us, "I will bless you. I will give you eternal life as a gift. I will provide and protect you. Where you go, I will go. In fact, I will never leave you or forsake you.' And it's not based on something we can do to earn salvation; it is based on His promise to us.

Read Genesis 31:4-5. So Jacob has a little talk with his wives, Rachel and Leah. And he wants to talk to them privately out in the fields. "God has always been taking care of me. He has been blessing us." Now, here is the truth. No matter what the situation, God is with us. We need to keep our eyes on our unchanging God and not the changing circumstances. Because things around change all the time. But Jesus Christ is the same yesterday, today, and forever. Look what Jacob goes on to say...

Read Genesis 31:6. Jacob's wives have come to love him. And respect him for the fact that he has worked 14 years for them. During those 14 years and the six years following that, they have seen their dad, Laban, take advantage of their husband. And Laban keeps taking the money that Jacob keeps coming up with. And they don't appreciate that. So notice what happens...

Read Genesis 31:7. Laban had changed Jacob's wages over and over and over. But Jacob says, "God didn't allow Laban to hurt me." In our lives, we can't control what people do to us, what they say about us, what they do to us. But one thing you can be sure of: God is in control. He is a sovereign God who will protect you and provide for you. So watch what Jacob says in verse 8...

Read Genesis 31:8. "No matter how many times your daddy changed the rules, it always worked to my advantage." Because He is with me, taking care of me.

Read Genesis 31:9. Question: Did Jacob deserve the blessing and the flock? Wonder why God did that? Based on the promises. God already promised him that he would bless him and take care of him. God's grace. Now he is going to tell about a dream that he had...

Read Genesis 31:10-12. Jacob tells his wives that he had a dream one time in which God came to me and told me not to worry. I know what Laban is doing. So all the animals that are going to be born will be yours. So don't worry. I am taking care of you.

Read Genesis 31:13. Remember Bethel means 'house of God.' It is from beit –el. Remember what the vow Jacob made to God at Bethel? Jacob said, "God, if you take care of me, I will go over and bring back a tenth of what I got." So God here in Jacob's dream doesn't let him forget. Remember, there is no Mosaic law yet. There isn't a tithe system set up. Jacob isn't under that law. It was a promise Jacob made to God. So now God says, "Leave at once and go back to your homeland." When he gets back, his mother is dead. And what about his father? Is he still alive? Is Esau still mad? And what will I tell my wives? Will they want to go back with me? They haven't lived anywhere but here.

Read Genesis 31:14-15. We have nothing here. We are slaves and foreigners. Our father, Laban, sold us to you, and we didn't get anything. Nothing.

Read Genesis 31:16. Now we got the money, let's leave. God has given us our father's belongings. So do whatever God has told you. Let's get out of here. We are ready to leave. Issac and Rebekah's household wasn't that great. Jacob and Leah's household isn't that great. Laban's relationship with his family isn't that great.

Do you see what this is a picture of? Fallen people. Picture of humanity. All have sinned and come short of the glory of God. We have to have a savior, or there is no possible hope for us.

Read Genesis 31:17-18. So Jacob loaded up the family station wagon along with all of his possessions and hurriedly drove his livestock to go back south to his father, Isaac, who lives in Canaan.

Read Genesis 31:19. Laban is away shearing his sheep. That is the reason that Jacob was able to sneak away. But notice Rachel steals her father's little household gods called teraphim. They were little dolls that were supposed to protect them from evil. Also, she thought she had the right to his possessions because she got her dad's dolls. Great relationships. Everybody gets along wonderfully, don't they? Do you see the contrast between Jacob's God and Laban's? Laban worshipped idols, and Jacob worshipped the true God.

Read Genesis 31:20-21. Jacob does the right thing in the wrong way. He was obeying God by going back to his homeland. But it probably would have been better to have told Laban he was leaving. I have been here for 20 years. I am taking my family and going home. But he didn't do that. And it says here "that Jacob deceived Laban." It has that idea of tricking him. So he fled, crossing the Euphrates River, and headed for the hill country of Gilead, which is in Moab. This is north of Jerusalem.

Read Genesis 31:22. They were gone three days before Laban even knew they were gone.

Read Genesis 31:23. So Laban pursues Jacob for seven days and catches up to him in Gilead. Can you imagine what Laban wants to do to Jacob? But watch what happens...

Read Genesis 31:24. God appears to Laban in a dream and basically tells him that he isn't going to stop him. Don't speak to him, either good or bad. Don't try to convince him to come back. Don't offer him money to come back. Don't say bad things about him. You are going to have to let him go. God is saying, "You don't have to get people back. You think Jacob has done you wrong. But it isn't your responsibility to do vengeance." And the truth is: people will do you wrong. They will say mean things about you. But don't get them back. Let God deal with them. Plus, God is telling Jacob that he is under His protection. You can't get him.

Read Genesis 31:25-27. Laban says to Jacob, "What have you done? You have deceived me. You have carried away my family like POWs. I wanted to give you a going away party. Yeah right.

Read Genesis 31:28. What do you think? Do you think Jacob should have allowed Laban to kiss his children and grandchildren goodbye? I think it might have been better if he had left waving goodbye, "See you next Christmas." I don't know.

Read Genesis 31:29. Laban tells him that he had the power to kill him, but his (Jacob's) God said not to.

Read Genesis 31:30. This is the second accusation. Laban first falsely accuses Jacob of stealing his family. He didn't because it really was his family. And now Laban accuses Jacob of stealing his little gods.

Read Genesis 31:31-32. Jacob was afraid that Laban would take his daughters back by force. Then Jacob says, "I didn't take your silly little dolls. But if anyone here did, then they shall die." Jacob didn't know that Rachel had stolen them. I imagine Rachel is thinking to herself, "This is not good." But you will have to wait until the next chapter to find out the conclusion to the episode of "As Jacob's World Turns."

Confronting in Love
Genesis 31:33-55

We are continuing our study of Jacob, which is found in the book of Genesis. He is a deceiver. He has deceived his brother Esau, his father Isaac, and his uncle Laban. But remember, Laban has also had his share of deceitful behavior. We are going to see Jacob as he travels back to the Promised Land. God has blessed Jacob as He promised. When Jacob leaves, he doesn't tell his uncle Laban. He just sneaks away with his family and property. But Laban finds out and gives chase. He catches up to him and accuses him of two things. First, he accused Jacob of taking his daughters like captives. Second, he accused him of taking his little gods (teraphim). But Jacob didn't know that Rachel had slipped into her father's tent and taken his household idols. Now, how does Jacob answer? Then, we will see that Laban refuses to accept any responsibility or blame, which fits him. Then, we will see God's protection of Jacob and a covenant that is made between these two men.

Have you ever been in that time of your life where you just want to get something off your chest? You know what I mean; you have been bothered by it and really need to just make it known. Sometimes, in counseling, there are people who come in to talk to me, and what they really want or need is just somebody to talk to. They just sort of want to get it off their chest. It is important that we have people to talk to and be open with. We can share and express our feelings. Remember, the first person you can always talk to is God. He is our savior. He loves us. He knows us. Hebrews 4:12 says that we can come "boldly unto the throne of grace. For help in the time of need." But there are also others that we can go to. Friends, family members, your pastoral staff. And if a person has offended you, go to them according to Matthew 18 and say, "This bothers me." We need to share each other's burdens and go to one another. Keep the lines of communication open.

We see Jacob dealing with his uncle Laban. He is going to spew out 20 years of frustration. He finally, after 20 years, tells his uncle (father-in-law) what he thinks of him. What he thinks about all that has happened. If you remember, he worked for Laban for seven years to have Rachel. Then what happened on the night he got married? Laban gave him Leah instead of Rachel. So then he worked another seven years for her. Then, he worked six more years for Laban's flock for a total of 20 years.

Last time, we covered chapter 31 up to verse 32. If you remember, Laban makes these accusations in verses 25-32. Well, Jacob responds in verses 36-42, and then we will see this covenant that they make in verses 43-55.

These people in the Bible that we know and love aren't living the way they should live. They aren't people of character right now. Jacob is living up to his nickname, which is a deceiver.

Read Genesis 31:32. Jacob tells Laban to go ahead and look through all his possessions, and whoever has stolen his little idols can be put to death. But Jacob doesn't know that it is Rachel who has stolen them. So Rachel is probably saying to herself, 'Don't say that.' Can you imagine how scared she must be feeling right about now? And that is where we ended last time. It is now time for the search. What in the world is Rachel going to do? She's got them. And he is going to search everywhere. Almost everywhere.

Read Genesis 31:33. Do you realize that if Jacob has a tent, Leah has her own tent, Rachel has her own tent, and the maids have a tent – then they are rich? So now Laban has entered Rachel's tent. Oh no. What is going to happen?

Read Genesis 31:34. You can just see her sitting in her tent on the camel's saddle. Underneath the camel's saddle is what? The false idols. And Laban is going all through that tent. Isn't he going to say, "Get up, Rachel? Let me see what's under there"? Well, he's not. Because look what she says.

Read Genesis 31:35. She tells him that she is having her monthly cycle. I can't get up. You see, it was customary for the women and children to stand in the presence of their father. So she says, "I'm sorry I can't get up. You know why." And Laban says, "Ok." She has picked up this deceiving stuff from whom, you think? From both of them. Her father and her husband is a deceiver. She has learned that "If the time comes and you have to lie, then lie." So, Laban didn't find his household idols. You know he's mad.

Now, we are going to see Jacob's anger. A 20-year anger. Let me just tell you. When you get angry, don't wait long to get it settled. What you need to do is communicate with the person you are upset with.

Read Genesis 31:36. What stuff have I stolen? You tell me. You can see him being mad. Did you find anything? What did you find?

Read Genesis 31:37. Whatever you found, just bring it on out here; let's look at it. Let's decide what's yours. Jacob is really upset. He is making fun of Laban right there in front of all these people. Now, watch what he does.

Read Genesis 31:38. Jacob says, "Listen up. Laban. I have taken care of you for 20 years. I have suffered all the losses. Every time an animal died, I didn't come to you and say, 'Uncle, you have lost another animal.' I just took it out of my flock and gave it to you. And if somebody stole an animal from your flock, you held me responsible for it. This is the way it's been for 20 years." You can tell he isn't happy. Look what he goes on to say.

Read Genesis 31:39-40. Look here; it has been tough. It has been hot during the day and cold during the night, and I haven't even slept that well for 20 years!

Read Genesis 31:41. Jacob is saying, "You have changed my wages over and over again." Every time I turn around, you change the deal. However, even though Laban tried to change the agreement for his benefit, it was Jacob whom God blessed.

Read Genesis 31:42. Jacob says, "If it hadn't been for God, I would have nothing." If it hadn't been for God, who came last night and scared you, you would have probably taken everything that I owned. And I would have nothing. But God has seen my affliction. And the toil of my hands, so God rendered judgment last night. God protected Jacob again and again. Does Jacob deserve to be protected? No. But by the grace of God, He keeps His promise, His covenant. In the same way, by the grace of God, He says, "I will give you eternal life through my Son, Jesus Christ, if you just believe and accept it by faith.

Well, you would think that after that tongue-lashing, Laban would be sorry. But that's not Laban.

Read Genesis 31:43. Laban thinks that Jacob's wives are his. That Jacob's flocks are his. Laban realizes that he could deceive Jacob. And Jacob could deceive him. But Laban can't beat God. There isn't anything he can do. Laban realizes that because Jacob is blessed by God if Jacob wanted to, he could harm him. So, deep down, he realizes that this isn't working out that well. I need some protection. So, he suggests that they make a deal. That they won't bother each other.

Read Genesis 31:44-45 So Laban wants to make a covenant with Jacob. A conditional covenant.

Read Genesis 31:46. Jacob makes a stone altar. A memorial. Then they ate by the heap of stones. Now they are acting like friends. But they are not. Jacob doesn't like Laban, and Laban doesn't like Jacob. They don't trust each other.

Read Genesis 31:47. Jegar Sahadutha is Aramaic, which means witness heap. Galeed is Hebrew, which means witness heap. So every time they see these piles of stones, we remember our covenant. Basically, this will be a boundary marker. You stay on your side, and I will stay on mine.

Read Genesis 31:48-49. Mizpah means watchtower. In the Bible, when you read "May the Lord watch over you," it is usually something good. But here it isn't good. He is saying, "May the Lord watch over you when we aren't together because I don't trust you." And Jacob says, "Well, I don't trust you."

Look what happens.

Read Genesis 31:50. Laban says to Jacob, "I hope God gets you if you do these things that are wrong."

Read Genesis 31:51-52. This pillar is a boundary marker. You don't cross over my side, and I won't cross over to your side.

Read Genesis 31:53. Jacob swore to this agreement. I'm leaving and going back home. Stay away from me. And I will stay away from you. They have a great relationship, don't they?

Read Genesis 31:54-55. That's it. It was over. Jacob worships God. And says, "Good riddance, that guy is gone." But Jacob's troubles are just beginning. Who is waiting for him when he gets back south? His brother Esau. What did Esau want to do to him 20 years ago? Kill him. So he thinks he is going right back into the hot zone. And we will see what happens in the next chapter.

CHAPTER THIRTY

Dealing With Crisis
Genesis 32:1-20

We are continuing our study of the life of Jacob, which is found in the book of Genesis. As you remember, I divide Genesis in this way – The first part in chapters 1-11 is the four big events: Creation, Fall, Flood, and division of the nations. The second part in chapters 12-50 deals with four big people, what we call the Patriarchs: Abraham, Isaac, Jacob, and then Joseph. Now, we are going to be in chapter 32 as we see Jacob's return to Israel, the Promised Land in the Middle East. If you remember, Jacob has lived with his uncle Laban near Haran for 20 years. And last time, we studied how he and Laban had a huge verbal fight. Because both of them had enough of one another's deceitfulness and trickery. Well, Jacob is on the way back, and God has shown His provision and protection. Jacob is going to face his brother, Esau, after all these years.

Question: How is Jacob going to face this crisis? And how do we face the crisis times in our own lives? Rest in God.

Three things that stand out in this chapter:

1. Jacob plans. He has some plans for what he is going to do.

2. Jacob prays. He is going to talk to God about the plans. And it is based on God's promises.

3. Jacob trusting God. And that is the part that we will see in the next lesson. As we see what happens.

As we look at this passage, there are some things that we can apply in our lives, especially as we deal with crises and problems.

Question: How do we deal with times of uncertainty, trials, and crisis? When Cindy and I made the decision to leave the International Mission Board, to leave our ministry in Chile to be closer to our family, it was really hard. I had a plan. I would get myself organized and send out my resumé. I had a plan. So I sent out my resumé but received little response. Then, I prayed and talked to God about this. And He reminded me to trust Him, and He will take care of me what I have to fear. And so I did. And then, I received a phone call from Kansas. And I talked with Bro. Tommy Hinson, the director of missions of the South Central Baptist Association, encouraged me. After being here at FSBC Arkansas City for a year now, I know God is the One that has led me here to be with you, serving alongside and with you at this time. I love you all.

Well, Jacob is going to make some plans because he is afraid of Esau. He doesn't know what is going to happen. He is going to pray. And we will see that prayer in this lesson. Next, we will see him trusting God as he wrestles with God. It will be a turning point in his life. God is going to change his name to Israel.

Read Genesis 32:1. The Angels met him. Can you imagine this? Who met him when he left home 20 years ago? Remember, God met him (Jacob's ladder) and told him that He would bless him, protect him and take care of him. He called the place "Bethel," the house of God.

Read Genesis 32:2. So Jacob, after seeing the angels of God again, calls this place "Mahanaim," which literally means two camps.

Question: Why would he call where he stopped "two camps"? Well, what he is saying is, "I'm not alone. Even though I am afraid, I'm not alone because God is with me." And here is a truth that you can't forget. As long as we are living on this earth, there are going to be trials and problems and uncertainties, but remember, 'God will never leave you nor forsake you. What should you fear.' Well, Jacob knows he is going to have to face his brother, Esau. Remember, Esau lived in the flesh. He did what he wanted when he wanted. He didn't think about the consequences. Well, the last thing that Jacob remembers Esau saying to him is - "I am going to kill you. When Daddy dies, I am going to kill you." So, does Esau still want to kill him? What's going to happen? Well, let's see Jacob's plans. Remember, it is okay to make plans but remember your plans should be based on what God wills. You don't say, 'I am going to do this.' You say, 'If God allows, this is my plan.'

Read Genesis 32:3. The first part of his plan is to send some messengers to Esau to let him know that he is coming. He didn't want Esau to think he was sneaking up on him. That is the last thing you want to do: sneak up on Esau.

Read Genesis 32:4. Jacob tells his messengers to go to Esau and say, "Your servant Jacob is on the way back." He is showing humility. He isn't coming as a conqueror. He is coming as a servant. All through the Bible, God humbles who? The proud.

Read Genesis 32:5. Jacob tells his brother that he has a lot of possessions. He doesn't want Esau to question, "Where did you get all this stuff? How come you are rich?" And Jacob's plan is to give his brother all his stuff so he won't kill him. What is going to be the response?

Read Genesis 32:6. And you can just see Jacob's face. Esau is coming to "meet" you with 400 men. I don't think this is going to be a party. "He must be coming to kill me." I am a dead man.

Read Genesis 32:7. The second part of his plan is to divide up all his stuff before he gets it all. "I need to figure out what I am going to do." I am to divide us into two groups because if Esau comes and attacks one of my companies, then the other company can get away. And hopefully, I will be in the one that runs off.

So now Jacob is going to pray. And notice his prayers are based on the promises of God. And that is the way we should pray. According to the Scripture. John Bunyan said in "Pilgrim's Progress" - 'Prayer is the sincere outpouring of your soul to God for such things that God has already promised according to His Word.'

Now, in Jacob's prayer, I see three things.

1. Jacob begins his prayer, showing his unworthiness to God. It is by God's grace that He doesn't kill us all. Salvation is made possible only through Jesus.

2. He makes his petition very clear. Realize that the more you make your petition specific, the more specific you will see the answer.

3. Claims the promises. Pray based on the promises of God.

Read Genesis 32:9. Jacob is reminding God of His promises. Promises to prosper him. 'God, you said you would take care of me.'

Read Genesis 32:10. Jacob is recognizing that he isn't worthy of all the God has done for him. "When I left, all I had was a stick in my hand. And now I am coming back with two companies of animals and possessions, two wives and twelve children. I am so rich now, and I am not worthy of Your lovingkindness (hesed in Hebrew)." And that is true of all of us. We are sinful; He is perfect. We are His creation; He is the creator. We are finite; He is infinite. We are unworthy of God's lovingkindness and His faithfulness. His loyal, unchanging love for us. His love provides for us and protects us moment by moment. It is His love that promises us that we will be with Him for eternity.

Now, Jacob's petition is very specific.

Read Genesis 32:11. "I am asking you, God, to deliver me from my brother's hand." Have you ever noticed that we only get specific in our prayers when we are in trouble? But what God wants is for us to get specific all the time.

Read Genesis 32:12. "Now, God, you promised me that I would have so many offspring that there will be too many to count. If I get killed and all these people with me, that isn't going to happen." And now Jacob is going to do what a smart person does when you want someone to like you. Give them money and stuff!

Read Genesis 32:13-15. Do you think it is wise to give things to someone you are trying to befriend? What does Prov. 21:14 says? "A gift subdues anger." So Jacob sends his brother 580 animals. Does anybody want to milk a camel? "Ok. That ought to do it. Send them on. Move them out."

Read Genesis 32:16. I want them to arrive in droves. Here, brother is a present, here is another present, here is one more etc. I want this guy to be happy by the time I see him!

Read Genesis 32:17-20a. When Esau says, "Who are you?" These animals are Jacob's, but he is giving them to you. Merry Christmas. (whisper) And Jacob is on the way.

Read Genesis 32:20b. Jacob is hoping to appease his brother, Esau. "Maybe he would accept me."

Next, we will see Jacob learning to trust in God.

Wrestling With God
Genesis 32:21-32

Turn in your Bible Genesis 32 as we continue our study of this book. Our focus, of course, at this time is Jacob's life. If you remember, he is on his way home from Haran after living with his uncle Laban for 20 years. He is returning to the Promised Land that God gave to his grandfather, Abraham. And he is going to have to face his brother, Esau. The guy who wanted to kill him for stealing his blessing. So what is going to happen when they meet? Well, you will just have to wait until the next lesson to find out. Now, we are going to finish chapter 32 with one of the strangest stories in the Bible. Jacob wrestles with a man who turns out to be God. And what does Jacob learn from this encounter? He learns to trust God. Powerful.

Spiritual growth is sometimes hard. I mean, it seems like we are just not growing. And we often don't have victory. One of the great truths that we need to learn as we have put our faith in Jesus Christ as Savior and Lord is that day by day and moment by moment; we need to learn to trust God. We need to realize that He is the strength and the power in our lives. That He works all things according to the council of His Will. We need to rest in Him, in His promises, rather than living in our power. It is easy to live our lives in the flesh. Now, think about Jacob. He has lived his entire life, as a whole, in the flesh. He has always tricked, always deceived, always tried to do his thing to get the advantage. One of the things that he is going to have to learn before he gets back to the Promised Land and before he can be the prince of God (Israel) is that he is going to have to trust God. And we are going to see that in this lesson.

Remember the last time Jacob prayed that God would remember his promises and protect him from getting killed by his brother? He also had a plan to give his brother lots of presents in hopes that he wouldn't be mad at him anymore.

Read Genesis 32:21. This verse tells us that he sent the presents to Esau ahead of time. He has prayed, he has a plan, and now he needs to trust God.

Read Genesis 32:22-23. Jacob has put his family on the other side of the river, Jabbok, which ironically means 'wrestling.'

Read Genesis 32:24a. So apparently, he went back across the river and is now alone. Why do you think he wants to be alone? Maybe he just needs time to think about what he is going to say to Esau tomorrow. We don't know. Watch what happens.

Read Genesis 32:24b. Isn't that weird? Out of the blue, some 'man' appears and wrestles with Jacob all night. Now, if we didn't read any more of the story, all we could say is, 'Who could it be?' The verse doesn't say. Could it have been Esau? Could it have been somebody living in the area? Or is someone just passing through? We are going to find out that this man - is God. This is called a theophany. Theos means God. Phanos means 'appearing.' So, a theophany is God appearing. It is when God made Himself known in a certain way. And there are all kinds of ways that God has made Himself known in the Bible, such as in the burning bush etc. And here, God appears as a man. A man who wrestles with Jacob. The word wrestle here is a unique word. It's not just the regular word for wrestle. It is the word to get dirty. It is like they were rolling around in the dirt. Notice what happens.

Read Genesis 32:25. I think what we see here is that Jacob is still fighting and coming to the realization that he is wrestling God. He is fighting against God. What has he been doing his whole life? Fighting against God. Making his own plans. Deceitful plans. And God is saying, "Quit fighting me. Let me handle things. Stop doing things on your own." And that is what God is saying to us today. "Let me control your life. Let me work things out. Rest in Me. Trust Me." So when he, God, saw that he, God, had not prevailed against him, Jacob, he, God, touched the socket of his, Jacob's thigh." God just reached over, touched his leg, and knocked it out of the socket. And what Jacob begins to realize is, "I am wrestling with God, and I am never going to win. How can you wrestle against God?" Have you ever felt like you are wrestling God in your life? Because you are doing things and just struggling. And what God is trying to say is, "Would you just quit worrying about all this on your own? Would you just stop trying to do all things and make it work out? Would you just hang on to me and rest and let me work it out?"

That is what God wants Jacob to do. Watch.

Read Genesis 32:26. God says, "It is time for me to go." And Jacob realizes that he needs to hold on to God from now on. Because he realizes where you get the blessings. From God. For hanging on to God and resting in Him. Trusting in Him. That is where you get a blessing. So Jacob has learned to hold on and not to fight. Notice the next thing.

Read Genesis 32:27. Why do you think God asks him what his name is? Don't you think God knew what his name was? What does the name mean? Deceiver. God wants Jacob to say, "I'm a deceiver. That has been my life."

Read Genesis 32:28. So God tells him that his name will now be Israel. Which means 'prince of God'. It could also mean 'to strive.' It could also mean 'the prevailing one. Like a ruler.' So God tells him that he is no longer going to be a deceiver but a victor with God. What a contrast. This is the biggest change in Jacob's life. From this time on, he learns that you don't fight God, and you don't have to trick to get your way; you rest in God, and you will prevail. Because it is God who gives the victory. And in our lives, when we finally realize that it isn't me that is making stuff happen, but the Sovereign God. May we rest in Him.

Notice what Jacob does.

Read Genesis 32:29. Jacob asks God his name. And God asks, "Why is it you ask my name?" You know what God is saying: "You know who I am. You don't have to ask." And God blessed him there.

Read Genesis 32:30. Peniel literally means 'the face of God.' Whenever you see 'el' at the end of a name, it is the word for God. For example, "Samuel means to ask of God. Daniel. Means God is judge." And so he saw the face of God and didn't die like he believed.

Now watch the next thing.

Read Genesis 32:31. He was limping because God dislocated his thigh. From that day on, he walks with a limp for the rest of his life. In fact, he has a cane that he uses. Every step that he takes now will remind him to trust God. It can't be your own strength, but it has to be God's strength. Then, the writer gives a little side note.

Read Genesis 32:32. So the Israelites decided not to eat this part of the hip ever, just to remember what happened there. I don't think we want something like a limp or an injury to cause us to remember that we have to trust God. But that is what he did for Jacob. And he can't run very fast now. He isn't very strong now. Who is he fixing to face in the morning? Esau. With 400 men. So Jacob isn't going to be able to fight him. So what is he going to have to do? Trust God.

CHAPTER THIRTY-ONE

Reconciliation – Humility & Forgiveness
Genesis 33:1-11

Well, in this lesson, Jacob meets Esau after 20 years of separation. When Jacob left, there was hurt, anger, and sin. Jacob had deceived and stolen the blessing. And Esau wanted to kill Jacob. And after all these years, they are going to meet. In this lesson, we will finally get to see what happens. Now, remember that God had promised Jacob that He would be with him. That He would protect him. And this lesson is one of the key events in Jacob's life. It is a truth – that all of us need to see, and that is the issue of reconciliation. The two brothers are reconciled and brought back together. And in our lives, we all need it. In fact, every person needs to be reconciled to God because we all have sinned and come short of the glory of God. And the second thing is many times, we need to be reconciled to each other. As we look at this passage, may we gain insight so that if there is an issue of reconciliation in our lives, if we need that, we will see the truths and principles that tie together.

You know, sometimes we get upset with each other, we get mad, we get hurt, we break fellowship with each other. And sometimes, it happens with our own families, friends, neighbors, people we work with, or other believers. Well, what do we do when this happens? Are we supposed to just have broken relationships with one another? I think one of the key truths in the Bible is the truth of reconciliation. The reconciliation of man to God. In fact, that is the story of the Bible. Perfect God brings sinful man back to Himself using His Son Jesus Christ.

As we look at this passage, you might say, 'It is a miracle.' In fact, wait to see what Esau does. It is incredible. There is humility. There is forgiveness. And it all ties together based on the grace of God.

Remember, we studied how Jacob learned that you can't fight God. You just need to hold on to God. And to trust God. And then God changes his name to Israel, which means prince of God.

Read Genesis 33:1a. You know what he is going to do? He is going to go back to being Jacob instead of Israel. You see, Jacob, the deceiver, always has to come up with a plan and figure stuff out by himself. Instead of trusting God.

Question: Why do you think Esau brought 400 men? Well, you will have to come back to the next lesson to find out. What does Jacob think? He thinks Esau is coming to kill him, right? So, look at what Jacob does.

Read Genesis 33:1b. You see, what he is going to do is divide up the two women and their children. He is going to take the two handmaids and their children and put them into four groups. Why is he doing that? Does he want to protect them, like we saw before? If Esau jumps on one group, maybe the rest can get away. Is that really his plan? Well, notice what he does.

Read Genesis 33:2. He put the least valuable to him up front, "Let's get the maids and her kids up there in front. So if Esau kills them first, maybe we will have a chance of escape." Then he puts Leah and her kids next. Then, finally, Rachel and Joseph last. Favoritism. It is always a problem in polygamy. When you look I the Bible, anytime a guy would have more than one wife, he always favored some over another. Conflict. Over and over.

Read Genesis 33:3. Maybe he is going to trust God on this one. He goes out in front of his family. And he bows down before his brother Esau. And Esau is getting a little closer, and Jacob bows down again. Seven times, Jacob bows down. This is an act of reconciliation. And there are two truths that stand out in the whole issue of reconciliation.

1. Humility.

2. Forgiveness.

And they go together. There has to be humility, where one is saying, 'I admit I did wrong.' And then there has to be the act of forgiveness. And forgiveness is always based on grace. You don't make people earn forgiveness. 'Well, if you act right, I might forgive you.' When you look at Jacob in these verses, you see humility. He bows down before his brother in respect seven times. He is hoping to be reconciled. Now, notice what Esau does. Now, if I hadn't read this, I would have assumed that Esau was going to kill him. Because Esau, who was openly rebellious to his parents, wanted to kill his brother for stealing his blessing 20 years back, he isn't going to forget, is he?

Watch what he does.

Read Genesis 33:4. Esau embraces his brother. Kiss him. And wept. What happened to Esau? Maybe he realized that some of his problems were his own fault. 'I am the one that married the foreign woman. I am the one that gave up my birthright.' Maybe there is the aspect that he wants to be reconciled as well. And these two brothers just hug and weep together. And there is forgiveness. And it is based on grace. Jacob hadn't done anything to desire forgiveness from Esau. But Esau, in grace – forgives. Look what happens.

Read Genesis 33:5. Now Jacob got the blessing. Sure enough, there is a blessing right there. Two wives, two handmaids, and twelve children. Jacob answers Esau by saying that, "God has graciously given me my family.' Always remember everything you have – the grace of God. Our salvation is the grace of God. Our Christian lives are the grace of God. Every possession we have is the grace of God. Our future is the grace of God.

Read Genesis 33:6-7. Now, everybody in Jacob's family comes up and bows down. They all come in humility. Now, watch Esau's question.

Read Genesis 33:8a. Remember what Jacob had already sent ahead of them? 580 animals. Present after present after present. Because he wants Esau to forget about killing him. But notice what Esau asks. Read Genesis 33:8a. Esau asks, "What did you mean by sending out all of those animals out to me?" And notice the Jacob's answer.

Read Genesis 33:8b. Jacob replies, "To find favor with you. I am seeking reconciliation and forgiveness." That's humility. "I have given you the gifts, I have bowed down before you, I brought my whole family here. I recognize it was wrong to steal the blessing." Now, watch Esau's response.

Read Genesis 33:9. Esau replies with, "That's ok, I have plenty. You just keep your animals." But that isn't exactly the answer that Jacob needs. Remember, Jacob is in need of forgiveness. He wants Esau to accept the gifts, which means he is forgiving him. But notice what Jacob says.

Read Genesis 33:10. Jacob says, "Now listen, if I have really found favor, then you need to accept the present. Because if you accept the present, you are forgiving me. I have to have this. I have to know that it's ok."

Read Genesis 33:11a. Now, if you look back at verse 9. Esau said, "I have plenty." Those are two different words in the Hebrew. The first plenty in verse 9 means, "I have a lot." But when Jacob says, "I have plenty" in verse 11, it means "I have all." Jacob is saying, "Take this because God has given me everything." He realized that under the blessing, under the covenant that God made with him, he had everything. Not just a lot of stuff. But he had everything. And sometimes, I think we make the mistake of thinking that we have a lot. Folks, we don't have a lot. We have everything. Everything that we need. For life and godliness. Sometimes we forget that we have everything. We go through life complaining, afraid etc. Jacob says to Esau, "You have to take my present because I have to be reconciled to you." Well, Esau took it. Look what it says in Genesis 33:11. Esau took the present. Which is saying, "I forgive you."

Now, we are going to stop here for this lesson. In the next lesson, we will finish this little passage. And we will focus on reconciliation between each other.

Reconciliation – Rejected
Genesis 33:12-20

Open your Bibles to Genesis 33 as we continue our study of the book of Genesis. And our focus at this time is Jacob's life. We are seeing the reconciliation between Jacob and Esau. We are seeing the whole biblical truth of reconciliation. And when we think about reconciliation, there are two things to remember

1. First of all, our reconciliation with God.

2. Second is our reconciliation with other people.

It seems that there is nothing worse than two people who can't get along. People who are at odds with each other. Maybe at one time, they were friends, family, or co-workers, but now they are at odds. Well, what needs to happen? Of course, we know, biblically speaking, they need to be reconciled. There are two key aspects that we saw when we started this chapter 33. Humility and forgiveness. Humility is when we humble ourselves, recognizing where we are wrong, and then the forgiveness aspect – the giving and acceptance of forgiveness.

Last time, we saw Jacob's return and the meeting of his brother Esau. We saw Jacob humbling himself before Esau, and we saw Esau forgiving. And it was a grace act all the way through.

Now, last time, we spent some time talking about reconciliation with God. Now, we are going to spend some time talking about reconciliation with others.

It is very obvious that as you go through life, you are going to have some problems. There are times we hit each other in the wrong way, so to speak. And we need reconciliation. As you think about your life, there are times in our lives when we have separation and breaking fellowship with other people. In order to have reconciliation with others, the same two aspects as we have in our reconciliation with God are humility and forgiveness. If you think about the lives of Jacob and Esau, we see the humility when Jacob was willing to come to Esau, bow down before him, and even call himself his servant, recognizing that he humbled himself before his brother. We saw forgiveness by grace in which Esau willingly ran to his brother, hugged him, and took the gift. And we are going to see in this passage that he is inviting his brother, Jacob, to come and live with him. And I want you to realize that Jacob doesn't want to go. Now, Jacob is glad that they are reconciled. But he doesn't want to live with him.

Question: When you are reconciled with someone, does that mean that you have to be friends with them? I don't think the answer is yes every time. In fact, the answer may be no. We are going to see that Jacob and Esau have never been friends and will never be friends. But they are reconciled.

Question: Is there somebody that you need to be reconciled to? Now, think about it. First of all, there is humility. And when dealing with another person, it comes from both sides. But sometimes we have this idea that if there is going to be reconciliation, the person who did us wrong needs to come to us and say, 'I did you wrong.' But that's not what the Bible says. We should be the ones who go and try to get things right. Humility. By the way, what is the thing that causes us not to be reconciled with someone? Pride.

The second aspect of reconciliation is forgiveness. Regardless of the situation, we have to forgive. Now, some people have this idea that they need to come and ask me for forgiveness, and I will forgive them. For example - if they did me wrong, then they need to come to me and ask for forgiveness, and I will say 'yes.' But I want you to understand that you must forgive whether anybody ever admits to you.

If you have been hurt by somebody, you have to forgive them. It is for your good. Whether they ever recognize it. There is an old saying that says, "If you bear a grudge, bear it before God." Make sure you give it to Him. If somebody asks for forgiveness, how many times do you forgive them? Every time.

The Greek word for forgiveness means to lift up and take away. To release the debt. Whatever you think they might owe you, whatever they have done wrong to you – you release them from the debt. You let it go. That is forgiveness. That's not to say that it didn't happen. That's not to say that it wasn't wrong. That's not to say that it really didn't hurt. It is releasing the debt. And it is for us. Ephesians 4:32: "Be kind to one another, tender-hearted, forgiving each other, just as God in Christ also has forgiven you ."

The basis that you forgive others is the basis that God has forgiven you. And it is for your good. Chuck Swindoll said, "The extent that you can envision God's forgiveness to you, to that same measure, you will be given the capacity to forgive others."

Sometimes, we forget all that God has done for us. And then get petty with someone else, maybe even another believer, because they didn't do us the way we thought they should do us. So here is the question for all of us.

Question: Is there a need for reconciliation in our lives with someone else? It takes both sides in one sense because there has to be humility.

Second, there is forgiveness, which is canceling the debt. You forgive the person whether they ever admit anything or not.

Third, it is all of grace. When we are reconciled with one another, we show the world how God has brought us to Himself.

Read Genesis 33:12. Esau is pretty happy, isn't he? First of all, I can't imagine Esau wanting to be with Jacob. To be really honest with you. But Esau does. Can you imagine Jacob wanting to be with Esau? No. And he really doesn't. Watch.

Read Genesis 33:13-14. So, I have to go slow. You go on ahead. See you at Seir.

But watch what happens. Read Genesis 33:15a. So Esau says to Jacob, "Ok, let me leave some of my men with you to help you. That is why I brought these 400 men." Is that why he brought the 400 men? I think he was afraid there might be a battle with Jacob. And, of course, Jacob was afraid because Esau did bring 400 men. But what is Esau going to do with the 400 men now? He is willing to lend Jacob some of his men to help them on their journey. But what does Jacob say?

Read Genesis 33:15b. No thanks. Question: Where does Esau think Jacob is going? Mt. Seir with him.

Read Genesis 33:16-17. Esau goes on to Seir. But Jacob stops at Succoth and builds himself a house on a ranch. Then, later on in this chapter, we see that he goes on west to the city of Shechem. Then, in chapter 35, he moves to Bethel because God tells him to do so.

Question: Where should he have gone to begin with? Bethel. Remember, he made a promise to God at Bethel. In Genesis 28:20-22. "If you take care of me when I come back, I am going to give you a tenth of all my stuff." And now we see that he tells his brother that he is going to Seir, but he really doesn't mean it. He instead is going to Succoth.

Read Genesis 33:18-20. 'El-Elohe-Israel.' Means God the God of Israel. So now he goes to Shechem, which isn't a good place to live. And we will see why in the next lesson. One of the most grossest stories in the Bible.

CHAPTER THIRTY-TWO

The Effects of Sin
Genesis 34:1-23

Open your Bibles to Genesis 34. This is one of the passages in the Bible that I wish we could skip. I wish we could ignore it. But it is there for a reason. We are going to get a good look at ourselves because, in this lesson, we see the effects of sin and dishonesty, and not only does it affect Jacob and his family, but it affects an entire city. As we study this passage, may we realize the effects of sin, and may we choose to live by God's Word and do what's right.

The question could be raised: Are people good or bad? Well, the Bible says in Isaiah 53:6, "All of us like sheep who have gone astray, each of us has turned to his own way..." Romans 3:10: "There is none righteous, not even one." Folks, we are sinful, and the only hope we have is Jesus Christ. Jesus Christ, who came and died in our place, who rose again and paid for our sins. Who gives us eternal life and changes us from the inside – out. We are a new creation. In this lesson, as we look at chapter 34, we will see some events at Shechem. This was a city named after a man named Shechem. In this passage, we clearly see the sinfulness of man. And I wish we could just skip this passage. Because it is such a gross passage. There is rape, lying, murder, stealing, slavery etc. The Bible never covers up the truth. What people are really like.

As we continue in our study, it will be a sad time. Last time, it was a happy time. The reconciliation of Jacob and Esau. But this lesson, and it is a horrible thing that happens at Shechem.

Read Genesis 34:1. Now remember Leah had six sons and one daughter by Jacob. It says here that "Dinah went out to visit the daughters of the land." This is the idea why she decided to start connecting with these pagan women. Remember, were they supposed to intermarry with anyone in the land? No. Was it because of racism? No. It was because of their false worship. God never said, "Don't intermarry these people because they are a different race." That isn't even an issue. God said, "Don't intermarry with them because they worship false gods, and they will turn you away from the true God."

Now, look what happened.

Read Genesis 34:2. Shechem was a very important man. Even the city is named after him. This event is written in Hebrew in such a way that shows that he came and he did this. It shows force. 'and he took her and lay with her by force.' He raped her. He saw her, took her, which has the idea of 'grabbed her,' and raped her by force. And we see the destructiveness of sin. This act is not going to just affect Dinah. But also Shechem. And it will affect Jacob. It will affect her six brothers. Plus five other half-brothers. You don't want to ever mess with a girl who has eleven brothers, right? But what is going to happen to Shechem, his father, and his family? Not only that, but the entire city is going to be affected. Sometimes, when we sin, we think, 'Nobody will ever know.' And it will only affect me. Sin never just affects you. It always affects others.

Read Genesis 34:3. Well, thanks a lot. It is a little bit late to speak tenderly after what he has already done. "Hey baby, you know who I am. I am the prince of this area. And I think you are really pretty. And I kind of like you. I think I will go talk to my dad; maybe we can work something out." By the way, she doesn't go home. He keeps her in his tent. He has raped her, and in a sense, she is a hostage who can't leave. Watch what happens.

Read Genesis 34:4. So Shechem goes to his father, and he is probably used to getting whatever he wants, "I want this girl. Go talk to her father and tell him so. Just go handle it for me, Dad.

Read Genesis 34:5. The news reached Jacob about what had happened to his daughter. And he doesn't say much. His boys were out in the fields. Why would he keep silent? Could it be he just needed to figure out what to do? How do you think the eleven brothers are going to feel? Well, you can imagine that they are going to be upset. Watch.

Read Genesis 34:6. Now Hamor doesn't approach Jacob with his head down low. "I am so sorry. I don't know exactly what happened. I just know my son made a big mistake. But I want you to know that he loves your daughter. Would you just accept our apology?" He didn't come that way at all. He came and said, "By the way, my son would like to marry your daughter. I would like for you to work that out."

Read Genesis 34:7. You know we live in a society today where most people think it is no big deal to have sex before marriage. It's okay if you just love them. It's okay if you use protection. Everybody is doing it. So many women have children by their boyfriends. Extra-marital affairs. What a society. So the boys came in from the field, and they were mad. "This is a disgraceful thing; such a thing ought not to be done." Literally, in Hebrew, "This is the kind of thing you don't talk about." It is always wrong. I want you to see the effects of sin. Everybody is upset. But where is Dinah? She is back at Shechem's tent. I bet the boys say, "Where is Dinah? Why isn't she here? Is she a prisoner? What have you done with her?" Notice what he says when he gets there.

Read Genesis 34:8. Where is the "I'm sorry." Where is the "This is a really bad thing, we are really upset by this, we want to make it right." As if you could make it right.

Now, look at the next verse.

Read Genesis 34:9. "I got a plan. This could be the start of something big. My son wants to intermarry with your daughter, so you can just intermarry with my daughters." Remember God's restriction. 'Do not intermarry with the Canaanites.' These people were the Hivites, who were part of the Canaanites. So, the Israelites needed to be separate people. They were not to compromise. By the way, once you start to compromise, It is so easy. Once you start the slippery slope, it just goes.

Read Genesis 34:10. Whose land is it? God's Who did God give it to? Abraham. Then to Isaac, then to Jacob. God has already come to Jacob and told him that this is his land. He doesn't need to make a deal with Hamor and Shechem to get the land. In chapter 35, God is going to come to Jacob to remind him again about His covenant.

Re-read verse 10. Does Hamor appear like he is coming across like, "Listen, we want you guys to be part of us." If you look at verse 23, Hamor goes back to his people and says, "Listen, if we can get these guys to kind of intermarry with us, we will take all their property." He is a deceitful man, just like his son. But on the other side, Jacob hadn't been a great champion of godliness, had he? Wait to see what his sons do.

Read Genesis 34:11. Shechem goes to Jacob and his sons and offers a dowry of whatever they want. Because he is the prince, he's got money.

Read Genesis 34:12. I wonder if he thinks that if he comes up with a large amount of money, then Dinah's family won't be mad at him. Do you think those brothers can be bought off? No way. They are mad! Do you know what the brothers are saying to each other? '"We are going to kill these people!"'

Read Genesis 34:13. They decided to lie to Hamor and Shechem because we know what he has done. And we aren't going to let him get away with this. Now, this is the natural response. Get them back. But folks, as Christians, we must live supernatural lives.

Read Genesis 34:14. Remember the Israelite's men were circumcised. So Dinah's brothers are being a little deceitful to Shechem.

Read Genesis 34:15-16 They are lying to Shechem. They don't really want him to be circumcised. And they don't really want to intermarry with Hamor's daughters. They want them to let their guard down. They are pretending to get on their side.

Read Genesis 34:17. Now, I want you to understand this is wrong for a number of reasons. The sign of the covenant was not something to be used to deceive people. The sign of the covenant wasn't just given to anyone. It was for those who believed in the true God of Israel and Abraham's descendants.

Read Genesis 34:18. So Hamor and Shechem thought this sounded pretty good.

Read Genesis 34:19-22. So Hamor and Shechem go to the city gate and tell the leaders and men of the city that they think it is a good idea to let the Israelites live in the area and intermarry. But there is just one condition.... And you can see the reaction of these grown men. I don't think so. Where did you come up with such a stupid idea? So how are they going to convince the city leaders to do that? Watch.

Read Genesis 34:23. We are going to take all their stuff. They are rich. Their possessions will be ours. We can take it away from them. Don't you want it? Greed overshadows pain, so to speak.

Read Genesis 34:24. They did it. And we will see in the next lesson how that becomes an advantage to Jacob's boys.

Jacob Gets Right With God
Genesis 34:25 – 35:12

We will see Jacob and his sons interact with Hamor and his son Shechem. Last time, we saw the depravity of man. We are seeing rape, lying, deceitfulness, and murder. We will also see Jacob getting right with God at Bethel.

I think one of the most misunderstood words is oftentimes worship. Because, say, 'We had a great worship this morning.' Question: What is worship exactly? The old English word comes from the word - worth-ship, which means giving worth to God. I think one of the most simple definitions of worship is - we respond to God. We worship as we respond to God, who He is and what He has done. It is the response of the creature to the creator. When we gather together, whether it is Sunday morning, Sunday evening, or Wednesday evening - our plan is to focus on our savior, Jesus Christ. We concentrate on Him; we adore Him, we praise Him, and we hear His Word.

So, how do we worship? Well, we gather together and sing, pray, give our tithes, and make application to the Word. Those are all aspects of worship because we are responding to God.

Question: Did you worship today? When we sang. Was that an act of worship for you?

When we took up the offering, did you give your tithe, not only as a responsibility of being a church member but also as commanded by God? When we prayed, did you voice your prayers to God or just let your mind wander? When we look at the truth and principles of God's Word, will you respond by saying, 'I want to understand this. I want to apply this in my life'?

In this passage, chapter 35, we are going to see Jacob coming to God and worshipping. He returns to Bethel, builds an altar, and worships. But before he can worship, he has to get right with God. Because remember what happened in chapter 34. Some pretty bad things.

As we study the last part of chapter 34 and the first part of chapter 35, it is kind of horrible and uplifting at the same time. Because in chapter 34, there is sin, lying, stealing, and murder. In chapter 35, there is the cleansing, the forsaking, and the blessing.

If you remember, last time, it looked like Jacob's sons really made a deal with Hamor, Shechem, and the men in town that if they got circumcised, then they would agree to intermarry with their daughters. And if you remember, last time, the men in the city thought this would be okay because then they could steal all of Jacob's possessions. So, do you think Jacob's sons really made a deal with Hamor, Shechem and the men in town? No.

Now, think about two things concerning sin.

1. It affects others. What Shechem did originally by raping Dinah, and now what Jacob and Hamor, and Shechem, and Jacob's sons are going to do affecting every one of them.

2. Sin is progressive. It gets worse and worse.

Read Genesis 34:25. The second and third oldest sons, Simeon and Levi, came into the city and killed every one of those men with their swords. But there is more.

Read Genesis 34:26. Now they killed Hamor and Shechem. And did you see what else? Dinah had been at Shechem's house all this time. I think he held her hostage.

Read Genesis 34:27-28. Simeon and Levi are now taking these people's stuff. Looting. They are now taking the possessions from the bereaved families.

Read Genesis 34:29. And now they have even taken hostages as slaves. Does this sound like the ones that God has chosen to be His representatives? When you look at this, don't you just wonder how they could do this horrible thing? The progression of sin just continues. People are capable of anything.

Now, watch what happens when Jacob finds out.

Read Genesis 34:30. What did he say? "You made me look bad, and now they are going to come after me." Did he say to them, "You guys have done a horrible thing?" Did he say, "How could you have done that?" He didn't say that at all. He only just said, "You have made me look bad. I stink." Their testimony is gone. Now, they are known for their deceit and cruelty. By the way, Jacob never forgets what happens here with these two boys. In Genesis 49:5-7, It is years later, and Jacob is blessing all of the sons except these two.

Read Genesis 34:31. Shechem treated our sister as a prostitute, so we thought it best to kill them. If it happened to you or a member of your family, you would probably feel the same way. The effects and progression of sin.

Well, it is time to get back right. 20 years back, Jacob stopped at Bethel and made a vow with God to return and give God a tenth.

Read Genesis 35:1. God comes to Jacob and says, "Would you mind getting back to where you are supposed to be? Go back to Bethel." It's almost as if Jacob is avoiding the place where he made his promise to God. You see, sometimes we do that. We tell God that we are going to do this or that. But we don't. Then we feel guilty. Then we get sin in our lives. And we don't want to do anything. When you get sin in your life, you don't want to read your Bible; you don't want to go to church and worship. As a pastor, I have seen this. Church members who just suddenly disappear. A week goes back, and they don't come. Then, two weeks. Then, a month. Then years. And if you see them in town, they see something like, "Well, I have been really busy, or I just haven't felt like coming anymore." And that can happen if you aren't careful. God is telling Jacob to get back to Bethel and worship Me. Get back in fellowship with Me. That's the plan.

Now, before Jacob can go worship. Do you know what he has got to do? Got to clean up your act. Get yourself right. And that is what he is going to do.

Read Genesis 35:2-3. What gods? Remember, Rachel stole the household gods of her father, Laban. And any others that they may have picked up along the way. The first thing that you need to do is get right with God. You have to deal with sin in your life. We must get the stuff out of our lives that may be stopping us. And we must do the same. If you have sinned in your life, if you have been doing something you shouldn't, if you have made a promise and haven't kept it, if you have been unsupportive or critical of others, then you need to reconcile and get right before God and before each other. Jacob also purifies himself. And we are going to look at that in a second. There is the idea of cleansing and confessing. Notice it says in verse 3 that God was with Jacob wherever he had been.

Question: Does God go with you wherever you go?

Yes. There is no place you can go that God is not with you. Incredible. God is there to provide and protect you. So look what happens.

Read Genesis 35:4. What was wrong with rings in their ears? Well, back then, earrings were often worn as good luck charms to ward off evil. False worship. Jacob's family needed to cleanse themselves of all pagan influences. So they dug a hole and put these amulets or charms in the ground.

Now watch. What was Jacob afraid of? Being attacked. But remember, God is the one who protects.

Read Genesis 35:5. Why? They were afraid of Jacob. Where did this great terror come from? God. God protected him.

Read Genesis 35:6-7. Jacob builds an altar. A place of worship. A place of sacrifice.

Read Genesis 35:8. Who is Rebekah? His mother. And now his mother's maid has died. Apparently, she had been traveling with Jacob. Since his mother had already died. So, he buries her at the oak of weeping (allon-bacuth).

Read Genesis 35:9-12. God reminds Jacob of his new name, Israel. The prince of God. And God confirms, once again, the Abrahamic covenant. In verse 11, God says, "I am God Almighty." Which means El-Shaddai. By the way, how much of the Promised Land does he have? None. He doesn't have possession. But notice, God is going to give it to his descendants after him.

CHAPTER THIRTY-THREE

God Keeps His Promises
Genesis 35:13-36:43

What are promises? It is something that we say we are going to do. I would say that most of the time when we promise we are going to do something, we really mean that we are going to try to do it. But sometimes we fail. Sometimes, we just don't really know what the future is going to hold or whether we will be able to complete what we say or not. But there is a great truth found in the Word of God. God always keeps His promises. He always does what He says. Whatever God says, it will come to pass. You can count on that. Well, we are going to see God coming to Jacob to remind him again of the Abrahamic promises. God promised the land, the seed, and the blessing.

We are going to finish chapter 35 and the story of Jacob worshipping God at Bethel, and then we will look briefly at the descendants of Esau in chapter 36. Next, we will begin a new character in Genesis, Joseph.

Now, there are four things involved in getting right with God.

1. Deal with sin.

2. Confess your sin.

3. Remember the promises of God.

4. The act of worship.

Remember, last time, God told Jacob to return to Bethel to worship Him. But before Jacob can do that, he has to get rid of all the foreign idols that were in the possession of his wife, Rachel. And then he told his household to purify themselves. And so they were preparing to go back to Bethel, to get right with God. And what God does is come to Jacob and remind him of the Abrahamic promises. And reminded him that his name had been changed to Israel, the prince of God.

Question: What has Jacob done to deserve the covenantal promises of God?

Nothing. In fact, the more we look at his life, the worse it is.

Question: What have we done to deserve the promises of God?

Nothing. That's why it is called grace. It is the grace of God that He sent His Son to die in our place. Giving us eternal life. It is according to His mercy that He saves us. We are saved through faith in Jesus as the Messiah, the Savior. I think the reason Jacob didn't want to go back to Bethel initially was because he knew he wasn't living right, so he really didn't want to face God. I think the reason many Christians who have sinned in their lives drop out of church, stop reading the Bible, and don't want to pray is that we have to talk to God. And that is not a comfortable idea if you have sin in your life.

Read Genesis 35:11-12. God Almighty means El Shaddai. El means God. And Shad (Shaddai is plural) means either God of the mountain or God of the breast. God of the breast means 'I am the one who provides.' God says in verse 11 that a nation will come from Jacob. What nation is God talking about? The Jewish people. The nation of Israel. His twelve sons became the twelve tribes. And God says that kings will come from Jacob. What kings? Well, how about Saul, David, Solomon, plus the 40 kings during the period of the divided kingdoms? Now look at the thing I love in verse 12. God gave the Promised Land to Abraham, Isaac, Jacob and to his descendants.

There was one conditional covenant, the Mosaic covenant, in which God said that He would bless them if they did what He said to do. There were also four unconditional covenants, of which three hinged on the Abrahamic covenant, the most important one. The other three are as follows:

1. The Palestinian Covenant, which is a restatement of the land.

2. The David Covenant, which is a restatement of the seed.

3. The New Covenant (Jeremiah 31), which is a restatement of the blessing.

Read Genesis 35:13. Now Jacob is prepared to worship God. He has dealt with his sin, he has confessed his sin, he has remembered God's promises, and now he is ready to worship God and will worship God.

Read Genesis 35:14. What is Jacob doing? What is a libation? It is a drink offering. Jacob took some wine or something and poured it out on the stone pillar and then took a high grade of olive oil and poured some of it on the stone pillar, too. So what's he doing? What did it mean to pour out something? It is the same if you say to God, "I give you my life." It is a dedication to God. Jacob is saying, "I'm yours." "I'm worshipping you."

Read Genesis 35:15. So Jacob names it again - Bethel. (Beit el). The house of God.

Now, in the rest of the chapter, there is some good stuff and some sad stuff. But once again, we will see the Sovereignty of

God, who works all the events. And may we rest in God no matter what events happen in our life.

Read Genesis 35:16. And the way this is written indicates that something is wrong. This isn't a normal birth. Maybe the baby is premature or something. They are moving from Bethel south to Ephrath (Bethlehem).

Read Genesis 35:17. The midwife tells Rachel not to be afraid, for she is having another son. Remember what she said when Joseph was born what she said (Gen. 30:24)? "May the LORD add to me another son." Well, she has another son, but she isn't going to live to see him grow up.

Read Genesis 35:18. Rachel names the baby Ben-Oni, which means 'son of sadness.' Probably because she knows she is dying. But Jacob instead names the baby Benjamin, which means 'son of my right hand.' By the way, who is Jacob's favorite son out of the twelve boys? Joseph. Why? Because he is the oldest son of his true love, Rachel.

Read Genesis 35:19-20. Even today, there is a little marker placed where the Jews think Rachel died. In our lives, there is going to be both the good and the sad. And the more years you have on this earth, the more you will have of both.

Read Genesis 35:21. Did you notice how Jacob is described at the beginning of this verse? Israel. A Migdal Eder is a watchtower built to discourage thieves from stealing sheep.

Read Genesis 35:22. It seems like when things are going well for this family, then all of a sudden, someone messes it up. They think they have their act together, the little gods are out of the house, we worshipped at Bethel, Benjamin is born, but then ka-pow a huge slip-up. Reuben is the firstborn son through Leah.

Remember, the oldest son got three things.

1. The blessing

2. The double portion (of the inheritance)

3. The priesthood of the family (this was before God set up the tribe of Levi to be the priestly tribe)

And now Reuban has committed this terrible sin, and we will see in chapter 49:3-4 that he won't get any of the firstborn rights because Jacob takes them away. So, who got the double portion? Joseph. He had two sons, Mannesah and Ephraim, who both became tribes. That is the double portion. If you notice, you won't see a tribe called Joseph. Who got the priesthood? Levi. Who got the blessing? Judah. Because the king and the Messiah come through Judah.

Reuben slept with Rachel's maidservant, Bilhah. Why? Well, it was symbolic in saying, "I want to take over this family." Because to have sexual relations with the women of the head of the family is like saying, "I am taking over."

Read Genesis 35:23-26. The writer of Genesis, Moses, lists the twelve sons again for us.

Read Genesis 35:27. Isaac is still alive. We haven't talked about him in a long time. He comes to see him after all these years.

Read Genesis 35:28. Isaac lived 180 years, which was more than his father, Abraham (175).

Read Genesis 35:29. Both Jacob and Esau helped bury him. Where? In the family tomb, the cave of Machpelah. Remember, Abraham bought this cave from Ephron the Hittite, along with the field. So Abraham, Sarah, Isaac, Rebekah, Jacob, and Leah were buried there.

Talking about Genesis 36. The entire Chapter 36 is a listing of the offspring of Esau.

The whole point of this chapter is to tell us that Esau and his descendants became the Edomites. Edom isn't part of Israel. It is southeast of the Dead Sea. And they ultimately become arch-enemies of the nation of Israel.

In verse 2, we see that Esau again takes wives from Canaan, which God said not to do. And in verse 8, we see that Esau moves away from Jacob to Mt. Seir, which is modern-day Edom. Remember, Jacob didn't go to Seir but instead went to Succuch, Schecum, and Bethel.

In verses 10-14, the author lists the descendants of Esau. Then, the author repeats the list in verses 15-19 but as a list of tribal chieftains. Esau and his descendants became a mighty nation with chiefs.

Esau also ruled over the people who lived in Seir after he arrived, as listed in Verses 20-29. Esau also ruled over the kings that lived in Seir, as listed beginning in verses 31-39. Esau becomes a very powerful man.

Then, in verse 40, there is a listing of the chiefs who descended from Esau. By the way, Edom is never friendly with the nation of Israel. In fact, when the Hebrews tried to enter the Promised Land, the Edomites refused to let them enter the land and later became bitter enemies of King David. Jacob and Esau were enemies in life, and their descendants are also. And still are. The Arabs are descendants of Ishmael and Esau.

In the next lesson, we will move into the great story of Joseph. A favorite character in the Bible.

CHAPTER THIRTY-FOUR

Joseph: Picture of Christ
Genesis 37

We are going to move from Isaac, Esau, and Jacob to the last big figure in the book of Genesis, and that is Joseph. You know, when I start thinking about these people, they're real. Sometimes, we ought to pretend that we are there at that time and we know these Biblical characteristics. What would it have been like to have seen Abraham and Sarah, to think about the 100-year-old man and the 90-year-old woman who is having a baby for the first time? What would that have been like? And now, we are going to zoom in on one of Jacob's 12 sons. Joseph. And why is he the favored son of Jacob? Because he is the oldest son of his beloved, Rachel. And Jacob loves Joseph. And everybody knows that he loves him and favors him. What happens in a family when you favor one child above all the rest? Big problems.

Sometimes, Joseph is compared to Daniel. Both got wisdom from God. Both had dreams and interpreted dreams. Both were imprisoned for obedience. And both became rulers in foreign lands. Think about it – Joseph became #2 in Egypt, and Daniel became #2 in Babylonia, as well as Medes and Persians.

Read Genesis 37:1-2a. Now, what this means by the way he is writing this is – "I am going to give you the summary about Jacob. Now, let's move to the next guy. Now, why do you think Moses, who is writing this, and of course is inspired by God, but why do you think the writer of Genesis makes the statement, "Jacob live in the land."? Because Esau left the land, Jacob lived in the land. Now watch what happens.

Read Genesis 37:2. So out of nowhere, here is Joseph, who is 17 years old. Now, some of you are younger than 17, some of you are a little older than 17, and some of you can't remember 17. But think about being 17 years old, and all of your brothers except Benjamin are older than you, and they don't like you. And not only that, but Joseph brings back to Dad a bad report about his brothers.

Now, the way this reads in Hebrew, his brothers did something evil. And the brothers are going to be mad. In reality, Joseph does four things that make his brothers mad.

1. He tells on his brothers.

2. And this one isn't his fault, but his father favored him above all the others.

3. And this one isn't his fault either, but his father gave him a special coat. And we call it the coat of what? Many colors. And we are going to talk about what that means, because in Hebrew it doesn't really say coat of many colors.

4. He had two dreams.

Read Genesis 37:3. Varicolored tunic in Hebrew literally means a full-length robe. Probably with long sleeves. In fact, it could have been a solid color. We just don't know. But something made it special. And none of the rest of his brothers got one. Also, did you notice that Israel loved Joseph more than all his brothers? Favoritism. By the way, do you think Joseph wore his coat very much? You bet. Probably wore it all the time. When he went out to the field to find his brothers, do you think he wore his coat? Yeah.

Read Genesis 37:4. Now you have seen where people in a family don't get along very well. But they don't usually hate each other. But here we read that his brothers <u>hate</u> Joseph. Now, when Joseph got that special coat, what do you think his brothers thought? This guy is going to get all the blessings, and he isn't the oldest son. The blessings should be going to Reuben. So, there is a rift between the brothers. So we have seen three reasons so far as to why they hated Joseph. Now comes the dreams.

Read Genesis 37:5. Joseph, don't tell them the dream. Now remember he is 17 years old. He is still a teenager. And this idea of telling his brothers about his dream isn't a good idea. Not a lot of wisdom.

Read Genesis 37:6-7. Hey brothers, "My sheaf rose up and stood erect, and your sheaves bowed down to my sheaf." What do you think that means? And look what they say?

Read Genesis 37:8. You think by that dream you are going to rule over us? Do you think we are going to bow down to you? Did they? Yes, they will. "Lord, we are your servants; please sell us some food." And so we see in this verse that his brothers hated him even more. But God is working through all of these things. Because one day, Joseph will be in a place of Egyptian leadership, his brothers will bow down before him. Well, he had another dream.

Read Genesis 37:9. Who do you think the sun, moon, and eleven stars are? His mother, father, and eleven brothers.

Read Genesis 37:10. You would think he would leave well enough alone. They all understood what he was saying. I mean, it wasn't this vague thing. He was acting like a braggart. His father asked, "Do you really think that I am going to bow down to you?" And he is beginning to think to himself, "What is going on here with this favorite son of mine?"

Read Genesis 37:11. So Joseph's brothers are angry and now jealous of him. But notice that his father is still pondering Joseph's dream. "I wonder; maybe he is going to grow up to be somebody." "I have always thought Joseph was pretty special." "Maybe God is working through Joseph." And He is. God has chosen to raise up Joseph. Not because he is better than the others. But because He just does by His will. It is the grace of God that He raises any of us up.

Grace is getting what you don't deserve. (Eternal life.) Mercy is not getting what you deserve. (we deserve separation). Justice is getting what you deserve. (and we don't want justice. You do not want the justice of God. You do want the justice of God to fall on Jesus Christ.) And that is why Jesus is our substitute. He died in our place. The just for the unjust, to bring us to God. Powerful.

Now, we are going to see the turning point in Joseph's life. Nothing will ever be the same after this day. Nothing will ever be the same in the lives of anyone connected to this family after this day. The eleven brothers will never be the same. The father, Jacob, will never be the same. And Joseph will never be the same after this happens.

Read Genesis 37:12. Shechem. What happened at Shechem? That is where Simeon and Levi killed all of those people. The best thing they should have done is stay away from Shechem. Remember what Jacob said: "We're in trouble around here because of what has happened." And these boys are once again in that area with the flock.

Read Genesis 37:13. Faithful. Faithful. I will do whatever you need me to do, Dad. "Are you going to wear your good coat?" "Yeah, I think I am."

Read Genesis 37:14. So Joseph goes looking for them. But guess what? They aren't there.

Read Genesis 37:15-16. I bet those brothers were famous, especially around Shechem. Why? Because they were known for killing all those men, looting their town, and taking women and children as slaves.

Read Genesis 37:17. Now think about how faithful Joseph is. He could have gone straight back to his father and said, "I went to Shechem and couldn't find them. They weren't there." But he didn't do that. He went on to Dothan looking for his brothers. And found them there. This is a picture of Christ. That is what Joseph is. The Son is faithful to fulfill the will of the Father.

Read Genesis 37:18. They really had to hate him to want to kill him. I mean, there they are out there, and they see Joseph coming. How do you think they spotted him from a distance? "here comes that coat." "You know what we ought to do; we ought to kill him."

Read Genesis 37:19. They are still mad about the dreams. They are mad that Joseph has told them that through his dreams, they are going to bow down to him. "Hey guys, do you want to bow down to this creep? I don't either; let's kill him so we don't have to think about him again."

Now, the brothers are at Dothan, which literally means two pits. Two holes in the ground.

Read Genesis 37:20. Isn't it sad that people think they can stop God's plan? They think they are going to kill Joseph. They aren't. Because won't allow it. God is working all this out for good. And sometimes, in our lives, difficult things happen. Bad things happen. And we say, "Wonder why this is happening?" And I guarantee that if you asked Joseph after his brothers grab him, and throw him down into a hole, and then ship him off to the Ishmaelites and then to Egypt. Would Joseph have said, "This is a good thing."? No. But later on, he could say, "God meant this for good." When you are in the midst of troubled times, God will take it and use it for good.

Read Genesis 37:21. Now, why would Reuben, the oldest brother, care what happens to Joseph? Maybe he realizes that it isn't such a good idea to kill Joseph. "I mean, I have already blown it once by sleeping with Bilhah (Rachel's maidservant), his father's concubine." "Maybe if I save Joseph's life and bring him back to father, maybe I could get back in good with him." "This may be my only chance to get back in favor with Dad."

Read Genesis 37:22. Reuben says to these brothers, "Hey guys, let's not kill him; let's just throw him in the pit alive." And he thinks, "I will come back later and get him out and take him back to Dad." But things don't work out like he thinks.

Read Genesis 37:23-24. Now, those pits were deep. And I imagine it hurt when he fell into it. Plus, I imagine Joseph's brothers probably roughed him up first. He was probably begging and screaming and trying to stop them. And couldn't. And they threw him down in that hole. And what do you think he is doing while down in that dark, damp hole? Probably hollering to get out. And what are his brothers doing?

Read Genesis 37:25. They are having supper! Now, I don't know why, but Reuben leaves for a while. And remember what Reuben's plan is? To get Joseph out of the pit later. So, while the brothers are eating, a group of Ishmaelites are traveling to Egypt to sell goods.

Read Genesis 37:26. Judah is the fourth brother. But because of the sins of his other brothers, Reuben, Simeon, and Levi, - he is probably next in line for the blessing. But he realizes that's not possible because Joseph has the coat, which shows that Jacob favored Joseph. Also, if they kill Joseph, they would be guilty of murder. Remember, Jesus will be from the kingly tribe of Judah.

Read Genesis 37:27. Listen up, brothers, if we sell him to these Ishmaelites, we still get rid of him, we won't be guilty of murder, and we can put a little money in our pockets, too. However, they will have to live the rest of their lives knowing that they sold their little brother into slavery.

Read Genesis 37:28. Joseph probably thinks his brothers are going to let him go. "Thanks, guys. I'm sorry to have been such a jerk with the coat." But they sold him for 20 shekels of silver, which was the normal price for a slave or a young boy. I guarantee you that when the Ishmaelites saw Joseph, they knew he wasn't any ordinary old slave. The brothers were willing to let the slave traders do their dirty work for them. Joseph faced a 30-day journey through the desert, probably chained, beaten, and on foot. Once he gets to Egypt, he will be sold as a piece of merchandise. And it doesn't look like a great thing for Joseph. But remember, God is in control. Joseph will save his people in the future. Which includes his brother Judah, in which the future kings come, and Jesus, the king of kings. Otherwise, they would have starved because of the drought. God's plans can't fail. He keeps His promises. The Messiah would come. And He did. Jesus will return. And He will.

Read Genesis 37:29. Reuben returns and discovers what has happened, and he tears his garments. This was their culture's way of showing extreme emotion. It was like saying, "I am so upset."

Read Genesis 37:30. What's going to happen to me? He should have been concerned about his brother Joseph. In a tough situation, are you usually concerned first about yourself or the other person?

Read Genesis 37:31. They killed a goat and put its blood on Joseph's coat to make it look like some animal ate him up.

Read Genesis 37:32. And this is the thing that gets me the most about the whole passage. This news is going to devastate their father. They bring Joseph's bloody coat to their father and say, "Examine this coat to see if it is your son's or not."

Notice they didn't say this coat, which was our brother's. They deceived their father. But what has Jacob done his whole life? Deceive others.

Read Genesis 37:33. The brothers are probably thinking to themselves, "We didn't even have to lie. Dad thinks a wild beast ate him up. We got out of that one."

Read Genesis 37:34-35. So now Jacob has torn his clothes. Because he was so sad, and his sons were there comforting him. Yeah right. Jacob says, "I will go down to Sheol in mourning for my son."

What is Sheol? The Hebrew word for 'The place of the dead.' The word is Hades in Greek in the NT.

Read Genesis 37:36. Now, that is a pretty powerful position. He was one of the most important men in all of Pharoh's camp.

And it just so happens that Joseph gets sold to this person. Not. God is in control. He is sovereign. There will be times when people who will on purpose mean to hurt you. They will mean to be evil.

Just remember God will take it and use it for good. Because God is a great God.

CHAPTER THIRTY-FIVE

Lineage of Judah
Genesis 38:1-30

Genesis chapters 37-50 basically focus on the life of Joseph, except chapter 38. This lesson is on the lineage of Judah. As we have been studying the book of Genesis, we have seen over and over again the depravity of man. We are going to see some interaction between Judah and Tamar, his daughter-in-law. And really in order to understand this passage, we need to know about Jewish culture, their marriage, and children. Now, when you think about the depravity of man, we have to ask the question: Where is our only hope? We will also see the Sovereignty of God because He is working in all events, even things that we see as bad.

Sometimes, when we study the Bible, we don't get all the information. This means that sometimes God just doesn't tell us everything. Think about it: when the Bible talks about the eternal state, and God says He will make a new heaven and a new earth in Rev. 21-22. We do realize that we are going to serve

God. The Bible says it in Rev. 22. But what will we do? How will we serve Him forever? What's it going to be like? He doesn't really tell us. The Bible says, "To be absent from the Bible is to be where? - Present with the Lord. Now, if your body is in the ground, and you are present with the Lord, - What do you look like? What kind of body do you have when you are present with the Lord? Do you realize that the Bible never tells us what we will be like at that time? Now we know that one day when Jesus comes in the clouds, that body will be raised from the grave and be transformed into a glorified body and meet that person. But what they are like up until then, He never tells us.

Well, we are going to look at a passage, and it is going to talk about one of Judah's sons named, Er. And it says that he did evil, and the Lord put him to death. But He doesn't tell us what he did. So, sometimes, when we study the Bible, it tells us everything. But we do have the information that we need though. We know that it is by grace that you are saved through faith. And Jesus died on the cross and paid for sin. And whoever believes in Him will have eternal life. And He has given us the power of the Holy Spirit for the Christian life and to help us understand the Word of God.

Now, in this lesson, we have another hard passage. We will once again see the depravity of man. The interaction is within the offspring of Jacob, and we will discuss the background of the tribe of Judah. This tribe is special because they came through Judah, David and Jesus Christ. This story is a break in the story of Joseph because, remember, Joseph has been sent off to Egypt, and we are going to see what happens back in the land of Canaan.

Well, we are going to see who Judah, one of Leah & Jacob's sons, marries, then we will see his sons, and we will also see who his sons marry. That means a good bit of time has passed by, probably at least 20 years.

Read Genesis 38:1-2. Is there anything wrong with that passage? Judah marries a Canaanite woman. And they aren't supposed to do that. God said not to mix in with the foreign people living in the area. Why, because they are a different race? No. It was because they worshipped pagan gods.

Why does Judah leave his brothers? It doesn't tell us. Now, who came up with the idea to sell Joseph into slavery? Judah. Maybe his conscience bothered him so much that he just had to move away. Just don't know.

Read Genesis 38:3-5. So Judah is married now, and he has three kids so far. Next, we will see his kids grow up. So this is a period of time. Probably between 16-20 years.

Read Genesis 38:6. So Judah has now found a wife named Tamar for his son, Er.

Read Genesis 38:7. Pretty powerful verse. The LORD took his life for being evil. What do you think he did? Don't know. The Bible talks about the fact that you can sin to death in 1 John 5. It's possible that you can commit sin and stay in that state so long that God judges you and you die physically. Think about the Great Flood. God killed the people because of their sins. Think about Ananias and Sapphira in Acts 5; they both lied to God and immediately died. 1 Cor. 11, some of the people were dying because they were taking the Lord's Supper drunk. Pretty powerful.

Read Genesis 38:8. This is where you need to talk about Jewish culture. There was the Levirate Law of Marriage. In that day and time, if your older brother died before he and his wife have children, the Levirate Law Marriage says that the next younger brother, who isn't married, is to marry her, have sexual relations with her, and the first son that is born is named after her first husband and the inheritance goes to him and not to the new husband. And this was to keep the family intact.

Now, look what Onan does.

Read Genesis 38:9. Because Onan knew that he would not perpetuate his own name, he selfishly avoided conception. He was stealing his inheritance. "I'm not going to raise up somebody else who is going to get the inheritance, get my brother's name, and not going to be my child. I'm not going to do it." So Onan decided to break the Levirate Law. So, he is doing wrong.

So watch what happens.

Read Genesis 38:10. Judah is 0 for 2 in sons. Ha ha. He has lost two sons because they did evil. Now, if you are next on the list, named Shelah, you would think, 'I don't want any of this.'

Now, when you look at mankind from this, does man look good or bad? Bad. People aren't basically good. If people were basically good, you could put your billfold down anywhere and come an hour later and there would be somebody waiting to return it to you. No. You come back, and it is gone.

Well, Judah now looks over to son #3, Shelah. But you know what, Judah says, "I think something is wrong with Tamar, my daughter-in-law. I have lost two sons who died after marrying her. I don't think I will let my third son marry her. Now, what is he supposed to do in the Levirate Law of Marriage? Tell his third son to marry her and have a child with her.

Read Genesis 38:11a. Does it sound like he is doing right? "Tamar, you are going to have to wait because my last boy is too young to marry you." So it seems that he is making a good fatherly decision.

Read Genesis 38:11b. He is lying. Judah tells her to just be a widow until Shelah grows up, but in his mind, he is thinking, "I am never going to give him to her. He might die, too." So he is really doing, right? No. Has anybody done right yet? Only Tamar, but she will do wrong in just a couple more verses.

Read Genesis 38:12. So Judah's wife now dies. And Judah then goes to see his long-time friend, Hirah the Adullamite.

Now, Tamar is no dummy. And Tamar thinks, "You know, I have been waiting for a while now, and Shelah is now a grown man, and I'm not married yet. I have been a widow for a number of years. Now the rules say, I'm supposed to that third son, so I can have children." Tamar has now figured out that Judah isn't going to give her Shelah. So she thinks, "One way or the other, I'm going to have a baby." Watch what she does.

Read Genesis 38:13. Tamar knows where Judah is going. So look what she does.

Read Genesis 38:14. So Tamar takes off her widow's garments, even though she is supposed to wear them until she gets married again. And the only person I am supposed to marry is that third son, Shelah. And I have had these widow's garments on for a long time; no other man has shown any interest in me because they know that I am a promised widow. And Judah isn't giving me his son, but I know where he's going. He is going west to Timnah to shear his sheep. So, I am going to take matters into my own hands. She takes off her mourning clothes and puts on her 'evening clothes.' Ha ha. She hides her face using a veil and sits at the gate where she would get picked up, so to speak.

Read Genesis 38:15. And so here comes Judah down the road, and he sees this veiled girl and thinks she is a prostitute.

Now, we are going to see in just a minute that he thinks she isn't just an ordinary prostitute but a temple prostitute. They were the ones that were connected with false Baal worship by the Canaanite people. So, if you wanted to have a good crop, you would have sex with a temple prostitute.

Read Genesis 38:16a. Judah wants to hire her for the night. A pagan prostitute. Great guy, huh? Huge contrast between the immoral character of Judah and the moral character of Joseph. But Judah doesn't know who she is. She is his daughter-in-law. But why do you think Tamar is deceiving him? Because she wants to have a baby with Judah's family.

Read Genesis 38:16b. She wants to know what he will pay her. "This is for your advantage. I'm a temple prostitute. What will you give me?"

Read Genesis 38:17. Now it is easy to say, "I will send you one of my little goats." And Tamar says, "How do I know that you will pay up? What will you give me as a pledge that you will come back with my payment?' Have you ever run out of gas and so you have to go borrow a gas can, and the store and the store clerk said, "Leave your driver's license here while you are gone? Because I need to keep something, so I know you will be back with my gas can."

Read Genesis 38:18. A seal was a form of identification used to authenticate legal documents. Usually, a unique design is carved in stone and worn on a ring or necklace, inseparable from its owner. The seal was used to mark clay or wax. So Judah gives Tamar his seal, cord, and staff for a deposit. And she had sex with him, and it says here that she conceived. She got what she wanted. A baby from this family.

Read Genesis 38:19. She went back home and put back on her widow's clothes. It is so easy to rationalize wrong. How many people have done wrong in this passage?

Everybody. Over and over. And we say something like this. "Everybody does it. Everybody else cheats on their income tax. Everybody else sleeps with their boyfriend before they are married. We really love each other. Listen, I am not really hurting anybody if I smoke pot or crack. What's so bad about going to see a rated-R movie? So what if I lied? No one really cares."

Read Genesis 38:20. You can see Judah's friend, Hirah the Adullamite, taking this little goat back down the road to the gate to find this 'temple prostitute,' and Tamar isn't there. She has already left.

Read Genesis 38:21. So he asks some men sitting there, "Hey guys, where is the temple prostitute who was here." And they reply, "There hasn't been a temple prostitute around here." Oh oh. Judah is in trouble.

Read Genesis 38:22. And I imagine Judah thinking, "Oh no."

Read Genesis 38:23. "Just let it go. This prostitute played me good. She got my stuff. And I fell right into it. But let's not make a big deal because it would be really embarrassing. I would be a laughingstock."

Question: Do we ever get away with sin? No. It doesn't matter what you do; if you sin and do something wrong, it will eventually come back. Sin has consequences. God has the law of sowing and reaping. And it works both in the positive and the negative. If you live according to God's Will, there will be blessings. If you live in sin, against God's Will, there will be discipline. Do you think Tamar is going to get away with this? No. Do you think Judah is going to get away with this? No. Look what happens.

Read Genesis 38:24. I'm a righteous, godly man. This daughter-in-law of mine has played the harlot! (whispering) And maybe this is the best way to get rid of her because I don't want to give her to my son, Shelah, anyway." I think we ought to burn her! Now, according to the law in Lev. 21:9, she could be burned to death.

Now, here is the truth – it is so easy to see other people's sins and not our own. Sometimes, people aren't spiritual by what they say they hold to, but it is how they live. Spirituality is living out the truths and principles from the Bible in God's power.

Read Genesis 38:25. As she is being drugged out to be killed, she says, "Would you take this signet, cords, and staff to Judah, because the owner of these things is the one that has made me pregnant."

Read Genesis 38:26. Notice he doesn't admit that he had sexual relations with her. He tries to ignore that truth. Remember when Rev. Jim Baker was caught having adulterous sex, and Rev. Jimmy Swaggart said on TV, "Any man that would do that sexual sin is a cancer in the body of Christ. We need to deal with him severally." And do you realize that at exactly the same time, what was Jimmy Swaggart doing? He was having sex with prostitutes and pornography. Folks, we can be blind to our own sin. We always see it in others but ignore it in our own lives. And so when Judah recognizes his stuff, he says, "She is more righteous than me because I didn't give her my third son, Shelah." But Judah, what about the illicit sex? Nothing.

Read Genesis 38:27-28. Twins. Why is it such a big deal who came out first? Because they get the birthright, double portion, and blessing. So one of the babies sticks his hand out, and the midwife ties a scarlet thread around it. But then he pulls his hand back in.

Read Genesis 38:29. So the boy who had the scarlet thread wasn't born first. His brother arrived first. And was named Perez, which means to break through. He broke through to be first. Maybe he was the one who pulled his little brother's hand back in. ha ha.

Read Genesis 38:30. The second boy born was named Zerah, which means 'brightening.' Probably because of the scarlet thread.

And it is through Perez that the lineage of Christ is found. Read Matthew 1:2

CHAPTER THIRTY-SIX

Joseph: From the Pit to the Palace
Genesis 39:1-6

Open your Bibles to Genesis 39. We are going to return to the life of Joseph. Remember, he has been sold into slavery and taken down to Egypt. Things looked bad for Joseph, but we saw that God was with him. Pretty incredible. God not only uses Joseph in Egypt, but He blesses him as well. Beginning with the passage and continuing all the way until the end of the book of Genesis, we will see that the slave becomes the ruler. This section is sometimes called Joseph: from the pit to the palace. Pretty powerful. As we look at this passage, several things stand out.

1. God is always with us no matter what. No matter what the situation. He will never leave us nor forsake us.

2. The issue of how God blesses us and uses us. And we are to be faithful.

3. The idea of stewardship. We are to use what God has given to us.

Let's begin by going to the Lord in prayer. Let's pray.

You know that TV set is something that is pretty powerful in our lives. 99% of Americans own at least 1 TV. And most own more than 1. It is such a strong medium. It comes into every home and shapes our culture. The message, for the most part, is the opposite of what the Bible teaches. It is a shaper of our society. In fact, TV eats books. Once people are out of school, about 70% of adults never read a single book. What they do is watch TV.

Well, it has been a period of probably more than 20-something years since Joseph was sold into slavery in chapter 37. So what has happened? We are going to see the continuing story of Joseph. In this passage, we are going to see the faithfulness of Joseph in his work.

Read Genesis 39:1. Now God has a plan. Something that we can't see at this time. But the plan is – He is going to have to preserve the nation of Israel. Because through the nation of Israel is going to come the Messiah, who is the Savior of the world. The famine is coming; there are going to be seven good years, and then there are going to be seven bad years. And when that happens, if something isn't done, the Jewish people would starve to death. God's plan, and it doesn't look like it at this time, was to get Joseph down to Egypt to save the nation. Now, if you ask Joseph, "Why are you down in Egypt?" He would say, "My brothers hated me and sold me into slavery." He doesn't know what is going to happen yet.

Now, here's a question. And things look bad. And sometimes, when things look bad, we raise this question. – Where's God? How could this happen to me? I have tried to do what God wanted me to do. I have tried to be a faithful man. And now I am down in Egypt as a slave. Where is God in the hard times? Sometimes, we think God isn't with us. But

Hebrews 13:5 says, "I will never desert you, nor will I ever forsake you." God is always with us. And God is with Joseph the entire time that he is there in Egypt.

Question: How do you respond when things go wrong? Well, we are going to find out about that as we go along.

Read Genesis 39:2. The LORD (YHWH), which means the ever-existing God, the Sovereign ruler of all things, is with Joseph. And that is an amazing truth to realize. That God is with every one of you. And He is with me. We don't ever have to be afraid. Notice what this verse says. 'The LORD was with Joseph, so he became a successful man, which means prosperous. It means that things are going good. By the way, what caused Joseph to be prosperous? God did. Everything that we ever have comes from God. All the success that anybody might ever have, all the blessings you might ever have, anytime that you are used, you are used by God. Watch what happens.

Read Genesis 39:3. Here is the second thing that we are seeing. That God blessed Joseph. Not only that, but we will see in the next verse that God blessed Potiphar because He blesses Joseph. 'His master saw...' You know, it is an amazing thing that everything that Joseph did, turned out right.

Read Genesis 39:4. I want you to understand that when Joseph first started, he just worked for Potiphar as his slave. Potiphar is an important man. He is the captain of the bodyguard for the Pharaoh. Potiphar notices that there is one guy out there, one of his slaves, who seems like everything he does turns out right and good, and he is blessed. And Potiphar finally says, "That slave Joseph is something. I am going to make him my personal bodyguard. I am going to make him my personal servant. He is going to do it for me." Notice what it says: 'He made Joseph overseer over his house and all of his possessions.'

We are going to see the stewardship of Joseph. He is faithful in the little things, and now he will be faithful in the big things. There is a truth in the Bible that you see over and over. That is, if you are faithful in that which is least, you will be faithful in that which is much. People want to do great things for God.

People say, 'I wish God would really use me.' Let me tell you, if you aren't faithful in the little things, then you won't be faithful to do the big things. It's just that simple.

So, we see that Joseph is a steward. The truth is that we are stewards of what God has given to us. Every one of us in this room has gifts, talents, possessions & finances, and time. It is all from God, and we are to use it for His glory.

Now, I want us to think about two things as you think about stewardship. Now, some of you may have grown up in churches, and every time you hear the word 'stewardship,' you think about some giving program. That's not what we are talking about at all. Stewardship is a wise use of someone else's resources. And what we realize is - God has entrusted to us certain resources. He has given you spiritual gifts, He has given you time, He has given you possessions, He has given you abilities. You are to use those for His honor and His glory. You are to be a faithful steward. We are to use what He has given as He pleases.

Faithful stewards of our lives. - 1 Cor. 6:19-20

Gifts and talents - 1 Peter 4:10

Possessions - Matthew 25:14-30 "Parable of the Talents"

Time - Ephesians 5:16

Well, look what happened.

Read Genesis 39:5. Do you realize that not only because Joseph was faithful, and God blessed Joseph, but also because those who are around Joseph actually got blessed because Joseph was getting blessed? And so God blessed Potiphar as well. Do you realize that when you are used by God, who uses you as a blessing, you are going to bless other's lives for Jesus Christ? It is pretty incredible.

Now watch what happens.

Read Genesis 39:6a. Potiphar says, "Joseph, everything that I have in my house – you handle it. You oversee the rest of my slaves; you oversee my fields and crops, and you take care of my children because it is obvious that in anything that you do, God is blessing you. And if God is blessing you, then He is blessing me. So I want you to take care of everything. I'm not going to concern myself with anything except – my food." Why? He is going to check out his own food because he doesn't want to run the risk of getting killed by poison.

Now, this verse ends with a statement that prepares us for the next sermon.

Read Genesis 39:6b. Not only how he looked facially wise, but that's also his appearance. But his form. He was probably a muscular-looking guy. Handsome. Why would the author just throw that in? Because of what is going to happen in the next few verses. And you will just have to wait until the next lesson to find out the conclusion to this episode of Joseph's life.

Dealing With Temptation
Genesis 39:7-23

Read Genesis 39:6. So we see here that Joseph was a handsome, good-looking guy. Now, this statement prepares us for this lesson. Now, before we move into the next section, remember that God is with Joseph. God blessed Joseph. Joseph was a faithful steward. God is with us. God blesses us. And we are to be faithful stewards.

We are going to see this whole idea of temptation. And here's the truth: just because you are living for Jesus Christ doesn't mean that you are exempt from temptations or problems. In fact, sometimes, when you are living for Christ, it just seems like this world tempts you and pulls you even more. So we are going to see Joseph, and it looks like things are going pretty well; it probably isn't that great being a slave, but if you are going to be a slave, you might as well be the top slave, who gets to tell all the other slaves what to do. So watch what happens.

Read Genesis 39:7. It came about after what has happened to him, from being sold as a slave, then put in place of responsibility of oversees the household of Potiphar, that Potiphar's wife began to look at him, and remember he is quite handsome and muscular, and she actually says to him, "Have sexual relations with me." She looked at him with desire, which has the idea of lust. Now, when temptation comes, there are several ways we can deal with it.

One of the ways we do not want is – rationalization. Notice Joseph didn't say, 'Well, she is pretty good-looking. I am a slave.

What perks do I have in my life? I didn't ask to be put here. Why not? Who is going to ever know? I mean, obviously, she wants to tell her husband. Sometimes in our lives, when temptation comes, whether it is a temptation to steal, lie, in a sexual area, or gossip, our minds immediately begin to rationalize. Nobody will ever know.'

So, how does Joseph deal with this? Notice what he does.

Read Genesis 39:8. He says, "First of all, I want you to understand. My master trusts me. He has put me in charge of everything. He doesn't even worry about anything. He told me, 'Joseph, I know you can handle my household. I trust you.'"

Read Genesis 39:9. "And secondly, madam, there is no one greater in this household than I am." He has withheld from me except you because you are his wife. Also, how could I do this great sin against God? I think there are two things when it happens.

He said, "First of all, my master trusts me." And second, "How could I sin against God and do this evil?" In your life, you will be tempted to do things wrong. And when the temptation comes, I want you to understand that most of us will say, 'How could I be tempted to do this when my boss trusts me, my wife or husband trusts me, my family trusts me, my church trusts me, my best friends trust me. They don't think I would do something like this.' And second, when it comes, you should say, 'How in the world could I do this evil against God?' That's what we are supposed to think.

You know, sometimes we think, 'No one will find out.' Prov. 15:3: "The eyes of the Lord go in every place, beholding both the good and the evil." God knows it all. Hebrews 13:4: "The marriage bed is undefiled. But adulterers and fornicators, God will judge." Is it right to have sexual relations outside marriage? No. If you have sinned in this area, confess it to God immediately. And repent.

Read Genesis 39:10a. You know the temptation is tough when it happens once. Temptation is tough when it happens occasionally. But temptation is Tough when it is there every day after day after day. You know what she thought, 'I am going to wear him down. I am just going to keep coming on to him, and eventually, he is going to give in. Because I know men.'

Read Genesis 39:10b. Notice there are two things that he decided. First, he said that 'he would not listen to her.' He refused to even consider the proposition. She would say, 'I want you to...' And Joseph would reply, 'I'm not listening. I told you already I would do that.' He refused to even put it in his mind. 'Whatever is pure, whatever is just, whatever is right, whatever is good - think on these things.' Let me tell you, when temptation comes, you know what you need to say: 'I am not even going to consider it. I am not even going to look over that way. I'm not going to think that way.' And second, it says here that 'he wouldn't even be with her.' He would not put himself in a position to be with her alone. Now we are going to find that as a slave in the household, I am sure she was in the house at the same time she was, but there were other servants around. And we are going to see in just a moment that she makes her big move when there aren't any other slaves in the house. All of us must protect ourselves, whatever the temptations are that will get us, and for every one of us, there are different things that tempt us. First of all - don't even think about it. You can't even consider it. You can't let it be a possibility. And second - you must get away from it. You can't be alone with it. Whatever it is.

Also, remember that God <u>never</u> tempts you to do wrong. But your flesh is the one that pulls you toward sin, and when you yield to it, it brings forth sin, and sin brings forth death. Now, before we get into the next section, I want you to realize that temptation isn't a sin. Temptation is the pull to sin. But it isn't a sin. If you give in to the temptation, then you have sinned. Now, I guarantee you that every single person was tempted in some way today. And some of you may have fallen. You may have yielded to the lust of your flesh; you may have yielded to the pride of life, the lust of the eyes etc. How do you deal with it?

Read Genesis 39:11. Why do you think none of the other servants were in the house when it was time for Joseph to do his work? Who do you think sent all those people out? Potiphar's wife. She's not a dummy. Temptation is never a dummy. It will try and get you in your weakest place. It will come right after you. Your flesh will say, 'That's exactly what I am looking for.' The lust of your eyes will go, 'That's exactly what I want to see.' It's such a hard pull.

Read Genesis 39:12. There is it again. 'Lie with me.' Just because you have victory doesn't mean you won't be tempted. Can you see Joseph – getting out of that coat and getting out of there? Let me ask you something. How do you think she felt? Humiliated. She is upset. She is the wife of the captain of the bodyguard of the Pharaoh of Egypt. Who is he? A Hebrew slave. He is nothing. And he walks out on her!

If you think you can handle temptation, you are only fooling yourself. There might be a time or two that you have victory, but if you don't flee from it, if you don't look at who trusts you and depends upon you, and that it is sin against God, you will fall. And let me tell you, nobody gets up in the morning to fall when the daily temptation comes.

Read Genesis 39:13-15. Lies. See, he was already taking off his clothes. "See, I have his coat. He tried to rape me." "I don't remember her screaming. Do you all?"

What else could she do?

Read Genesis 39:16: Have you ever been a kid and got into trouble, and your mother said, "Wait until your father gets home." She is saying, "Just wait until Potiphar gets home. Joseph is going to be in big trouble."

Read Genesis 39:17-18. "The Hebrew slave whom YOU brought wanted to rape me. I screamed, and he fled, but I got his coat here to prove it." What do you think the captain of the bodyguard of the Pharoah of Egypt would do to a slave who did something he didn't want him to do? Probably kill him. Right?

Read Genesis 39:19-20 Yes, he got pretty mad at Joseph, but did you notice that he only put him in jail? He didn't kill him. Why? Well, God protected Joseph. Because in the sovereign plan of God, Joseph will be the one who will feed the nation of Israel soon. And the Messiah will come from the nation of Israel. Is it also possible that Potiphar knows about his wife's promiscuity? Yes. Probably. "I have never seen Joseph do one thing wrong. Why would he suddenly do this?"

Do you think Potiphar really didn't know what to do? Because he didn't, Joseph would never do that, but he also just can't say to his wife, I don't believe you. I mean, Joseph is a Hebrew slave. So Potiphar is going to have to do something.

Can you think of any other reason that Potiphar didn't kill him? They didn't want to lose the blessings that had been happening since Joseph arrived. He may be thinking, 'I will put him in king's jail for a little while, then pull him back out, and will get blessed again.'

Think about it. What did Joseph do to deserve being thrown into prison? Nothing. He was just obeying God. He didn't violate the Word of God. What did Joseph ever do to become a slave? Nothing. He basically just told his brothers the truth about the dream he had received.

Sometimes we say, "Why is this happening to me? What have I ever done to deserve this?" Just because you obey God doesn't mean that everything is going to turn out in the way you think is right. Because sometimes in our lives, things go wrong. Remember, all things work together for good for those who love God, those called according to His purpose. We just have to trust Him. Well, let's see what happens.

Read Genesis 39:21. No matter where Joseph goes, the LORD is with him. And the LORD blesses him. Everywhere he goes. So watch what happens.

Read Genesis 39:22. You just can't keep a good man down. So now Joseph is in charge of everyone in the jail. Joseph is thinking, "If you are going to be your father's son, be the best one; if you are going to be a slave, be the best one; if you are going to be a prisoner, be the best one." Wherever you are, be the best that you can be. Why? Because your life is for who? The Lord.

Read Genesis 39:23. Again, the Lord is with him and made him prosper. God is working in Joseph's life. Even in the bad times of life. And the bottom line is to preserve the nation of Israel.

Now, I want to raise one question. What if you fail? I will guarantee you, starting with myself, that every one of us – has failed. What do we do when the temptations come and we don't do these four things? We give in to the temptation and sin.

Well, the first thing you need to do is – deal with the sin. Confess it. And when you do. God is faithful to forgive us and cleanse us.

The second thing we do is – stop doing it. We get out of there and get on with our lives. Repent and sin no more.

And thirdly, make a decision that you are going to live for God. Make your life count for Him. You say to God, "Take my life. Use me for your glory." May we live for Christ.

CHAPTER THIRTY-SEVEN

Joseph: From Prison to Prominence
Genesis 40

Open your Bibles to Genesis 40. We are continuing our study of Joseph's life. Things look bad. He has been thrown into prison by his master, Potiphar. But we see, as always, that God is continuing to work. He plans to raise Joseph up to a place of authority. He is putting Joseph in the right place at the right time. And that is a key. We must realize that God is working in the events and circumstances of our lives, putting us in the right place at the right time to do the right things. Well, we are going to see some dreams. God uses dreams not only to reveal information but also to advance Joseph. Joseph is able to interpret these dreams because God gives him that ability.

You have heard the phrase, "The Lord works in mysterious ways." Isaiah 55:8: "For My thoughts are not your thoughts. Nor are your ways My ways," declares the Lord. He does work in a sense in a mysterious way. Joseph, who was sold as a slave by his brothers and then raised to leadership status by his master, is now in prison for a crime he didn't commit. How can this man be used by God? And what we realize is God has put Joseph in Egypt for a reason – to save the nation of Israel, and in reality, to save the world because the Messiah will come through the nation of Israel.

God uses Joseph to interpret two dreams of two prisoners and then two dreams of the Pharaoh next week. Remember, they didn't have the written revelation at this time.

Now, as we study this passage, we realize that almost 13 years have passed. Joseph was 17 years old when he was sold as a slave and taken down to Egypt.

He will be 30 years old when he is raised up to power in the next chapter.

Read Genesis 40:1. After what things? After Potiphar's wife came on to him, and he refused her advances, she lied to her husband and accused Joseph of rape. So Potiphar put him in prison. And Joseph is put in a leadership position in prison. Now, it doesn't tell us what the cupbearer and the baker did. Now, a cupbearer's original job was to test the drink for the king because if it had been poisoned, you had to die. Now, as time went by, the cupbearer was so trusted as a servant that eventually, he became almost like an advisor. Now the baker cooked the food. And, of course, he had to be a trusted man, too, because of the safety, preparation, etc.

It says here that they offended their Lord; literally, in Hebrew, it says that they sinned against him. You know the truth is that, especially back in that day and time, whenever you were under someone of that kind of authority, you always wanted to stay on the good side of the king because he could have you killed immediately. Because the Pharoah had absolute power. He was even considered a god. The people thought he was. And his oldest son, when he died, would be God. That's why when you get to the book of Exodus, all of the plagues against Egypt were against the gods of Egypt, and the very last plague was the death of the firstborn son of Pharaoh, who was considered a god. That is probably why it was the death of the firstborn.

In Romans 1, the Bible tells us that man rejects the true God and worships the creation.

Read Genesis 40:2-3. It just so happens that Potiphar puts them in the same jail where Joseph is imprisoned. Coincidence? Actually, we know there is no such thing as coincidence or chance. God is working out all things according to the council of His Will. In our lives, there are no coincidences. There are things that are happening in your life today, and tomorrow, and in the past that you might not even realize that God is working all that in His tapestry of your life to work things out in the way that He wants, to conform you to the image of His Son, and to bring out His perfect plan in your life.

Read Genesis 40:4. It tells us how long. But it is amazing that Joseph, the slave, ends up overseeing these officials. Think about the providence and sovereignty of God. He works in all of these events.

Read Genesis 40:5. Can you imagine the next morning when these two guys wake up and say, "Man, I had a weird dream last night." And the other goes, "I did, too. "what was your dream?" "Well, it was pretty good, but I don't have a clue what it means." "Hey, I don't have a clue either."

And they probably talked about their dreams with each other. "It must be something from the gods."

Read Genesis 40:6. Wouldn't you think they would already be dejected since they were in prison? But apparently, there is more dejection than normal. So Joseph walks in and asks, "What's the matter with you guys?"

Read Genesis 40:7. Literally in the Hebrew, "Why do you have bad faces today?"

Read Genesis 40:8a. In that day and time, dreams meant what? Something important. Maybe it is a message from one of the gods. What would Joseph say? Hey, I have had dreams all my life. Tell me the dream; I will tell you what it means. Because you see, God lets me know these things. Read Genesis 40:8b. What's he implying? That God is going to tell him what it is. I am connected with God. I know Him. So tell me your dreams. How are they going to know if his interpretation is right? It has to come true.

The key here in this passage is that God is making Himself known, which is called Revelation. Now, here are some other theological terms you need to know. Inspiration is a revelation in written form. The Bible is an inspiration. Illumination is what the Holy Spirit does to help us understand the written revelation, which is an inspiration.

Then there is the word interpretation, which means – what does this revelation, inspiration mean? Now, usually, there is only one interpretation in a passage. Occasionally, in the OT, especially on a prophecy, there is what we call a near and a far interpretation. However, sometimes, the prophet would say something, and it would be fulfilled in a short time with an ultimate long-distance fulfilment. The last key theological term is application, which means taking the interpretation and applying it in your life.

In this passage, we have God-given revelation, not in a written form, but through a dream. And Joseph is there to give them an interpretation of what the revelation means.

When you think about how God has revealed Himself. He has revealed Himself really in three big ways. Romans 1:20 says He has revealed Himself through the creation. God has also revealed Himself through His Son, Jesus Christ. Thirdly, God has revealed Himself through the written revelation, which is what we call the Bible.

The Bible is to you from God; it is authoritative, it is truth, and it is to be applied in your life. Now, let me clarify that. Not everything in the Bible was written to you. Not everything in the Bible is for you to apply. But the parts that are – live those out, making your life based on the Scripture.

Read Genesis 40:9-11. Here's what happened. What does it mean?

Read Genesis 40:12-13. Joseph says here's what your dream means. You see the three branches. That's three days. Three days from now, you will get to go back to being the Pharoah's cupbearer just like you used to do. Wow. Good dream.

Read Genesis 40:14. Joseph says to the cupbearer, "Hey, don't forget about me. I want to get out of this prison cell too." And probably the cupbearer said to him, "Don't you worry. I will never forget you after you have told me this good news." Do you realize that this is the first time that Joseph has ever said something like, "Hey, help me get out of here."

Read Genesis 40:15. This is the first time that he has ever defended himself in everything that we have read so far. Now, if you are the baker, what do you want to know? When he gets out of prison and goes back to work for the Pharoah, he says, "Hey, how about telling me my dream?"

Read Genesis 40:16-17. Hey Joseph, what do you think that means? Am I getting out of here in three days? What do you think?

Read Genesis 40:18-19. Are you sure? This doesn't seem fair. My dream was just as good as the Cupbearer's dream. But Joseph says, "The three baskets of bread are three days, but the Pharoah is going to kill you, hand you on a tree, and the birds are going to eat you up." Wow. That's not nearly as much fun as the other guy's dream.

Sometimes, things don't always turn out the way we wish they would. Well, look and see what happens. Because if Joseph is really from God, and he is, then his interpretation of the dreams will turn out just like he said.

Read Genesis 40:20-22. It came true exactly right. Now how could it come true exactly right? Because God told him. God gave Joseph the ability to interpret these dreams. It is always going to be exactly right. When Jesus says He is going to prepare a place for you, - He has gone to prepare a place for us.

Is there going to be a 1000-year reign of Jesus Christ? Yes. Because He told us. He is trustworthy. All of His promises have been true, are true now, and will be true.

Well, look how this passage ends. It is sort of sad.

Read Genesis 40:23. Can you picture Joseph the day they leave? Which was three days later. And the Cupbearer is restored just as Joseph predicted. And the Baker is killed just as Joseph predicted. So Joseph is probably thinking, "Well, I imagine the cupbearer is telling the Pharoah about me. I should be getting out pretty soon." But it doesn't happen because the cupbearer forgot about him. What would we say if we were in this situation? What is going on? Why is this happening to me? All I have ever done is what God wants me to do. What happened to me? - I got sold into slavery. What happened to me? - I became a slave. What happened to me? - I got in prison. What happened to me? - I gave these two interpretations, and they came out right, and I am still in prison. But we don't see Joseph saying those things.

Have you ever said to yourself? How come things aren't working out the way I think they ought to? Do you know why they don't? Because the way you think they ought to, is not the best way. Or it would be working out that way. We need to understand that truth. God knows what is best. Just trust Him.

CHAPTER THIRTY-EIGHT

Pharaoh's Dream
Genesis 41:1-36

Open your Bibles to Genesis 41. As we continue in our study of Genesis and the life of Joseph, This lesson we will begin to see that God is going to raise up Joseph. We have seen some tough circumstances in Joseph's life. He was thrown into a pit. Sold into slavery by his own brothers. Falsely accused and thrown into prison. But now God will raise him up, use him to interpret the dreams of the Pharaoh of Egypt and give him the position of power. And there is a reason for all of this. Isn't it amazing? God is putting him there to save his own people from starving to death so that the Messiah will be able to come. God has put Joseph in the right place at the right time. Sometimes, when you look at your life, you say, "Why is this happening? This isn't right." And yet, even though we may not be able to recognize it, God is working.

Famine. No food. Nothing. In this lesson, we are going to see the warning. Egypt, at this time, was the most powerful nation in the world. Pharoah was the most powerful ruler in the world at that time. And God is going to warn them that a famine is coming that will last for seven years. God uses Joseph to warn the nation. But also to protect the nation of Israel.

Remember, Joseph had two dreams back in Caanan. He interpreted two dreams from the Pharoah's servants in the Egyptian prison. And now, he is going to interpret two dreams of the Pharoah.

Read Genesis 41:1. What two full years? Two full years since the cupbearer went back to work for the Pharoah. Restored to his former position. But remember, the cupbearer forgot about Joseph. Sometimes, in our lives, people will forget about us. But also, we think God forgets us. "God, I have been praying about this for months; don't you even care? Why is this happening, or why didn't this happen?" But God doesn't forget you.

So Pharaoh had a dream, and in it, he was standing by the Nile River. This river is very important because it is the center of agriculture in the country.

Read Genesis 41:2. Seven good-looking cows.

Read Genesis 41:3: Seven ugly-looking cows.

Read Genesis 41:4. Probably would wake up anybody. What in the world is that dream? No more steak sandwiches before bedtime. Ha ha.

Read Genesis 41:5. Seven good ears of grain.

Read Genesis 41:6. Seven bad ears of grain.

Read Genesis 41:7. Again, he wakes up after having a disturbing dream.

In the Bible, there were times when God actually gave revelation through dreams. Now, here God is giving Pharoah a dream. But he doesn't know it is from God. And I think we are going to find out why the interpretation isn't being answered by his 'wise men' because his dreams are actually from God.

Read Genesis 41:8. So Pharaoh is really bothered about his dreams that he just had, so he calls in his so-called wise men, his magicians. He then tells them his dreams, but they don't know what they mean. This dream came from God, so only the interpretation is going to come from God. And in that whole place, there is only one person who knows God and can interpret the dream. And it is going to be Joseph.

Now, right then, the light probably went on in the cupbearer's head. "oh, wait a minute. I just thought of something." Look at what he says.

Read Genesis 41:9. "I just remembered something. Do you remember the time that you were angry with me and sent me to prison? Well, something happened while I was in there."

Read Genesis 41:10-11. We, both me and the baker, each had a special dream and a special interpretation. You can almost see Pharoah's thinking, "Well, you had a dream; I have had a couple of dreams, so what? What is your point?"

Read Genesis 41:12. Joseph was 17 years old when he was put into prison, and he was in there for 13 years. He will be 30 years old when he begins to rule. And now it has been two years since the cupbearer left prison. So the cupbearer calls Joseph, who is 28, a youth. And this Joseph knew what my dream and the baker's dream were all about.

Read Genesis 41:13. And his interpretations happened exactly as he said.

So what is the Pharaoh going to want to do? Call up Joseph. None of this is a coincidence. In our lives, there is no such thing as coincidence. Nothing ever just happens. God is Sovereign. He is in control.

Read Genesis 41:14. What do you think Joseph thought when they came to get him? Probably the worst. Things haven't really worked out so great for him. What did they have him do when they got him out of the dungeon? Shave and change his clothes. Wonder why? Because if you were going to stand before the Pharaoh, you were clean-shaven. The Egyptians didn't like facial hair. They cleaned him up so as not to offend the Pharaoh.

Read Genesis 41:15. Joseph is now 30 years old. He is standing before the most powerful ruler in the world. He has been a slave for a long time. 23 years. And remember that Joseph had a couple of dreams back in Canaan, where God made it known to him that his brothers would bow down before him. Has his brothers bowed down to him yet? No. He may be wondering how that is going to happen now. He doesn't know that in the next chapter, his brothers will be standing in front of him, bowing low. Ha ha. And when his brothers come, they won't recognize him because he is clean-shaven, which is the Egyptian culture. But in the Hebrew culture, the men wore beards. So the Pharaoh tells Joseph that he had heard that he could interpret dreams.

But notice how Joseph answers the Pharaoh.

Read Genesis 41:16. Notice he didn't even tell Pharaoh about being falsely accused and put into prison by mistake. The word favorable answer doesn't mean it will be a positive answer; it just means that he is going to give the right answer, the correct answer. Joseph says, "God will tell you what the dreams mean." Let me ask you a question. When do you think God tells Joseph what the dream means? Do you think Joseph knows right now what the dream means? Joseph makes it clear that it is God that gives the interpretation of the dreams. He is just the instrument. And sometimes we forget that. We need to realize that we are just the instrument. If God does something good through us, we must give God the glory. If you get to teach the Bible, if you get to lead someone to Christ if you get to help participate in VBS if you get to work with the youth in the church, who gets the glory? God.

Read Genesis 41:17-24. Powerful. If you hadn't read this before, you wouldn't know what it meant either.

Now, Joseph probably already knows exactly what dreams mean.

Read Genesis 41:25. God has revealed to you what He is about to do. Who is in control? God. But does Pharaoh believe in the God of the Jews? No. He is going to.

Read Genesis 41:26-28. Seven good cows and seven good ears of grain are seven good years, and the seven bad cows and seven bad ears of grain are seven years of famine.

Read Genesis 41:29-30. First, the seven good years were followed by the seven years of famine. But just like you couldn't even tell the difference when the seven bad cows ate up the seven good cows, nobody will even remember the seven good years. But all of the crops will be gone.

Read Genesis 41:31-32. Joseph tells the Pharaoh that God gave him the dream twice so that he wouldn't miss it. God wanted you to remember your dreams because God is going to bring this about very soon. The seven good years are starting.

Joseph tells Pharaoh 4 times that this dream is from God. He is warning them. Let me ask this question. Why in the world does God even care about these Egyptians? To save the Israelites. So why doesn't God just leave the Israelites in the land of Canaan and protect them there from the famine? Because He has to get them out of the influence of those pagan Canaanites. Judah has already moved away from the family. We see a deterioration of the people. They are getting further and further away from God. So, He is going to take them out of that land and move them into Egypt in order to keep them alive. How many Israelites are there? About 70-75. They go into Egypt with 70; how many do they come out with 400 years later? 2 million. Slaves. They walk out of Egypt rich. How? God. Never fought a battle. And they take the Promised Land. How? God. He is in control.

Well, look what happens. He is going to give some advice. God does not only tell Joseph what their dreams are; he also gives Pharaoh some advice on what he should do.

Read Genesis 41:33. Now, when Joseph told Pharaoh to find a wise and discerning man to be the overseer of the land of Egypt, was he implying that Pharaoh should pick him? No. I don't think Joseph was looking for a position. I just think he was giving advice.

Read Genesis 41:34. Listen, just start taking 20%; everybody has to bring in 20%. Normally, Pharaoh got how much? 10%. But Joseph says to Pharaoh, we need to get more than normal. We need to get 20% and store it up.

Read Genesis 41:35. So you need to pick out somebody wise to be an overseer, and then let everybody bring in 20% of the produce every year for the next seven years; we need to store it up in the cities and under Pharaoh's authority guard it. And you can almost see Pharaoh think to himself "Man, why didn't I think of this? What a great idea."

Read Genesis 41:36. Store up one-fifth of the food for seven years so that when the famine comes, and it is coming, we won't perish.

In the next lesson, we will see Pharaoh's response.

Famine in the Land
Genesis 41:37-57

Turn in your Bibles to Genesis 41. As we continue in our study of this powerful book of beginnings. And in this last section, our focus is on Joseph. And we have seen that he was sold into slavery at the age of 17 by his brothers. First, he served in the household of Potiphar, then was falsely accused and thrown into prison. Why would God allow all of that to happen? And when we think about our own lives, and some bad things happen at times, we say, "Why does God let this happen to me? Has God forgotten us?" And the answer, of course, is NO. We must remember that God is in control. He is working out His plan. This lesson is as we look at the life of Joseph, and we realize that He is working in Joseph's life, just like He works in our lives. This lesson, from the prison to the palace. Because Pharaoh has two dreams, and Joseph is called to interpret these dreams, and in all of this, God is working. Not only to deliver Joseph but also to deliver His own people. And we will talk about it as we go through it. But why would God take Israel, the family, and the 75 people out of the land of Canaan, which is the Promised Land, over to Egypt?

Chance, fate, luck, lottery. Take a chance to come to the casino. Sometimes, people look at life that way. That life is a game of chance. They hope things are going to turn out their way, and maybe they will be lucky. But the truth is - there is no such thing as luck. God is in control. He works all things according to the council of His will.

Now, what are the chances, what is even the possibility, that a nomadic shepherd, a Hebrew man who is sold into slavery and then thrown into prison, is going to move from that position to being second only to the Pharaoh of Egypt? What is the possibility of that happening? Probably not any chance whatsoever. But yet, God is in control. And He is working.

All the way through last Sunday's story about Joseph interpreting the Pharaoh's dreams, he gave God the glory. He was basically saying, "I am just an instrument for God; it is God who has given you these dreams. And it is God who is going to tell me the interpretation of your dreams." It is true for us: no matter what God allows you to do, it is God who gets the glory. It is God using us. God is the one that gives us the power, gives us the spiritual gift and talents, God is the one that puts us in the opportunities. So, anything that we get to do for God, we can all turn it back and say, "It is God who gets all the glory."

Read Genesis 41:33-36. Take a really wise person who will then take 20% of the grain for the next seven years and store it up. So that when the famine comes, the people will survive. And we ended last time with "What will Pharaoh's response be?"

Read Genesis 41:37. You can see him go, "Hey, that's a pretty good idea. Let's go with that one."

Read Genesis 41:38. Now, what he means by that, and he doesn't mean like a god or a spirit inside of him, the idea is somebody who is really smart, wise, and can handle the situation. Now, who so happens is standing there? Not so happens. Joseph is at the right place – at the right time. Is it so happens that he is the one who interprets the dream? No. There is no such thing as chance or just so happens. The right place for Joseph had been a prison. How else would he have met the cupbearer and the baker? Are you trying to tell me that when I went through THAT, that was the right place at the right time? Obviously, if it is God's plan that He is working in our lives.

Read Genesis 41:39-40. Wow. What a turn of events. Pharaoh says, "Since you figured all of this out, and since you are wise, so here is what I am going to do. I am going to put you on the payroll. I am going to put you in my household; I am going to put you second only to me. You will control everybody else.

Everybody else will bow down to you as they do me. Except me because I am Pharaoh."

Can you imagine a Hebrew slave moving to #2 in Egypt? You say that's impossible. Well, what is impossible with me is possible with God. Think about it – this isn't going to happen unless God does it. What do you think some of those main Egyptian leaders thought about this? They probably thought, 'That guy isn't an Egyptian.' But Pharaoh's plan is to make him an Egyptian. Because if Joseph is going to be in a place of responsibility like this, he needs to look like one of us.

Read Genesis 41:41. That is what he did. Joseph rose to power from the prison to the palace.

Read Genesis 41:42. Now, what was so important about that signet ring? It meant that Joseph had the same authority as the Pharaoh. That is power. I am getting you some good clothes, a gold necklace.

Read Genesis 41:43. Pharaoh had Joseph ride in his second chariot. Usually, the person who rode in the chariot behind the Pharaoh's chariot was his son. But here, at this time, they were all concerned about approaching famine; the second chariot now belongs to Joseph. And all bowed to him because he was second overall in Egypt.

Do you ever think about a change that happens to us? We were dead in trespasses and sins. We were children of the devil. Now, we are alive in Christ. We are now children of God. What a change! What did we do? Nothing. Just believe in the Messiah. Salvation is a free gift from God. Who knew the interpretation of those dreams? Joseph or God. God used Joseph. We are now clothed in righteousness. From death to life, raised up as God's children, no longer slaves to sin, but heirs of God raised up to serve our Savior and Lord.

Read Genesis 41:44. Pharaoh says, "Even though I am the supreme leader in Egypt, you make the decisions. This whole issue of the famine, and the grain, and the storage – nobody does a thing except you say it." Powerful. Joseph was faithful to do whatever God had called for him to do.

Let me ask you a question. If God can take a Hebrew slave who is in prison to second-in-command in all of Egypt in one day, what do you think He can do in your life? You never know how God will use you.

Read Genesis 41:45. Pharaoh gave Joseph an Egyptian name. Which means 'God speaks – he listens'. Joseph is the one who knows what God says. Pharaoh also gave him a wife, the daughter of a priest. A prominent Egyptian official. God oversees all things. The providence of God. And God does the same thing for us. Are you trusting God in all things?

Read Genesis 41:46. How old was David when he became king of Israel? 30. And now Joseph becomes a big leader in Egypt at how old? 30. How old was Jesus when He began his earthly ministry? 30.

Read Genesis 41:47. Just like he said. The food is coming in. There is so much grain. Joseph will be faithful in the small things, and he will be faithful in the big things. And that is the key. Are you willing to do little things for God? Be faithful. We want to hear Him say, "Well done, my good and faithful servant."

Read Genesis 41:48-49. They had so much grain stored up they couldn't even count it.

Read Genesis 41:50. So in the 6th good year, Joseph's wife, Asenath, gave birth to two sons.

Read Genesis 41:51. The name of the firstborn son, Manasseh, literally means 'making me forget.' Joseph is saying, "I have forgotten all that has happened to me. I have forgotten about being put into a pit at the age of 17. Being sold into slavery. Being falsely accused and thrown into prison. Look at me now. I have authority. I have a wife. And now I have two sons."

Read Genesis 41:52. The name of the second-born son, Ephraim, literally means 'fruitful.' He says, look at what I have. God has blessed me. And it is true for us. God has blessed us. So forget the past and be fruitful in the Present. Some people or even some churches never do anything because they are so dragged down by their past failures. They even live for God in the Present. They keep thinking, "Can you believe what I did?" If you confess your sins, He is faithful and just to forgive you and cleanse you from all unrighteousness. Forget the things that are behind and press on to the things that are ahead. And serve Him faithfully for His glory.

Read Genesis 41:53-54. Why is there bread in all of the land of Egypt? Because they had saved for it. They had planned. God had warned them. And this is just exactly what He said. Where is the famine? In all the lands. That means Egypt, also back there, where Jacob and Joseph's brothers are starving.

Read Genesis 41:55. Pharaoh tells the people, "Go to Joseph. Whatever he says – do. Joseph is handling the project."

Read Genesis 41:56-57. Joseph opened storehouses full of grain and sold it to the Egyptian people. And people around the world heard that Egypt had grain. And people started traveling to Egypt to buy it. And that is where we will get into chapter 42.

CHAPTER THIRTY-NINE

Joseph Tests His Brothers
Genesis 42:1-38

I am sure that Joseph's brothers worshipped as they were supposed to. They affirmed their Hebrew heritage. But they were not really children of God. They were outwardly religious but inwardly unchanged. We heard the account of their assault on their brother and how they sold him as a slave. We read about the deception of their father. We have heard the witness in months past of the reckless nature of their lives. They were outwardly religious but inwardly lost.

As we move into Genesis 42, the long-awaited reunion between Joseph and his brothers will finally take place. In this chapter and the ones to come, we are going to see God bring these men to faith. We are going to see what it took for these men to truly become children of God. And as we do, we will be able to see the process that God generally uses to awaken those who are spiritually lost.

As we look at our text, we see three different scenes. We see the brothers at home, the brothers before Joseph, and the brothers as they talk amongst themselves. And in these three scenes, we see God doing three things:

1. He awakens the brothers to the fact that there is a problem.

2. He shows them the nature of their sin

3. He brings them to a point of repentance.

A. The first part of the story takes place back in Jacob's home. The predicted abundance and famine in Egypt was not confined to Egypt. It was worldwide. Jacob and his family in Canann (which is north of Egypt) are facing the same problems. For a while, I imagine this family is able to live on what they have in reserve. But the weather is not changing, and the supplies are almost depleted. The situation is becoming serious.

Read Genesis 42:1-5. I get the impression that Joseph is frustrated with his sons. In a crisis situation, they don't seem to be doing anything. It sounds like things are getting tense. It is important that we see what God is doing. For years, Jacob and the boys were living life without having to think about God. Life went on as normal. They got up, did their work, came home, and the next day started all over again. They were content with their routine. Their needs were met, and life went on as it always had.

But with this famine, God gets their attention. Now, "Life as it always is" is not enough. It is easy to avoid God when we feel self-sufficient. It is easy to feel that you have no need for God's touch when everything is running smoothly. These men were comfortable in their denial and their deceptions. As long as the status quo remained, they would never change. So, God provokes a crisis. This crisis would either harden them further or wake them up. This is the way God often works.

In the book of Amos 4:6-8, God tells the Israelites, "But I gave you also cleanness of teeth in all your cities. And lack of bread in all your places, yet you have not returned to Me," declares the LORD. "Furthermore, I withheld the rain from you while there were still three months until harvest.

Then I would send rain on one city, and on another city, I would not send rain; one part would be rained on, while the part not rained would dry up. So two or three cities would stagger to another city to drink water, but would not be satisfied, yet you have not returned to Me, "declares the LORD.

God could have simply washed His hands of these folks. He could have said, "Fine, forget it." But that's not what he did with the Israelites . . . and that's not what He does with you and me. God loves us too much to let us go without a fight. So, at times, He exercises "tough love". He brings a crisis into our lives that forces us to address ultimate issues. It may be,

- An unexpected diagnosis
- A financial emergency
- An overwhelming situation
- A family crisis

In these situations, God often seeks to awaken us out of our spiritual lethargy. God lovingly put Jacob and his family in the midst of a famine . . . in order to draw them to Him. You can't be treated for a disease until you are made aware that there is a problem. God is forcing these brothers to see that they need help.

So here's the question we need to ask? Are you going through tough times? Is life a struggle right now? Could it be that God is trying to get your attention? Could it be that He is trying to awaken you out of your spiritual slumber? Is it possible that God is trying to move you from a profession of faith to a possession of faith? Is it possible that God loves you so much . . . and that He wants you to be His with such intensity that He will stop at nothing to turn your heart to Him?

B. Now, the second part of the story. Read Genesis 42:6-17. Joseph and his brothers hadn't seen each other for probably 20+ years. Joseph was 17 when he was sold into slavery, 30 when he was brought before Pharaoh, then there were seven years of abundance, and it probably would have taken a year or perhaps more to use up all the reserves the family may have had. During this time, Joseph and his brothers had certainly gotten older. They had lost some hair and gained some weight. They were grey, and the older brothers were probably starting to show signs of the wear of life.

Can you imagine the scene? Joseph looks up and sees his brothers. He recognized them, but they didn't recognize him. And why would they? I suspect you have been to class reunions and had a hard time recognizing people you grew up with. Or maybe you have run into someone who recognizes you in the supermarket, but you don't recognize them because you are seeing them in a different setting than normal.

The last time the brothers saw Joseph he was covered with mud from being thrown in the cistern, he was wearing tattered clothing, and he was in a position of weakness, pleading for his life. Now he is dressed in royal attire, he's clean shaven, confident and powerful. And he is speaking Egyptian. This is the last place they would have expected to find Joseph.

When they have their turn before Joseph, they bow before him (remember Joseph's dream?). And Joseph does something that may strike us as a bit odd. He doesn't tell his brothers who he is . . . he doesn't even give them a hint that he knows who they are. Joseph begins a period of questioning. "Where are you gentlemen from?" They reply that they are from Canann and they have come to buy grain. Jacob accuses them of being spies!

The brothers argue that they are not spies. They are just brothers who have come to get grain for their family. Joseph pretends not to believe them. Their response, "Sir," they said, "there are twelve of us brothers, and our father is in the land of Canaan. Our youngest brother is there with our father, and one of our brothers is no longer with us."

Now, why would they say all these things? First of all, they are trying to be honest. Second, they are pleading that it is absurd to think they are spies. What spy would travel with his brothers and in a group of ten! A good spy wants to blend in and be inconspicuous.

Joseph remains calm. He is not after revenge . . . but he does want to know if his brothers have really changed. He is concerned for his brother Benjamin and for his father. If they treated him shamefully . . . .what did they do to Benjamin? Besides, I think Joseph (who had lived his life listening to God) realized that this was an opportunity to reach his brothers. So, Joseph proposes a test.

One of the men is to be selected to go home and return with Benjamin before the others will be set free! So, Joseph throws them all in prison for three days.

So Joseph decided to accuse his brothers of the very thing they had held against him. Back in Dothan, Joseph had protested his innocence but had been treated with harsh words, imprisonment in a cistern, and, finally, deportation to Egypt as a slave. Now, the brothers were protesting their innocence, and Joseph responded with harsh words and imprisonment.

Joseph is subjecting his brothers to the same charges and a taste of the same experience that he endured. He is not doing this for punishment . . . he is doing this in the hope that his brothers will wake up to the nature of their actions. He is hoping this treatment will make them "come clean."

It is unfortunate but true that often we:

1. Do not appreciate the effect of words until we have felt their sting ourselves

2. Do not sympathize with the one who struggles until we have struggled

3. Do not comprehend the pain of indifference until others have ignored us

4. Do not understand rejection until we have been rejected

5. And we do not understand sin until we see the way it hurts God and destroys others

Joseph was not being cruel . . . God was using these events to awaken the conscience of his brothers. He was stripping away the pretense and exposing the horror within. You can't treat a disease until you know what disease you are dealing with. A person can't be saved until he realizes he is lost. The brothers needed to see, to feel, to understand their own wickedness.

C. Read Genesis 42:18-38. The third part of the story follows the three days in prison. For three days, they thought about their situation. For three days, they experienced some of the horrors that they had inflicted on Joseph. And now they are brought before Joseph again. The brothers are given a reprieve of sorts instead of one brother going home and the others staying . . . one stays, and the rest are able to return home.

Joseph wants to see if the brothers are willing to desert one of their own again. Will they abandon Simeon as they did Joseph? What is most interesting about this scene is the conversation that takes place between the brothers. They thought it was a private conversation . . . they didn't know that the Egyptian leader who sat before them knew Hebrew and knew very well the situation they were talking about.

They said to one another, "Surely we are being punished because of our brother. We saw how distressed he was when he pleaded with us for his life, but we would not listen; that's why this distress has come upon us." Reuben replied, Didn't I tell you not to sin against the boy? But you wouldn't listen! Now, we must give an accounting for his blood." They did not realize that Joseph could understand them since he was using an interpreter. He turned away from them and began to weep but then turned back and spoke to them again.

What this conversation shows is something very significant. Twenty years had passed, their lives had gone on . . . but their past sin continued to haunt them. I suspect they had agreed to never talk about the incident. They certainly resolved many times to "move on" and to all appearances, they did. They seemed unaffected by the past. But it was like a paint job on a moldy wall . . . you can cover the problem, but you don't get rid of it.

Do you have a place in you that has stored bad memories? We try to bury them, but they keep creeping back into our conscience:

- We try to forget the people we made fun of as kids.

- We try to forget the people we used for our own advantage.

- We try to hide the lies we told to people we loved

- We try to forget the people in need that we ignored

- We try to forget the things we did in secret that we knew were wrong.

But we can't forget. Slowly, these things eat away at our joy and our heart. We may work hard to be better people than we used to be . . . but we cannot escape the fact that others are living with scars that we are responsible for. We cannot escape the fact that no matter how holy we try to pretend to be . . . there is a cancer called sin that is buried inside of us. We present ourselves as good and righteous while living in fear that someone will learn the truth.

Looking squarely at our sins is painful, embarrassing, and, at times, makes us sick. But without a recognition of sin . . . there can be no forgiveness. Without seeing our need, we will never need a Savior. It's a road we don't like . . . but it is a road that must be traveled. We are not "All okay" We are anything but okay. We are wicked people who have done horrible things, and no matter how good we are at hiding these things . . . we know the truth.

What we need is something we have long believed we could never receive. We need to be forgiven. Joseph's brothers found that forgiveness. You can too. You may not be able to go back to the person you hurt (but if you can, you should). What we can do, and must do is turn to the Lord, He is the one we are ultimately accountable to.

We are foolish to pretend these sins of our past are nothing. We kid only ourselves when we act like we "have it all together". The only way to come to God is with a heart that is broken and hands that are open, pleading for mercy. And when we do, we find arms open to receive us and embrace us. If you come honestly, confessing your sin with a sorrow that makes you want to change . . . His arms will embrace you.

What I hope you see is that before we can be made new in Christ, we have to come to grips with our own sinfulness. What about you? Does your faith come out of your realization of sin, or are you still playing games with God? Are you still pretending that you are self-sufficient? Are you still trying to sell everyone on the fact that you don't need God . . . Does he need you? If so, you may look like a believer, but you aren't. You are just a phony who is playing "church".

If we are ever going to find the salvation which we desperately need and inwardly crave, we have to be honest with God. We have to see the wrongs of the past as sin. We need to expose our denials. We need to face the truth.

And if you are unwilling to do so, God will pursue you. He will work to get your attention. He will haunt you with the past. He will pursue you with relentless determination. Not because He is cruel . . . but because He loves you, and because He knows that until you recognize that you are sick . . . you can never be made well.

But if you come to Him, the message of the gospel will stagger you. Jesus died for the very sin that haunts us. If we turn to Him, God will cover our past with the blood of Christ. Our wickedness will be forgiven. We will be given a new beginning. We will be able to stop running from the past and start living the life we were created to live.

Do we deserve this mercy? No. Can we earn it? No. Can we ever repay what we ask to receive? No. But when we confess, repent and ask . . . God forgives, heals, and makes new. The Bible calls that - grace.

Are you going to ask forgiveness for your sins? Are you going to trust God to save you? Do you believe that Jesus is the Christ, the Messiah who died on the cross, paying for your sins, raising from the dead, and conquering death? Will you place your faith in Christ right now? If you do, then make your decision known publicly. Step out right now and come to the front. I will be here to greet you.

CHAPTER FORTY

Rebuilding Trust
Genesis 43:1-15

There are some things that reveal our character. Let me ask you a couple of questions for you to think about.

1. What would it take for you to violate the Word of God? You say, 'I wouldn't.' You might – put you in the wrong situation at the wrong time.

2. Are your words and your walk the same? Can you be trusted? If you bought something for $12, and you gave the clerk a twenty, and the clerk gave you a ten and 2 ones in change, what would you do? Would you say, 'Oh, wait, wait, you gave me too much change?'

In this lesson, we are going to see Joseph continue to test the character of his brothers. Are they honest? Remember, he put extra money in their bags of grain. When they left Egypt, having paid for the grain, Joseph put their money back in the bags. And on the way back, they opened up their bags and discovered the money. 'oh no. what do we do?' And some other questions. What are they going to do about Benjamin? Are they going to go get him and bring him back? And what are they going to do about Simeon, who they left there in prison in Egypt? So Joseph is testing them.

Jacob is going to have to trust God. Will he? The brothers are going to have to trust God. Will they?

Read Genesis 43:1. It didn't end. It is that seven-year time period. Boy, it's tough. So what happens?

Read Genesis 43:2. Now they have run out of the grain that they had purchased in Egypt. So Jacob says, "Go back." Has he forgotten? Or does he think maybe they will forget? You see, Jacob doesn't want to face the fact that when the food runs out, and he has to send his sons back to Egypt, Benjamin is going to have to go with them. Even though we read in chapter 52:38 that he said 'no way. He can't go because he might get harmed.' What happens?

Read Genesis 43:3. So Judah reminds his father that the man said, "You won't even get to see me, you won't have a chance to get any food, you won't have a chance to get your brother out of prison until you come back with your youngest brother." Now Judah is saying things that Jacob, his father, doesn't want to hear, "I don't want to hear that. I told you he isn't going."

Read Genesis 43:4-5. "Listen, if you let Benjamin go, we will go back and get some food." Notice they don't ever mention who in all of this? Simeon. Wouldn't you be saying, "What about poor Simeon? He is in prison in Egypt. How long has he been there?" We don't know. But it has been a while because they are out of food once again. And we are going to see in verse 10 that Judah says, "We could have gone down and back twice." Can you imagine Simeon in prison going, "Where are they? They should have been back way before now." And he is marking the days on that wall. And I imagine Simeon thinking, "Something isn't right here." And Joseph is thinking, "Are they going to leave Simeon like they did me? Have my brothers changed? Where are they?"

Read Genesis 43:6. Notice what the author of Genesis is calling Jacob in this passage. Israel. And Israel is saying, "What an idiot thing for your guys to do. How could you treat me so badly by telling the man that you had a younger brother?" Notice how they respond.

Read Genesis 43:7. "Look, father, we had no way of knowing the man in Egypt would say, "Bring your brother down."' Well, Judah is going to take the lead. Judah knows that things are bad. They are all going to starve to death. So, look what he does.

Read Genesis 43:8-9. Judah says to his father, "Listen, we have to do something. I am willing to take the risk. I will take charge. If you will give me Benjamin, he can go with me. I will be responsible for him coming back. And if for some reason he doesn't come back, God forbid, I will take the blame.'" That's a curse. He is saying, "I will take the curse on me for you losing your son." Pretty powerful. He is willing to take the responsibility. You know, in our society, there are a lot of people who don't want to take any responsibility. On anything. Well, Judah continues his stirring words with his father.

Read Genesis 43:10. We could have already gone and come back twice. We could have had food already. We need a decision, so we can go.

Well, the ball is in Israel's court. What would you do? We say we love all of our kids the same. But remember, Jacob didn't love all his sons the same. He favored Joseph, who was gone. Remember he things Joseph has been killed by wild animals. He is now favoring Benjamin. So now Israel is going to have to trust God. That God will protect Benjamin on the trip over to Egypt and get him back home safe. Remember Jacob thinks everything is going bad. But he doesn't realize that the near future is going to be the best it has ever been in his life. He is about to see his son Joseph, who he thought was dead. He about to live with him the rest of his life in luxury. With plenty of food to eat. And also he is about to meet his Joseph's son, his grandsons for the first time. Simeon will be released from prison. And he is going to live in the best land in Egypt. Things are about to become absolutely wonderful. But his thinks right now that everything is terrible.

You see, sometimes we are right on the verge of something being better than we can imagine. But we get afraid and say, 'I don't know if that is going to work. Are you sure? I don't want to do that.' And yet, we don't know, but we might be on the verge of something great as God works all things ultimately for the good. God is in control.

Look what Israel does.

Read Genesis 43:11. You don't go back to this powerful man in Egypt without some kind of presents. Always a good idea.

Read Genesis 43:12. "Listen when you go back down there, go back with your money; you don't want this Egyptian ruler to think that you are dishonest. Just explain to him that you don't know how the money got into your sacks; this is money we paid the first time, we are bringing it back, and here is some more money to purchase more grain. And we have brought some presents for you." They have to be men of character. They must take the money back. In our society, honesty is rare. 'Steal at the office. Cheat on our taxes. Plagiarize. Pad the expense account. Cheat on the test. Break your promises.' Happens all the time.

And then Israel continues.

Read Genesis 43:13. Take Benjamin with you as the Egyptian ruler asked.

Read Genesis 43:14. God Almighty, El Shaddai. I must trust Him. 'If I lose my sons, I lose my sons' I just pray that when you get there, the Egyptian ruler will listen to you, release Simeon, and not take Benjamin, and you will all be able to come back safe. I must trust God. He is in control.

One of the hardest things for parents to do is to entrust their children to God. I remember when we first arrived in Costa Rica, we had to leave little Stephen, age 1, with total strangers the day after we arrived in the country. It was hard. But we had to trust God. And you do, too. God gives your children to you as a gift. Psalm 127:3. They are His. We only have them for a short time. We are to train them to love. To teach them the Word of God. The rights and wrongs. Jacob is saying, "I don't want to let go of Benjamin. But I have to. I don't have a choice. Because for my family to survive, I got to trust God."

Look what happens.

Read Genesis 43:15. We are going to stop there. In the next lesson, we will see what Joseph does when he sees Benjamin and his brothers. He is going to continue testing them.

Passing the Test
Genesis 43:16-34

Open your Bibles to Genesis 43. We are continuing in our study of the book of Genesis. And the focus of this section, of course, is the life of Joseph. If you remember, Joseph has risen to power and is now overseeing the selling of the grain during those seven years of famine. And we saw that his brothers came from Canaan to buy grain. But Joseph didn't reveal himself to them. They think he is an Egyptian. He looked out and saw his brothers and began to test them to see what kind of men they were now. And now, in this lesson, we are going to study the brothers' second visit. What will Joseph do? Will he continue to test them? How are they doing? Are they passing the test or failing the test? Will Joseph reveal himself to his brothers? Joseph sees his brother Benjamin after all these years.

We have tests throughout our lives. Whether in school, at work, or just in our life. Sometimes tests come and what we have to do is - trust God. Sometimes, things don't turn out exactly the way we think they should. Last time, we have seen Joseph testing his brothers. Why? He wants to see what kind of men they have become. He remembers what they were like 20 years ago. How they hated him. How they were jealous of him. How they sold him into slavery. How they came back and lied to their father. But how are they like now? Do they hate his younger brother, Benjamin? Are they honest?

Last lesson we saw three tests.

Remember, Joseph told them that they couldn't come back to get any more grain unless they brought their younger brother, Benjamin. And remember that Joseph kept their brother Simeon in the Egyptian prison. And finally, remember that Joseph put their money back in their grain sacks. And remember that Joseph kept their brother Simeon in the Egyptian prison. And finally remember that Joseph put their money back in their grain sacks.

Now, in this lesson, did they pass the tests? Do they trust God?

Read Genesis 43:15. And that is where we left off last time.

Read Genesis 43:16. This is incredible. They have come back with Benjamin. And they are just nobodies. This man, who is the second most powerful man in Egypt, there are people coming every day wanting food, and he decides who gets what food, and suddenly there are the brothers, they don't know him, and he looks down and says to his steward, "They are going to eat with me." If you were one of these brothers, and the word came to you, "Prepare yourselves, you are going to eat with Zaphnath-Paaneah (Joseph)" (the new name given by Pharaoh - Gen. 41:45), What would you think?

Read Genesis 43:17-18. They probably thought, "Oh, oh. He knows about the money in our sacks! He probably thinks we stole it. We are in big trouble. They are going to jump on us and beat us and take our donkeys." Their donkeys were the most important possession they had. So they said, "We had better talk to this steward." By the way who is this steward? We are going to see that this steward knows a lot. A steward is sort of the law of the house. An overseer of a wealthy person's property. Remember, Joseph was a steward for Potiphar.

And now, ironically, Joseph has his own steward. The Bible calls us stewards. 1 Cor. 4. The things that we have, everything that we have, is what God has given to us to use, and we are to be wise stewards of all of the time we have left, possessions, spiritual gifts, talents, etc. Use them for His glory. Well, the brothers are going to talk to Joseph's steward because they don't know what to do.

Read Genesis 43:19-21. We just want you to know that we didn't steal that money. We are honest men. You see, they think they are going to that house because they are in trouble.

Read Genesis 43:22. We just don't know how the money got into our sacks. That's pretty honest, isn't it? That is what Joseph is hoping they would do. That's his plan. He is testing them. Will they bring back Benjamin? How do they treat him? Do they fuss at him? Do they make fun of him? Do they leave him out?

Watch what the steward says.

Read Genesis 43:23a. The steward is the one who put the money in their sacks. Because Zaphnath-Paaneah (Joseph) told him to do so. The steward knows they are telling the truth. Joseph knows they are telling the truth. But I think the incredible statement is – 'Your God and the God of your father has given you treasure in your sacks.' Do you know what he is saying? 'This is all from God.' God is working on this whole deal. And he is talking about the true God. Not some Egyptian false deity. Here is this Egyptian steward talking about God. How would he know about YHWH? Because he had been with Joseph.

Read Genesis 43:23b. Can you imagine this scene when the brothers get to see Simeon again? All eleven of them together again. And what they don't know is that all twelve of them are together again.

Now watch what happens.

Read Genesis 43:24-25. They had the present ready. Remember that their father, Jacob, said to bring some presents to give to the Egyptian leader? I can imagine the brothers are really beginning to wonder what is going on. I mean, they are inside the Egyptian leader's house. And they have been given the royal treatment.

Read Genesis 43:26. They bowed down to Joseph. What did they say 20 years ago? We never are going to bow down to you. How many times have they bowed down so far? At least twice, and they will again before this thing is over. God's Word said they would bow down. In the vision, in the dream that God gave Joseph. And one thing about it, we can always say – if God's Word says it, you can count on it.

There are times when we get afraid, and we don't know how we are going to make it; I don't know how we will have enough. I don't think I can afford to tithe. Listen, you can't afford not to. You need to tithe so that you will have enough. God always takes care of us. Trust Him. Be faithful.

Well, look what happened.

Read Genesis 43:27. Did you see what Joseph asks? He wants to know if their father, Jacob, is alive and well. I mean, it took them a while to return. And Joseph is wondering why. Are they going to come back? Are they just going to leave Simeon in prison? Are they going to bring Benjamin back?

Read Genesis 43:28. They bowed down again. You know that Joseph is just dying to tell them who they are bowing down to. But he doesn't.

Read Genesis 43:29. There are some deep emotions happening here. He sees his brother, Benjamin. After 20 years. His brother. Not his half-brother. All the others are half-brothers. This is his own flesh and blood.

Read Genesis 43:30. What do you think he said to those guys when he left? Be right back, excuse me. Of course, he can do anything he wants. He is the second most powerful man in Egypt.

Read Genesis 43:31. Now, I want you to notice something. Do the Egyptians eat with the Hebrews? No. That would be detestable. They are just uncultured shepherds.

Read Genesis 43:32. The brothers ate by themselves. And Joseph ate lunch by himself. Because it was loathsome for the Egyptians to eat with the Hebrews. It makes the Hebrews feel really good, doesn't it?

Read Genesis 43:33. Can you just see the brothers' faces when they were seated from oldest to youngest? Reuben, Simeon, Levi, Judah, Dan, Naphtali, Gad, Asher, Issachar, Zebulun, Benjamin. I am sure their mouths were wide open. Because that could not have happened by coincidence, there is no way this Egyptian ruler could have known who was the oldest and who was the youngest.

Read Genesis 43:34. Everybody got a chicken leg. But Benjamin got five chicken legs. Everybody got a tablespoon of mashed potatoes. But Benjamin got five tablespoons of mashed potatoes. Everybody got a scoop of cookies and cream flavored ice cream. But Benjamin got five scoops of cookies and cream-flavored ice cream. Why did Joseph do that? Again, Benjamin was his blood brother. And maybe because he wanted to see their response to their youngest brother. Did they hate Benjamin? Were they jealous of Benjamin? Will they treat Benjamin like they treated him? He continues to test them. And what did they do? They feasted and drank freely with Benjamin. They are passing the test. All night long, they have passed the test. But he has more tests for them. But you will have to go to the next lesson to find out what happens.

CHAPTER FORTY-ONE

Joseph's Final Test
Genesis 44

Open your Bibles to Genesis 44. We are seeing the life of Joseph. He of course is the main character in the last part of this book. We are seeing his interaction with brothers after 20 years. They have come to Egypt to buy food during the famine. They don't recognize Joseph. But Joseph recognizes them. And we have seen something that is incredible in these last couple of chapters. And that is – Joseph is testing his brothers. What are they like? Are they honest? Are they loving? Do they care about each other? How do they relate to the youngest brother, Benjamin? Are they jealous of him in the same way they were jealous of Joseph 20 years ago when they sold him into slavery? He is testing his brothers. And we have seen so far that they have passed the tests. They have shown to be honest men. They brought back the money that was in their grain bags. They even did what Zaphnath-Paaneah (Joseph) asked them to do. They brought back their youngest brother, Benjamin. Now, we are going to see the final test. How will they treat Benjamin? That's what he wants to know. Because that is his real brother. We are going to see one of his half-brothers stand out, and that one is Judah. We are going to see one of the great truths in God's Word, and that is the idea of substitution. Judah is willing to give his life to Benjamin. When we study this chapter, we think about the greatest truth in the Bible, the substitution of Christ for you and for me, and how He was willing to give His life for us. He took our place. So that we would not have to be separated from God. He took the penalty of sin. The wages of sin is death. Jesus Christ died so we don't have to be separated.

Who would you give your life for? Your husband, wife, your children, your parents? Romans 5:8: "But God demonstrates His love for us, that while we were yet sinners, Christ died for us. Christ didn't die for perfect people. There aren't any. He died for sinners. Us. Substitution.

Now, remember last time, Joseph gave Benjamin 5 times the amount of lunch than the rest of the brothers. How did they act? They didn't seem to be jealous. So far, so good. Let's see what happens.

Read Genesis 44:1. He isn't going to give them a little grain to take back. He said, "Put as much into those sacks as you can put." Then, they put their money back inside, just like we did last time. He wants to know if they are still going to be honest. Will they bring it back again?

Read Genesis 44:2. He tells his steward to put his silver cup in the sack of the youngest brother, Benjamin. Why? Why is he coming after Benjamin? He is making it look like Benjamin stole the cup. How are his brothers going to respond? Will they say, "How could you steal the cup, you idiot! You are on your own." Or are they going to say, "Wait a minute. We defend him." What is going to happen? Will they protect him, or will they leave him? That is what Joseph wants to know.

Read Genesis 44:3. It looks like everything is going well. They were able to buy more grain. They got Simeon out of jail. Benjamin didn't get hurt or anything. They even got to eat at the head guy's house.

Read Genesis 44:4. Joseph says to his steward, "Go after them. And when you catch up to them, say, 'You have done evil. Why would you do this? We gave you food; we let you eat with the vice president. Why would you do evil to us?' And, of course, they are going to look around at each other confused. What in the world are you talking about?"

Read Genesis 44:5. Joseph then tells his steward to say "When you overtake them, say this cup belongs to my master. This is the cup he uses for divination. He can predict the future with this cup. You have returned evil for good." Let me ask you a question. You know Joseph right? Godly man. Do you think he used a silver cup for divination? Nah. He is just saying that. So that they will really be worried about this Egyptian ruler. So watch what happens.

Read Genesis 44:6-7. He caught up to the brothers and said, "You have stolen the master's cup." And they looked around and said, "We would never steal any old cup. We didn't even know he had such a cup." "We are honest men."

Read Genesis 44:8. "Now listen here. We brought back the money that we found in our grain sacks. We are honest men. We would never do this." "you can check us out. Nobody got it. We aren't that dumb."

Read Genesis 44:9. "We are so certain that we didn't steal this silver cup, that whoever has the cup, you can kill him. And the rest of us will be your slaves. We are that sure we didn't do it." I think I would have looked around first and asked, "Did any of you guys get this cup?" Before making such a serious statement.

Read Genesis 44:10. Notice the change of words. The steward softened the penalty contained in the brothers' proposal. In verse 9, one would die, and the rest would be slaves. But here, in verse 10, one would be a slave, and the rest would be innocent. Now, who is going to get caught? Benjamin. Now, what is going to happen to him? Are they going to say, 'Hey kid, you are on your own.' 'You shouldn't have taken that cup.' 'See ya' That is what they probably would have done to

Joseph 20 years ago. Are they going to do it to Benjamin? He wants to see what they will do to Benjamin. He is tricking them.

Read Genesis 44:11-12a. So, each brother opens his sack of grain while Joseph's steward searches for the silver cup. He starts with the oldest brother, Reuben, on down. 10 out of 10 so far. Doing great. But notice that they didn't mention the money in their sacks. It wasn't the most important issue at the moment. But then...

Read Genesis 44:12b. What would you do? If you lived in that day and time, you would tear your clothes. 'Oh no!' This was the way that you should have been extremely upset. 'This can't be happening to us.'

Read Genesis 44:13. I imagine Benjamin is probably pleading, 'I am telling the truth. I didn't steal it. I don't know how it got there. Somebody must have put it there. Please listen to me. I didn't do it!' Benjamin is caught as a thief. We are nearing the test now. What are they going to do when they get back to the city? The steward says, "Load up. Everybody back to town." And Joseph is waiting. What is he going to do?

Read Genesis 44:14. So now we see that Judah is taking the lead. And notice what the brothers do when they get back to Joseph's house. Fall down to the ground before him. Remember the dream 20 years ago? And Remember that the brothers said they wouldn't bow down to him. This is the fifth time mentioned here. Probably more than that.

Read Genesis 44:15. Do you know what Joseph is saying? You think you can get away with stealing from me? Again, I don't think Joseph practiced divination. But he is probably just tricking them in thinking this silver cup was really important.

Now, look what Judah does. He becomes the spokesman. Now, watch this statement because it is powerful.

Read Genesis 44:16a. Judah basically says to Zaphnath-Paaneah, "What can we say to you? We don't have an answer. We can't justify ourselves. We don't know how it got in there."

Now, watch the next statement.

Read Genesis 44:16b. "God has found out the iniquity of your servants." What is Judah talking about? He is saying, "We have done wrong in the past. And God is judging. We have been lying to our father all these many years about Joseph. Whatever a man sows, he shall reap."

Read Genesis 44:16c. That isn't part of the deal. The steward said that only the one caught would be a slave. But Judah says here, "All of us are your slaves." Did you see that? He didn't say, "Well, Benjamin stole the cup. See ya. Walk like an Egyptian." But Judah offers all of the brothers to be slaves. We are all in this together. And that is what Joseph wanted to see. Would they leave Benjamin behind, or would they stick with him? Would they defend him or not? This is the test. And they passed.

Read Genesis 44:17. So Joseph says, "Leave your brother and go back to your father." And in his mind, he is asking, 'Are you going to do that to Benjamin, just like you to me?' 'Have you changed?'

Read Genesis 44:18. Judah asks to speak to Zaphnath-Paaneah alone. He doesn't want the rest to hear this. "And don't be mad at me. I know you are equal to Pharaoh and could kill me like that."

Read Genesis 44:19-26. Judah is telling Joseph the whole story.

Read Genesis 44:27-31. In verse 28, Judah tells Zaphnath-Paaneah about the one brother, Joseph, who was surely torn to pieces by a wild animal, which is a lie. He isn't telling the Egyptian ruler the whole truth of the story. He is just telling him what his father thinks. Judah then pleads with this Egyptian ruler that his father would just die if something happened to his youngest son, Benjamin.

Read Genesis 44:32. Judah then tells Zaphnath-Paaneah about how he personally took responsibility for Benjamin and put a curse on himself if something happened to him.

Read Genesis 44:33. Judah has now asked this Egyptian ruler to please consider taking him instead of his brother Benjamin. Because he don't want his father to die in sorrow. "I will do whatever it takes. I am a surety for him."

Read Genesis 44:34. "Please take me instead. I just can't bear to see my father suffer in grief over the loss of Benjamin." Would you have done it? Would you die for your brother? Your wife? Your children? The test has been passed. Judah cares enough about his brother to become a slave in his place.

Do you know what he is saying? "I don't know how the cup got in the sack. But if Benjamin stole it, I will bear his punishment." The wages of sin are - death and slavery. If Benjamin is going to have to be a slave for the rest of his life, I will be a slave for the rest of my life. Substitution.

Every one of us in this room - sin. Let's face it. We all have sinned and come short of the glory of God. The wages of sin is - death. Every one of us is supposed to be separated from God. If we think about the mercy and the grace of God, and the justice of God.

Grace is getting what you don't deserve, mercy is getting is not getting what you do deserve, and justice is getting what you deserve. If everyone got what we deserved, we would be doomed to hell. But God is such a great God that He sent Jesus Christ to die in our place. Because we owe God - death. We are supposed to be separated. And there isn't one thing we can do about it. And we weren't coming to God and saying, "Show us mercy."

We were going the other way. And God, in His grace, sent Jesus Christ. And Jesus Christ became a human being so that He could become our substitute and die in our place. 1 Peter 3:18. "For Christ died for sins once for all, the just for the unjust, which is called substitution; why? So that He might bring us to God."

Substitution. It is all through the Bible. It is the greatest story of all time. The story of Reconciliation. How God brings sinful man back to Himself. How? Using His Son, Jesus Christ.

He became our substitute. He is the satisfactory payment. We can never get over the fact that Jesus took our place.

So, what is Joseph going to do? He now knows that his brothers are honest and are willing to die for one another. They have passed his test.

What is he going to do?

You will just have to wait until the next lesson to find out.

CHAPTER FORTY-TWO

Redemptive Love
Genesis 45

Open your Bibles to Genesis 45. We are going to finally see Joseph reveal his identity to his brothers. It has been 20 years since he was sold into slavery by his brothers. We have seen how he tested them to see if they have changed, to see if they have repented. And they did pass every test. So we get to see the big event!

The theme of this lesson – forgiveness and sovereignty. Here are some theological terms that you need to know:

Justification – to be declared righteous. When we put our faith in Jesus as Savior, the Bible says we are justified; we are declared righteous. Gal. 2:16.

Imputation – means to credit from one account to another. When we put our faith in Christ, He makes us righteous. Romans 4:5

Propitiation – means a satisfactory payment. 1 John 2:2

Sanctification – means to be set apart. The moment you put your faith in Jesus Christ, you are positionally set apart in Christ. At the same time, over the process of our life, we are growing to be more like Christ, which is progressive sanctification. 2 Peter 3:18.

Redemption – to purchase by paying a price 1 Peter 1:18.

Expiation – means to suffer the punishment or pay the penalty for someone else. It is really another word for substitution. We see a great truth in the Bible – we have all sinned and come short of the glory of God, and the wages of sin is death. And yet Jesus Christ came, and He died in our place. He became our substitute. He died on the cross to pay for our sins.

We ended our study with Judah offering to be the substitute for his brother Benjamin.

Read Genesis 45:1. It says here that he couldn't control himself any longer. He has played this game with them. He has hidden himself from his brothers all this time. Don't you imagine the first time that those ten half-brothers showed up, and he knew exactly who they were? He wanted to tell him who he was. But he needed to know what these brothers were like now. Are they any different than they used to be? And he tested them at least five times. He wants to see if they are repentant. He is trying to redeem them out of love. And every time, they passed the test. And so he tells everyone to leave the room. You see, he is a very powerful man in Egypt, and he doesn't want the people to see him crying.

Read Genesis 45:2. But the Egyptians heard him crying anyway and apparently told some of Pharaoh's people. Because they had heard of it. Do you think Joseph was weeping for joy or for sorrow? I think it was a joy. 'Something is up with Zaphnath-Paaneah.'

Read Genesis 45:3. He probably takes off his Egyptian headdress. And began speaking to them in Hebrew. If you were one of the step-brothers, Is this a good day or a bad day? You probably are thinking, "Oh boy, my sins have found me out. This is the most powerful man in Egypt other than the Pharaoh, and this is the guy I sold into slavery. This is the guy I didn't care anything about. This is the guy that I waved goodbye to as he was pleading for life as they were taking him off as a slave. And now this is the guy that has the power of life or death over me. And he is not happy." That is what you would think. And you know what else? If I get to live, which is doubtful, what are we going to tell Father? Because we made our daddy believe 20 years ago that an animal ate him up. And surely Joseph is going to tell Father what we did 20 years ago.

Read Genesis 45:4. You can just picture these brothers standing there in shock with their mouths open. And so Joseph calls them a little closer. "I am your brother Joseph, whom you sold into Egypt". And I imagine they are probably even more afraid and dismayed at this point. Now, what would you do if you were Joseph? For 20 years, more than half of your life, you have been in a foreign country. Originally sold as a slave. And a good bit of that time a prisoner, too. Would you be tempted to get your half-brothers back if you ever got the chance? And now Joseph has the chance. What is he going to do? He is going to forgive them based on the sovereignty of God.

Read Genesis 45:5. Joseph says, "Listen, yes, you did bad when you sold me into slavery. But God was using your actions to preserve life. He sent me ahead to keep not only the Egyptians alive but all of us." How does sovereignty and freedom fit? Joseph says, "You sold me, but God sent me." Joseph was certain that it was God's will, not man's will, that controlled every event. And notice that Joseph forgives them. 'don't be angry with yourselves.' We all have been done wrong by somebody else, and you probably thought, "I am going to get them back if I am ever #2 in Egypt." But Joseph realizes that even with somebody's evil action, God is working to bring about His plan for your life. Even when bad things come into your life and other people make choices that hurt you, you have to understand that in the Sovereign plan of God for your life, He is working in all things to conform you to the image of His Son. Can you forgive those who have hurt you?

Read Genesis 45:6. He is letting his brothers know that the famine still has another five years to go.

Read Genesis 45:7. He tells his brothers that the whole reason he is there in Egypt is because the covenant promise of God that He made with Abraham is to keep us alive so that His ultimate plan can work out. Because the Messiah will come through Abraham and specifically through Judah.

Listen, folks, we had better be thankful that Joseph ended up in Egypt and was able to interpret the dreams through God so that he could be in a place of leadership, so that he could save his household, so that the Jewish people could stay alive, so that the descendants of Judah could come all the way down to David and then all the way down to Jesus of Nazareth. Aren't you glad God is Sovereign? Aren't you glad we have a savior? Who is our substitute?

Read Genesis 45:8. Now, Joseph isn't saying that the brothers aren't off the hook. He isn't saying that there aren't consequences for their actions. They have already suffered some consequences. Now your heavenly Father loves you, and there are natural consequences to some sins, and sometimes God, because you disobey Him, deals with you and me as a Father to a child. Joseph is saying that it is the Sovereignty of God that has made me an advisor (father) to Pharaoh and put me in a position as ruler over the land of Egypt.

Read Genesis 45:9-10. Joseph says, "Go back and get my dad and come back. Everybody come back down here because you can live in the best part of Egypt, called Goshen, which is the northeastern part of Egypt." Pharaoh told him that his family could live in the best area.

Read Genesis 45:11. Tell Father that he must come and live here because there will be five more years of this terrible famine. I will take care of you. Everybody must come, or you won't make it. By the way, about 70 came down.

Read Genesis 45:12. Joseph is still trying to convince them who he is. "Can't you hear me? You know my voice. Look carefully in my eyes and face. It's me."

Read Genesis 45:13. Why do you think Joseph is in such a hurry for them to go get Father and bring him down? Because Jacob is old. How old was he when he arrived in Egypt? He was 130 years old. How many years did he live? 147. He is going to have 17 years with Joseph in Egypt.

Read Genesis 45:14-15. His brothers talked with him. Had his brothers talked with him when he was growing up? What did they say to him when he was a boy? Why don't you just shut up, you dreamer? They didn't talk to him back then. They didn't like him. And now, after all these years, they are talking. And they are hugging one another and crying. This is an event that is beyond comprehension. Joseph forgives. There may somebody in your life that you are holding a grudge against. It may be your mother or father. It may be a brother or sister. It may be your former best friend. And you have lost months and maybe years over this broken relationship. Forgive. Don't let any more time slip away. Go to them and reconcile.

Read Genesis 45:16-18. This is Pharaoh talking. Get your brothers loaded up and send them back to Canaan to get your father and his household, and come back to me, and I will give them the best of the land.

Read Genesis 45:19. Pharoah continues with, "I am going to let you take some wagons in order to help you move everybody. I know it is kind of tough with little ones."

Read Genesis 45:20. And Pharaoh then says, "Don't even worry about your goods. You can have the best goods in the land." Do you think the Pharaoh respected Joseph? Yes. Can you imagine a Hebrew slave who is a prisoner and has become #2 in Egypt and has become so powerful that even the Pharaoh says, "Now listen up, you tell your family to come on down here because we will take care of them totally. Don't worry about a thing."

Read Genesis 45:21-22. Why would Joseph give them clothes? It wasn't like it was that long of a journey. A set of brand-new clothes in that culture meant a brand-new start. And he is saying, "It is a brand-new start. You need to forget about the past. We are starting over as a family." And notice that he gave Benjamin 300 pieces of silver. How much does it cost to buy a slave? 30 pieces of silver. And remember, there were ten brothers involved in him being sold into slavery. And he also gave Benjamin five changes of clothes.

Read Genesis 45:23. Joseph sent his father gifts and a whole bunch of food so that he wouldn't have to stop at the QuikTrip on the way down. He can just keep his foot on the pedal and keep on trucking.

Read Genesis 45:24. And finally, Joseph tells his brothers not to fuss at each other. "Remember, it is over."

Read Genesis 45:25-26. The word stunned in Hebrew almost means 'heart attack.' It means that he became dull on his insides. It was almost like he couldn't breathe for a second. "This is too good to be true. My son, who was eaten by an animal 20 years ago, is actually alive? And not only that, but he is the ruler in Egypt?"

Read Genesis 45:27. And the brothers say "Hey dad, what kind of wagons are those? How do you think we got all of this stuff?" And Jacob's spirit is revived. He is leaping for joy. Don't ever give up hope that God has a wonderful future in store for you.

Read Genesis 45:28. Come on, let's load up and go. Now, remember that Jacob watched his boys leave. He is pretty sad because he has already lost his wife, Rachel, and his son, Joseph, to a wild animal. His son, Simeon, is in an Egyptian prison, and now they are taking Benjamin to an unknown fate. But he doesn't know that it is about to be the best time in his life. He is going to be reunited with all of his boys including Joseph. And live in the best place with plenty to eat. God does beyond what we can imagine.

Wouldn't you have loved to have been there when the brothers come back to their father, and they come back with all this stuff because Pharaoh said, "Oh, don't send them back empty-handed." Wouldn't you have love to see Jacob look up and see this caravan of possessions coming and all these

Egyptians, and the brothers walk up to Jacob and say "Joseph is alive and is a ruler over Egypt."

Is God's blessing beyond what you can imagine? Everything in our lives is beyond what we can imagine. In our lives, we forgive because of God's sovereignty. God provides for us day in and day out. Aren't you thankful? Are you worshipping Him and praising Him for what He has done and is doing and will do?

CHAPTER FORTY-THREE

How Do We Know God's Will?
Genesis 46:1-30

The nation of Israel left the Promised Land and went to Egypt. Is it okay for Jacob to do that? Because in the past, it was wrong. Years ago, when Abraham left Canaan for Egypt, he got into trouble. Not only did he lose his testimony down there, he picked up Hagar, the handmaiden, which got him into trouble later on. Then we saw Isaac wanted to leave; God told him, "You can't go to Egypt." So now, is it okay for Jacob to leave the Promised Land and go down to Egypt? And how is Jacob going to know? As we look at this passage, how do we know God's Will? How do we know right from wrong? How do we know where our authority is? How do we find out this kind of thing? As we see the great blessing of Jacob seeing his son Joseph once again. We also want to think about some of these issues.

Are certain things right and wrong? Of course, they are. Where do you go to make decisions? What exactly is our authority? Is right and wrong based on what we think is right and wrong? George Barna has become the guru in Christian circles concerning the beliefs of Americans and also the beliefs of people in our churches. On an extensive survey polling thousands of people, he finds that most believe there is no absolute truth. Different people can define truth in conflicting ways, and both think they are correct. Some people say this is wrong, but others say no, it is right. Whatever people think is right, is right. In fact, over 80% of Americans believe in God, and a large part of that percent claim to be Christian. But the problem is that of that percentage of Christians, 53% of the Christians in the U.S. say there is no absolute truth. That the Bible does not contain absolute truth. Only 16% of those people make moral judgments based on the Scripture. So where do those go? 45% base their moral judgments on their own personal experience. I don't know. I believe in the Bible! It is the absolute truth! I am so glad that I am part of a church that is founded and based on the written Word of God. God has revealed Himself to us.

Now Jacob is going to base his decision on whether he goes to Egypt or not, not based on the fact that Joseph said to come down, not based on the fact that Pharaoh said it was okay to come down. He bases it on the fact that he goes to Beersheba and worships God, and waits for the Word of God to tell him to go or not.

Now, in this lesson, we are going to see that Jacob, who is 130 years old, is going to go down to Egypt to see his son for the first time in 20 years.

Read Genesis 46:1. Now there is a reason he went to Beersheba, and there is a reason it says the way it says it. Because most of the time, when it talks about it says the God of his father, Abraham and Isaac. But this verse here just says, "To the God of his father Isaac." He is on his way down to Egypt and when he reaches Beersheba which is the southernmost place in Israel, he stops. This was a very special place for his father, Isaac. Because at Beersheba, he had set up an altar and worshipped God. And God had worshipped God there. So now Jacob is going to stop there and also worship God. Now, you can't tell it in this verse, but Jacob is afraid to go to Egypt. He knows that Abraham was never supposed to go to Egypt, but he went, and he got into trouble. And his father, Isaac, was never allowed to go to Egypt. And we are going to see in verse 3 that he is afraid and God is going to confront him. And so he is going to offer sacrifices to God, a memorial of where both Abraham and Isaac had worshipped. God appeared to my father at this same place. The Bible is full of memorials. The Tabernacle, the altars, and the feast days were always built to remember what God has done. Do we have anything that God has given to us as a memorial to remember what God has done? The Lord's Supper. That is what it is. "Do this in remembrance of me." This is a memorial. "Until Jesus comes back." Remember the death and resurrection of Jesus Christ.

Read Genesis 46:2. Have you ever noticed that when God calls a person, he usually calls him twice? "Jacob! Jacob!" God spoke to Jacob in a vision at night. "How much of the Bible was written at this time," so he could have opened the Bible to see what to do? None. He didn't have a written revelation. God wanted to give him His Word, so He did in a night vision, like a dream.

Read Genesis 46:3. God tells Jacob that He is the God of his father, Isaac. Then tells him not to be afraid to go down to Egypt. Was he afraid? Apparently so. Then tells him that He will make him into a great nation there. What was the promise to Abraham? I will give you land, give you a seed, I will give you a blessing. I will make of you a great nation. And the same promise to Isaac. And the same promise to Jacob. And instead of making the great nation in Canaan, He is going to take down to Egypt with 70 people and bring them out with 2 million. They will be a great nation when they come out.

Read Genesis 46:4. What that mean? Jacob is going to die. Because when they died, they closed their eyes. Notice what it says. "And I will surely bring you back again." Now if Joseph closes his eyes, where is he going to die? Egypt. But what is God going to do? Jacob will be buried where? In Israel. Now this is prophecy here. And it all came true. How did Jacob know whether to go down to Egypt or not? God told him. He had the Word of God. This is the 8th time that God appears to Jacob.

Now the question is for us – how do we know what the right thing to do is? Well, we have the same thing. We have the Word of God. It is in written form. Ours is even better. You know it is true. It never changes. So, where do you go to learn about right and wrong? The Bible. How do we know how to worship and pray? The Bible. How do we know about end-time events and what God is going to do in the future? The Bible. How do we know the roles of husbands, wives, parents, and children? The Bible. How do we know how to treat one another? The Bible. How do we know how to grow in the grace and knowledge of Jesus our savior? The Bible.

So when we seek to make decisions both individual decisions and in decisions in our church – we need to go to the Bible. May we know God's Will.

So what happens? What does Jacob do?

Read Genesis 46:5-7. Why so much detail? I think the point is that he wants us to understand that what we call the Jewish people are leaving Canaan. The land that God promised them. And they are pulling out of there based on the fact that God told them to do so. And that is an incredible thing. But remember, it is still their land. God gave it to them. Forever. It belongs to them. In May, 1948 When they became a nation, that was the first time since 70 AD that they possessed the land, which they also owned but now possess.

Now, the whole reason that God is taking them down to Egypt is for protection. He wants to get them away from the pagan Canaanite influence and to preserve them during the famine. And He is going to grow His people even in the midst of persecution and slavery. God gave us, through the Jewish people, the Messiah. Also, God gave us the Bible through the Jewish people. In fact, it is a Jewish book. They are God's people. As Christians, we need to stand by our Jewish brothers and sisters.

Now in verses 8-25 God lists for us the sons of Israel. The 66 people that go down to Egypt. 33 came from Leah. 16 from Leah's handmaid, Zilpah. 14 came from Rachel. And 7 from Rachel's handmaid, Bilhah.

Read Genesis 46:26-27. God cares about every human being. He cares about every detail. He knew you would be studying this book. He wants us to know about Jacob's family. The twelve boys and their families. Aren't you glad God about you too? And that He cares about every detail of your life, too?

He knows about every little detail in your life. So talk to Him about the stuff in your life. There is nothing in your life too small and nothing in your life too big for God.

Now, I want to close with the reunion. And we get into it more in the next lesson.

Read Genesis 46:28. Can you imagine the excitement that is building? How long has it been since Joseph has seen his father? At least 20 years. The last time he saw his father, Jacob asked him to go check on his brothers to see if they were okay. And he always obeyed his father.

He said, "I sure will, see you later." Never saw him again until now. And Jacob thought his son was dead. Attacked by wild animals. All those years as a slave. All those years in prison, do you think Joseph thought he would ever see his family again? To see his father again?

Read Genesis 46:29. It says that Joseph fell on his neck which means that he gave him a bear hug. They just grabbed each other. Crying. Weeping for joy.

And finally, look what Jacob says to Joseph.

Read Genesis 46:30. There are a lot of people in this room who have lost people that you love. They were Christians. But have now died. "To be absent from the body is to be present with the Lord." And you miss them. And you think about them sometimes. But do you realize that one of these days, there is going to be a reunion? The Bible says that Jesus Christ will appear in the clouds, and with a shout, the archangel and the dead in Christ will rise first, and that is their bodies. We who are alive and remain will be caught up together with them to meet the Lord in the air.

One of these days, I am going to see my grandparents, whom I haven't seen in many years. All of us will get to see people who have died before us. You talk about a reunion! And Joy! They aren't dead. They are with Him. They just aren't with us. God *is* the God of Abraham, Isaac, and Jacob. God is the God of the living, not the dead! Oh, happy day! When Jesus comes!

How Do You View Life
Genesis 46:31-47:12

Go ahead and turn in your Bibles to Genesis 46 as we continue in our study of this wonderful book of beginnings. We are nearing the end of our study and our focus now is on the life of Joseph. He is the man raised up by God really in a sense to provide for the nation of Israel during the famine. And you remember last time the sweet reunion between Jacob (Israel) and his long-lost son, Joseph.

Now as we look at this passage in the Bible I want you to think about a few things that stand out.

1. The reunion of Joseph and his family

2. The family meeting before the Pharaoh.

3. How does Jacob view life?

How do you view life? Good or bad? I counsel people sometimes as a pastor. They come by the church office and need to talk. One of the things that I have noticed is that people look at life in different ways. There are some people who come in and say, "I hate my life. It is so hard. Things are always bad. There are a lot more downs than there are ups." Then there are others who come in and say, "Life is so good. Yes, there are some bad times, but there are more good times than there are bad."

So, how do you view life? Do you love life, or do you just mope around all the time?

Remember the old saying – 'Is the glass half-empty or is the glass half-full?' How should we, as believers, look at life? When the trials and the problems come into our lives, do we say, 'I am going to trust God.' I know that He says, 'Count it all joy when you fall into various trials, knowing that testing of your faith works patience.' When the good things come into our lives, do you say, 'This is the grace of God? I must praise His name.'

In this lesson, we are going to look at how Jacob looked at life. Is he going to look at life as something good or bad? Much good from God or much bad from God?

As we saw in the last lesson, there was a reunion between Joseph and his father. And there is going to come a time when Jesus Christ will come with the shout of the archangel, with the trump of God the dead in Christ shall rise first, and we who are alive and remain will be got up together with them. And thus, we will meet the Lord in the air. There is going to be a reunion one of these days. And the longer you live, the more you are looking forward to the reunion. You will get to see people who have died. Your grandparents, your mother, or your father, your sisters and brothers. And you can hardly wait to see them. One day. One glorious day.

Now Joseph is going to give his brothers some advice. "I know about the Pharaoh and these Egyptians. I know how they think. So let me give you some advice when you go see the Pharaoh." Watch what Joseph says...

Read Genesis 46:31. Joseph tells his family that he will go to Pharaoh and that you are here.

Read Genesis 46:32-34. Now, when you get to speak to the Pharaoh, and he asks, "What do you guys do for a living?" They don't like shepherds, so you guys tell him, "We take care of livestock." That way, you won't offend them. You need to know about the Egyptian culture. And that is the truth. Before Cindy and I went overseas as missionaries, we studied the culture for months prior to leaving. How do you do certain things? And how do you greet one another? And what do you say in certain situations? We needed to know about their culture. We needed to know about such things in order to communicate the message of Jesus Christ.

So Joseph has given his advice. Watch what happens...

Read Genesis 47:1. Now, if you remember, the Pharaoh had already told him to do that. "Go get your family and bring them down; they don't need to bring all your goods because we have plenty here, and they can live in the region of Goshen, in the northeastern part of Egypt." I am doing this for you, Joseph.

Read Genesis 47:2. He didn't take all his brothers.

Let me ask you a question. Which five brothers? I think the five oldest. Of course, we really don't know.

Read Genesis 47:3a. What are they supposed to say? Keepers of livestock. What are they not supposed to say? Shepherds. Don't say you are shepherds.

Read Genesis 47:3b. Wrong answer. You can just see Joseph over here saying to himself, "You meatheads. Did I not teach you anything? What in the world are you thinking?" He had already told them that being a shepherd was loathsome to the Egyptians. "We are shepherds, both we and our father."

Read Genesis 47:4. They come up to the king of Egypt and tell him that they are involved in the worst occupation and then request the best land. "Can we live in the land of Goshen because we got sheep?" Now you know that if God isn't in all of this, it isn't going to work. Now watch what the Pharaoh does...God is working...

Read Genesis 47:5-6. Do you know what Pharaoh is saying? "Take some of your brothers and let them oversee some of my livestock." Let them live in my best land, and if they need a good job, put them in charge of my animals." That's grace. Pharaoh trusted Joseph. Because Joseph saved the Egyptians during the famine. He interpreted the Pharaoh's dreams. Think about the blessings in the life of Joseph and his family. First of all, God raised Joseph to be a ruler of this nation. He found favor with the Pharaoh. He has brought his family to Egypt for protection and for provision. And that is one of the reasons that God took them out of the land of Canaan, even though it was the Promised Land. He took them out so that the influence of the pagan Canaanites wouldn't corrupt them. And he has given them the best land and said, "I will use you if you want to work for me." God blesses His people.

Let me ask you a question. Does Jacob and his family deserve these blessings? No. Does anybody deserve any blessings from God? No. Have you ever thought about if these are God's children, and they are, and we are God's children because we have put our faith in Christ? How has He blessed us? Do you realize that He has given us eternal life? It is called an inheritance. There are two types of inheritance in the Bible. There is an inheritance that is earned, and there is an inheritance that is given to us. The inheritance is given to us, and Peter says, "In it, an inheritance kept in heaven and never fades away, but kept by the power of God." He has given us a home in heaven, eternal life, and a new, glorious body. All these things and more. And it is the grace of God. He has just given it to us. He has also given us spiritual gifts, the power of the holy spirit, and opportunities to serve Him. And if we do that, He will actually give us rewards for serving Him in His power through His gifts. That is all the grace of God.

Do you believe that you <u>get</u> to serve the Living God? I mean sometimes we act like, 'Man, I <u>have</u> to do this or that at church.' Folks, you get to serve God, not that you have to. We look at life sometimes like, 'I am here for me and my desires and pleasures.' And what we need to be saying is, 'I belong to the living God. He saved me, He created me, He has given me eternal life. He has gifted me. He has empowered me. What do you want me to do? I want to serve You!'

Now it is time for Jacob, 130 years old to meet the Pharaoh. How did he look at life?

Read Genesis 47:7. Jacob blesses Pharaoh. Here is this really old man blessing the king of Egypt. What a contrast. Jacob was the lowly shepherd before the mighty ruler of Egypt. You see, one is a child of God, and the other is a child of the world. Jacob is God's representative.

Read Genesis 47:8. "You are really old. How old are you? Gosh, you look old."

Read Genesis 47:9. What did Jacob say about his life? "I have lived 130 years, but they have been few and unpleasant." "Jacob, how's life?" "Not too good. I haven't lived long, and they have been pretty bad anyway." That's what he is saying. And we would say, 'Wait a minute, how could 130 years be few?' It's not. But to Jacob, he thinks it is. Because it is less than his father's, but is it unpleasant to be one of the chosen people. The one God came and gave your grandfather a covenant, which was passed down to your father and then passed down to you. And remember, God changed his name from Jacob (deceiver) to Israel (prince). And God has given you twelve sons and a daughter. And through you, this mighty nation will build. And God has appeared to you eight times. This is an unpleasant life.

Read Genesis 47:10. Jacob is acting as God's representative to bless the Pharaoh. Why would he do that? Because Pharaoh is going to be God's instrument to protect His people during the famine. And they are going to grow from 70 people to 2 million before it is all over.

Now, we can look at life believing that God is Sovereign and in control. Or we can look at life in a negative way and say, 'Oh, my life is so hard. So many problems. And look at all I don't have.' Jacob looked at life from a negative viewpoint.

Now everyone of us in this room could start complaining about bad things in our life. We all could look at life in a negative viewpoint. We all could say things didn't work out like I thought they would. And what you don't have. What car you don't have. What clothes you don't have. What family you don't have. Life is so bad. Or you could flip it around the other way and say, 'By the grace of God, He chose me before the foundation of the world, He has given me eternal life, He has given me gifts, He has given me family, He has given me clothes, He has given me everything that I need. And I don't have to worry about a thing. He will never leave me nor forsake me.' I guarantee you that all of us really can say, 'You know, life is pretty good. Because the creator of the world loves me.'

How do you look at life? It's not the length of your life that makes the difference. It's not the influence that you have. It's not the popularity that you have. Life is measured by the relationships - and the key relationship is your relationship with the living God. He is the creator, your savior, and your heavenly Father.

Here is a little summary at the end of this Bible lesson.

Read Genesis 47:11. What everybody needed was provided. Joseph took care of them.

CHAPTER FORTY-FOUR

Do You Keep Your Word?
Genesis 47:13-31

Open your Bibles to Genesis 47 as we continue to see Jacob's family settling into Goshen, Egypt. We are going to see the severity of that famine. We are going to see what happens to the Egyptians and how God uses Joseph not only to provide for them but also to bring the whole nation into one thing. And then, at the end of this passage, we are going to see Joseph make a promise to his father. And so we are going to talk briefly about keeping our word. And the question is - when you make a promise, do you keep your word?

Well, what I want to do is begin by making a promise to you. I plan that from now on - whoops, I had better stop. I had better be careful with what I said. Because if I promise something, then does it matter if I keep it or not? If I say I am going to do something, do I do it? If I say I will be there, am I there? How binding is a promise? If I say I will do a certain thing, is it okay not to do it? Is not keeping our word a reflection of our character? People today make a contract, and then they try to figure out a way to get out of it. People make vows, then if difficulty arises, they just break them. We expect others to keep their word when dealing with us, but how about our keeping our word to others? One of the goals is to be faithful men and women of character who can be trusted to keep our word. Joseph makes a promise to his father. And it is a fairly simple promise. But will he do it? How do you view your promises? We make promises all the time. Do you keep them?

Read Genesis 47:11-12. We saw last time that Joseph settled his father, Jacob, who is 130 years old, and his entire family in the wonderful land of Goshen, Egypt. And provided for them everything they needed. God moved the Israelites to Egypt to provide for them and to protect them during the famine. And God is going to turn them into a great nation as promised. God has really blessed them. And God has blessed each one of us so much.

Now, we are going to see what happened during the remaining five years of the famine.

Read Genesis 47:13. This was really a severe famine that affected the entire world. People from all over the place are coming to Egypt looking for food. And Joseph is the one who decides who gets to buy the stored food that belongs to the Pharaoh.

Read Genesis 47:14. So now the Pharaoh is getting all the money because people are buying grain from Joseph.

Read Genesis 47:15. The people are spending all of their money on food. But what is going to happen when the people run out of money?

Read Genesis 47:16. How much will you give me for this camel? So Joseph is now trading grain for whatever the people owned.

Read Genesis 47:17. Now, who has all the grain? Pharaoh. Who has all the money? Pharaoh. Who has all the livestock?

Pharaoh. So what is going to happen when the people run out of livestock?

Read Genesis 47:18. So what is the Pharaoh going to get next?

Read Genesis 47:19. They are now offering themselves as slaves to Pharaoh.

Read Genesis 47:20. So now, who has all the land? Pharaoh. He has everything. So what is he going to make them do?

Read Genesis 47:21. So now the Pharaoh makes the Egyptian people move and not be all scattered out because the land wasn't theirs anymore. He makes them live in certain places now.

Read Genesis 47:22. Why do you think the Pharaoh didn't make the Egyptian priests give up their land? And he gave them an allotment and fed them? Who do the Egyptian priests represent? Their gods. And you don't want to make the gods mad. I mean, there is already a famine. Some god is already mad. So you want to keep the people who talk to the gods happy.

Read Genesis 47:23. Now Joseph has a plan. He says, "You now belong to the Pharaoh. He has all of your money, your livestock, your land, and we got you." But here is what we are going to do for you. Here is some seed for you to sow on the Pharaoh's land.

Read Genesis 47:24. You belong to the Pharaoh, but I am going to take care of you. I am going to give you seed, but what I want you to do is - work Pharaoh's land, and when his crops come up, you give back to him 20% of the yield. I am going to allow you to keep 80% for yourself to support your families.

So what do you think they are going to say to that idea?

Read Genesis 47:25. You saved our lives! We were starving, and you saved us over and over again. Not only that, but we get to keep 80% of the profit that doesn't belong to us. We will be Pharaoh's slaves.

Read Genesis 47:26. I imagine Pharaoh was very grateful to Joseph, who not only saved his people but the Egyptians and made the Pharaoh a very powerful, wealthy ruler. Folks, the Bible says that all have sinned, and then the Bible goes on to say that the wages of sin is death. We owe God death. What are we going to do? But someone has saved our lives. Jesus of Nazareth has come and died in our place. To be the provision for us. And just like these Egyptians said to Joseph, "You have saved our lives!" When we wake up in the morning, we ought to say, "Jesus, you have saved our lives!" "In your grace, not anything we could do, you took our place. You have saved our lives!" Joseph was a man who was faithful to fulfill the responsibilities that God raised him up to do. Jesus Christ, the Son of God, was faithful in fulfilling the responsibilities that the Father raised Him to do. Are each one of us, as children of God, faithful to fulfill the responsibilities that God has for us?

Read Genesis 47:27. Why? That's the plan of God. He is fulfilling his promise to Abraham. They are becoming very numerous. Now know that when we get to the end of this book, and you begin reading the book of Exodus, that being very numerous becomes a problem. When another Pharaoh becomes a leader who does not know Joseph, and he sees all of these Hebrew people living in Goshen, he is afraid of them, so he decides to make them slaves. So, part of the blessing becomes a curse in that sense.

Read Genesis 47:28. Jacob lived in Goshen for 17 years. And died at the age of 147.

Read Genesis 47:29. Placing a hand under a thigh was a symbol promising to do what is requested. It was like saying, 'Cross your heart, hope to die, put your right hand up, put your hand under my thigh.' That isn't one we use in our culture today. But that is what they did back then. Jacob asks his son, Joseph, not to bury him in Egypt. When the resurrection comes, when the Messiah comes into his kingdom, I don't want to be in Egypt. I want to be in the Promised Land.

Read Genesis 47:30a. Anybody remember what their burial place was called? Cave of Machpelah. This is the one that Abraham bought years ago for 400 shekels of silver from Ephron the Hittite back in Genesis 23 as a burial place for Sarah. Sarah, Leah, Isaac, and Rebeccah are buried there. Jacob also wants his bones to be buried there too.

Read Genesis 47:30b. Did you see what Joseph said? I promise. Is he going to do it? Yes. We will see it in chapter 50.

Read Genesis 47:31. Jacob (Israel) worships God. Do you know what he is saying? "God you said I was going to die, and that my son would close my eyes. You said that I would be brought out of here. And I know that my son, Joseph would never leave me in Egypt. Because this isn't my home. And I believe his word."

If you said something, could somebody walk out of the room where you said you would do it? Would they walk out of the room and say, "I guarantee he is going to do it? Because he always does what he says." It is a sign of character. When you make a promise, do you consider it binding? Most of the time, in our society, they don't. Folks, God takes us at our word.

CHAPTER FORTY-FIVE

Passing On the Truths
Genesis 48:1-22

Go ahead and turn in your Bibles to Genesis 48. We are continuing our study of this first book in the Holy Bible, the Book of Beginnings. The focus of this lesson is on both Jacob and Joseph. Jacob is going to give out his final blessing before his death. And really, there are two aspects to this Bible lesson. Chapter 48 deals with Jacob blessing Joseph's two sons. Then, the next lesson, chapter 49, deals with Jacob blessing his own sons, the twelve. We are going to see the whole idea of passing on the truths and the faith. Jacob wants his sons and their sons to take the truths of the God of Israel. Passing on your faith is your responsibility. The truth about Jesus Christ. And our first responsibility is to our children. We will also see how Jacob views God. It is a very powerful thing. How do we view God?

Read Genesis 48:1. Now we know that Jacob died when he was 147 years old. And apparently, Jacob is about to die. Word has come to Joseph: "Your father is really sick." We are going to find that when Joseph gets to his father, he is in bed and can hardly get up. So, in Joseph's mind - his father must be dying. So Joseph took his two sons, Manasseh and Ephraim, with him. Why? He wants his father to bless those two boys. There is a symbolic aspect all the way through, from Abraham to Isaac, to Jacob, and on down to these two boys. Abraham had two sons, Isaac and Ishmael. However, the younger Isaac got the blessing, and everything was passed through him. Isaac had two sons, Jacob and Esau. But the younger, Jacob, got the blessing. Now, here is Joseph wanting to bring his two sons to his father to be blessed. But something special is going to happen during this blessing. Now, last time, we looked at the issue of how you view life. Do you look at life as everything bad? Or do you look at life and say good things are? Jacob looked at life as pretty bad when, in reality, it was pretty good.

Read Genesis 48:2. So Joseph is coming with his two boys. And here is old Jacob struggling to sit up in his bed to see his favorite son and his grandsons one more time.

Read Genesis 48:3. Now, the first thing that Jacob tells his son isn't, "Let me see those grandsons of mine so I can bless them." No. He says, "Son, I want you to remember that God Almighty (El Shaddai), the all-powerful and the all-eternal, appeared to me at Luz, and then Jacob changed its name to Bethel. (house of God). And God blessed me."

Read Genesis 48:4. This is the same Abrahamic covenant. Jacob is once again telling his son, Joseph, the story of how God revealed himself to me and promised to me the same promise He gave grandfather Abraham. And God has kept His promise. Is Jacob (Israel) fruitful? Yes. Twelve sons and one daughter. Is the nation a large generation? Not yet, but they are on their way. And notice that the Holy Land belongs to the nation of Israel - forever. It is an everlasting possession. I don't care how many peace pacts or roads to peace there are. I don't care if the UN gets involved. The bottom line is - that the land is Israel because they gave it to them - forever.

Now, Jacob is going to do something that is very special, unique and different. He is going to give Joseph something that will affect these boys. Remember, in a family, the oldest son has three things. Remember what they were?

1. Got a double portion.

2. Got the priesthood of the family.

3. Got the blessing.

Jacob is about to give Joseph a blessing, but the blessing is going to go to these two boys. The double portion he is going to give to Joseph. Now, watch what he does and how he does it. The father of the household had the right to give these to anyone he chose. Who got the priesthood in the family? Levi. God set them apart. And God is going to bypass the oldest. And He has done it every time. Who is the oldest? Reuban. But Jacob is going to bypass him and instead give his blessing to Joseph. And Joseph has two sons, and who is the oldest? Manasseh. But who do you think Jacob is going to give it to? The youngest is Ephraim.

Read Genesis 48:5. Jacob is telling Joseph that he is taking his two sons, his grandsons, and is counting them as his own sons. And by doing that, they are going to count on the eleven brothers. And so after 400 years of being in Egypt and they are returning to the Promised Land, the Ephraim tribe and Manasseh tribe get part of the land. Only Levi didn't get a region of land. But God told them that He would take care of them, but they would get 48 cities (Joshua 21), and everybody would bring their tithes (3 of them) to support them and the sacrificial system.

Read Genesis 48:6. Did you ever notice that when they divided the land up (Joshua 13) when they entered the Promised Land, there wasn't a tribe of Joseph? What's it called? Ephraim and Manasseh.

Read Genesis 48:7. Why did Jacob bring this up? Where is Rachel buried? Bethlehem. Where is everybody else buried? Cave of Machpelah. (Genesis 23) Rebekkah, Isaac, Abraham, Sarah, Leah, Jacob. Where is Jacob going to be buried one day?

Cave of Machpelah. (Genesis 50) He isn't going to be buried with his beloved wife, Rachel.

Read Genesis 48:8. Now do you think that he couldn't see them? I think he wanted Joseph to say who they were. His eyes were getting bad.

Read Genesis 48:9. Here comes the blessing. Now, even though Jacob couldn't see well, he knew who these boys were.

Read Genesis 48:10. He grabs them, hugs them, and kisses them.

Read Genesis 48:11. This is better than I imagined. He actually had a great life, didn't he? Yes.

Read Genesis 48:12. Why? Joseph is showing respect to his father. The mighty ruler in Egypt is bowing down to his lowly-aged father. Kids respect your parents.

Read Genesis 48:13. So Joseph puts Ephraim on his father's left. And Manasseh is on his father's right because he is the oldest.

He is pushing them up in that way so that Jacob will know what to do. But things don't always happen like we think.

Read Genesis 48:14. He swapped! Now, what is going on?

Read Genesis 48:15-16a. Now Jacob starts the blessing for Joseph (instead of Reuben) and says three things about God.

1. "The God before whom my fathers Abraham and Isaac walked." Jacob is saying, "I am talking to God, the God of the covenant. And that is how he saw God. The one who promises and keeps it. The land, seed, and the blessing. Do you see God as the God of promises that He keeps?"

2. "The God who has been my shepherd all my life to this day." Now the word shepherd in Hebrew is raha. The one who provides and protects. Now, to any Jewish person, if you said 'shepherd,' it always brought out a good idea.

Because the shepherd is the guy who takes care of the sheep. He loved them. He provided for them. He protected them. Do you see God as your shepherd?

3. "The angel who has redeemed me from all evil." Jacob is calling Him the angel of Jehovah. That is a term for God in the OT. He is the God who has redeemed me. He is the go'el. He is the one who paid for sins. He is the one who purchased him. (and us). Do you see God as your redeemer?

Read Genesis 48:16b. His name is now what? Israel. (Prince of God). He is no longer Jacob the deceiver. They will be known as the tribes of Israel. He is wanting his faith in God to be passed down to his sons and grandsons. Every one of us in this room wants our children and grandchildren to believe in God. Obey Him. Trust by faith in His Son, Jesus, as the Messiah. And to know the truths of the Bible. And just as we pass on these truths to our children. May they also do with their children. That's the plan. If you don't pass on your faith to your children, how will they know? There is an old saying, 'Christianity is one generation from extinction.' If you don't pass it on, what happens?

Here are four things we are to do as a parent:

1. We need to see our children as a gift from God. Psalm 127.

2. We have been entrusted with authority over our children. We have a great responsibility. Moms and Dads, you are the boss. Kids obey your parents. Do what they tell you.

3. We need to pass on our faith to our children. Eph. 6 and Deut. 6. Let them know what you believe. Train them up in the truths of the Word of God. The character of our children tomorrow depends on what we teach them today. We must never be content with simply protecting our kids from the world; rather, our goal is to equip them to help change the world.

4. How do we do it? By our message and by our lifestyle. Col. 3:17. 1 John 4 – 'As Christ loved us, we are to love one another.' A child is more likely to see God as his Father, when he sees God in his father.

Here's one thing for our children:

1. They need to come under the authority of their parents. Obey and honor your mom and dad. Obey them as long as you are under their authority. And honor them as long as you are alive. Honor their position because God placed them there.

Well, watch the reaction when Joseph realizes that Jacob crossed his arms there.

Read Genesis 48:17. The Right hand is the main blessing. You have it switched around. The main blessing goes to the oldest son, who is Manasseh, and he is on your right side.

Read Genesis 48:18-19. Jacob knew what he was doing. He is diligent in obedience to God's will. He reminds Joseph that God is sovereign and that He has chosen this course of action. By the way, during the divided monarchy, Ephraim's descendants were the most powerful tribe in the north. In fact, oftentimes, the northern kingdom was referred to as Ephraim.

Read Genesis 48:20. Israel blesses both boys. Israel says, "One of these days, you are going to be so good that they will start saying in the future, 'Boy, I hope we turn out like Ephraim and Manasseh.'" This was a big event. And it shows the faith of Israel. By faith he believed the promises of God. The God of covenant.

Read Genesis 48:21. There is no doubt whatsoever. After Joseph dies, these people, his family, will be slaves for 430 years. But God will bring them back to the Promised Land.

Question: Why do you think God allowed His people to be slaves in Egypt? All things work together for good. Was slavery good? No. Could they have become a great nation without becoming slaves? If you were living in the best part of the land of Egypt. You have plenty to eat. Life is going great. Why would you want to go back to Canaan, where you have to take it by force from a bunch of scoundrels? Why go back and fight when I can just stay here in comfort? Remember when they were in captivity in Babylon, and after 70 years, now you had your family, housing, and a nice life? And someone says, "You can return if you want to; it is over 500 miles back to Israel, which is desolate, and the cities are ruined." Would you want to go? Only 50,000 went back out of millions that stayed. And out of that 50,000, only 43,000 were Jews because 7,000 were non-Jews that went with them. That is the book of Ezra and Nehemiah. So, if the people had stayed in Egypt in that great place of Goshen, they might not have ever gone back.

Read Genesis 48:22. Now Jacob talks about that double portion. In the twelve tribes listed, Joseph is never mentioned. But Ephraim and Manasseh are. That is the double portion for Joseph.

CHAPTER FORTY-SIX

How We Live Now Not Only Affects Our Future, But Others as Well
Genesis 49:1-28

Go ahead and turn in your Bibles to Genesis 49. We are almost through. Can you believe it? We have gone all the way through this first book in the Bible. After this lesson, I will have only two more messages to complete Genesis.

We are in a powerful section because we are seeing the blessings. The blessings and the prophecies of Israel right before his death. He calls in his sons, he deals with their past as well as their future. It is very powerful if you think about it. How we live now not only affects our future, but others as well. Including our children, our family, our descendants.

How we live, what we do, how we believe has a bearing on ourselves and others both now and in the future. So in this lesson we will see what Israel says to these boys, how they lived. And what they did will affect the future.

Now, in our modern 21st century, in our culture today, our dying fathers don't call us in to give us a blessing. But we do expect the approval aspect of the blessing. We want to know that our parents love us and approve of us and that we are okay. And we need to hear that we are okay. Many struggle with their relationships with their parents or guardians because they never received the blessing. Oftentimes, parents never realize the impact that they have. And the whole idea of the blessing. There may be some of you in this room who are still waiting for the blessing from your parents. I have known grown men, 45-50 years old, doing their jobs, still hoping that somehow their father will take notice. Been out of the house for 25 years. And yet they are still waiting for their dad to say, "You know, son, you can do it. I have faith in you." They are still waiting for someone in their family to say, "We know you can make it."

I have known women who have gone from one relationship to another, still looking for that love from a father that they never had. How important is this blessing? In this lesson, we see Jacob giving his blessing to his twelve sons. He is about to die; he calls them in and gives them his final remarks. And they are prophetic remarks. And, of course, they are in the Scripture.

This is basically dealing with the nation of Israel because, from these twelve boys, their descendants will come the twelve tribes of Israel. This was the promise, the covenant made with Abraham. "I will make of you a great nation." Jacob is going to tell these twelve men what will befall them in the future. In the days to come. We are going to see the statements that Jacob makes about his sons, how they lived, and what will come to pass. We need to realize that our future is shaped by our past actions.

What you are now is based on what you have done in the past. The actions of the individual will affect the lives of their descendants. You see, sometimes we say things like, "I do whatever I want to do. It doesn't affect anybody." The Biblical principle is 'What you do affects not only you but also those who come after you. Those you are in contact with every day.'

Now Jacob is going to give details on five of his sons, Reuben, Levi, Simeon, Judah, and Joseph. And the other seven sons there are just little short sayings about their future. Not much details. And some of them we just have to kind of guess what Jacob is saying.

The writer of Romans says that, "The things that were written in the past, were written for our instruction." Both the OT and the NT is given by inspiration of God and is profitable for doctrine, teaching, reproof, and correction, training in righteousness.

The entire Bible is for us. Now, not everything written is something that we can apply, but there are a lot of great things in the Bible that give us truths and principles of life and about how we live - so that we can make an application.

Remember the movie "It's a Wonderful Life" where George Bailey learned that his life touched so many others. Do you realize that if you were not here, things would be different? Because your life touches so many, both the positive and negative? Jacob will be making the blessings and the prophecies, and he is doing that as an act of faith because it is actually prophecy. He is basically lining up the nation of Israel to come and talk about each one of these boys, and the prophecies will be fulfilled in the Promised Land as the nation grows. How you live right now and what you pass on to your children and grandchildren is going to affect the future. The future of your name, your family, and those you come in contact with.

Read Genesis 49:1. Jacob calls his sons together; apparently, he thinks he is about to die. He wants to talk about the prophecies. He says, "Let me tell you what is going to happen to you." In the days to come... In the Hebrew mindset, "The days to come" not only meant, 'What's about to happen' but also, 'Way in the future what is going to happen through you, so to speak.' This is that blessing time. This is what every son waited for – the father's blessing. And this is what every one of us in this room wants and needs from our parents. And some people go through life struggling because they don't get that blessing.

Read Genesis 49:2. He used both of his names in that one sentence. When you think about Jacob you think about the guy who started off as a deceiver who didn't trust God, but depended upon himself. And when we look at our lives, we say, "That's me sometimes." We depended upon ourselves thinking that we can do it. Then he says, "Listen to Israel, your father." He is the prince of God that has changed. He is the one who wrestled with God and learned that you go through life resting in God and not in yourself. You see, Jacob never limped, but Israel did. Well, he starts with the oldest son, Reuben. Now, usually, the firstborn got the birthright – the double portion, priesthood, and blessing. But remember, he has already given the double portion to Joseph. And we are going to see later on that the priesthood goes Levi. And who will get the blessing? It won't be Reuben. It will be given to Judah.

Read Genesis 49:3. Now, if you were Reuben, you would be going, "Yeah, that's me. Firstborn. Strength. Power. Thank you, Dad."

But notice...

Read Genesis 49:4. He lacked control in dealing with sex and anger. Jacob says to Reuben, "Son, don't you remember? Do you think I am going to give you the firstborn blessing? You are uncontrolled." One of the marks of maturity is self-control. The fact that you do what you are supposed to do when you are supposed to do it. "Because you went up to your father's bed." Genesis 35:22. 'But remember, be not deceived, God is not mocked, whatever you sow you shall reap.' By the way, Reuben was one of the tribes that decided to remain on the east side of the Jordan River. Let's stop and think about your life. Are you and I self-controlled people? Are we disciplined people with the fruit of the spirit? God gives us the power if we depend upon Him to be self-controlled. Do you want to do great things for God? Then, you must be a self-controlled person. Jacob says to Reuben, "You lost your position."

Read Genesis 49:5. Jacob lumps Simeon and Levi together because of what they did. Remember what they did with their swords? Genesis 34:25 They took revenge against Shechem for defiling their sister Dinah, killed lots of men in the city, looted the city, and even took the women and children as captives. Anger, revenge, violence.

Read Genesis 49:6-7. Because you did those terrible violent things years ago back at Shechem, I don't want to be a part of you. I don't even want to be identified with you. In fact, I am going to scatter you. And you know what happened? After the captivity, Simeon was near Judah and was assimilated into Judah. In fact after the division of the Northern and Southern Kingdoms, Simeon is never even mentioned again. Just Judah. And what about Levi? They never got any land. They were scattered throughout Israel in 48 cities. The prophecy came true.

Read Genesis 49:8-9. Now, through Judah will come the Messiah. The blessing comes through Judah. There are three aspects here. Judah gained victory and strength, and Judah was going to be the ruler. Jacob says that Judah is going to be a lion. Does that sound familiar? Is there someone who is like a lion out of the tribe of Judah? The Messiah. The Messiah is going to come through Judah.

Read Genesis 49:10. This is one of the great verses in the OT. But most people don't even know it. "The scepter shall not depart from Judah." What's the scepter? A long stick with a thing on the top. And the king had it. Now, what would the king have a scepter for? It was his rule and authority. Where is the king of Israel going to come from? Tribe of Judah. Until Shiloh comes. Shiloh could mean the name of a town. But the word Shiloh comes from the Hebrew word "shalom," which means peace. So the scepter is going to be there until the peace comes. Who is the peace? The Messiah. He is the prince of peace. The king of kings. The Lord of Lords.

Read Genesis 49:11. What is the world is Jacob talking about? You don't wash your clothes in wine do you? What he is saying is that there is going to be so much blessing when the king comes that everybody's got a vine. And there is going to be so much wine and so much blessing, that is will be like washing your clothes in it. There is so much.

Read Genesis 49:12. Literally, his eyes are 'dark' from wine. And his teeth white from milk. All he is saying is – when this guy is the king, everybody is blessed. Everybody has all the milk that they want. Everybody has got everything that they want. And that is true. When the king of kings and Lord of Lords comes to set up his Kingdom (1000-year reign), everybody will be taken care of. Jesus is the king! The Gospel of Matthew and Matthew presents Jesus as the king. He is the descendant of Abraham, Isaac, Jacob, Judah and David. The first time that Jesus came to this earth, He offered Himself as the king of the Jews; he offered Himself as the king of kings and lord of lords. He was rejected. He came to seek those who were lost. He came to die and pay the penalty for sin. And that is His first coming. But the second time He comes, according to Psalm 2 and Matthew 25, Revelation 19, He will come as the king to rule in righteousness and justice with a rod of iron. He is coming!

Read Genesis 49:13. Jacob prophesies that Zebulun will live in the northern part of the land near the Sidonians on the ocean side. Now, remember this was a prophecy long before they ever came out of Egypt. I mean, first of all, he is going to die, then Joseph will die, then they are going to be slaves for 430 years, then come out with Moses, then wander around for another 40 years, then Moses is going to die, then Joshua is going to lead them in and divide it up. Does it just so happen that the tribe from Zebulun gets this certain piece of land? It was a prophecy hundreds of years before.

Read Genesis 49:14-15. What does that mean? I don't know. But notice that the land that Issachar's tribe gets is just south of Zebulun's land, which is a good area for growing crops. "He bowed his shoulder to bear burdens and became a slave at forced labor." Now, this could refer to the fact that when they built the temple a number of years later, the people from the tribe of Issachar were the main groups that came down and helped build the temple. But just don't have enough information to know for sure what it means.

Read Genesis 49:16-17. Dan got to the land kind of in the middle of the country, but they didn't think it was big enough for the people, so they said, "Well, if you want more land, then you will just have to go out and find you some more land." But everything else was taken, so they went way up north, and there were some people living there who weren't Jewish, so they killed them all and took the land. Now Dan means judge. So Dan becomes a leader and a judge. "A horned snake in the path that bites the horse's heels so that his ride falls backward." And Dan was a fighter tribe. And history proved that. Dan was strong and liked to fight and kill. Look at the end, though. Jacob makes this statement...

Read Genesis 49:18. Daniel means that God is my judge. Looking for the salvation. Daniel gives all the prophecies of the coming Messiah. He gives the exact years and the exact days that the Messiah will come.

Read Genesis 49:19. This seems to indicate that there will be people who attack the tribe of Gad, and he will attack them back. That's all we know. By the way, Gad was one of the tribes that decided to remain on the east side of the Jordan River. And they were vulnerable to raids by the Moabites to the south.

Read Genesis 49:20. Asher's land was the northwestmost division of the land. Historically, people say that the tribe of Asher was famous for its rich food, and they grow good crops.

Read Genesis 49:21. Beautiful words. Thank you for coming. That's it. East of Asher's land is Naphtali's land. This is the hill country north of the Sea of Galilee. Beautiful words. How about 'good news.' Matthew 4:13 tells us the beginnings of Jesus' ministry. Where did He begin it? Jesus preaches in the region northwest of the Sea of Galilee. Matthew quotes that the light of the Messiah will come from the region of Naphtali.

Now for Joseph. He has already got the double portion. His two sons, Ephraim and Manasseh, get portions of the Promised Land.

Read Genesis 49:22. This means that there is going to be so much blessing from Joseph. "Its branches run over a wall."

Ephraim and Manasseh, in fact were some of the biggest tribes and got the biggest section of the land.

Read Genesis 49:23. What could that be referring to? Nobody really knows. But it could be referring to when his brothers came up against him because they wanted him dead. But he held firm.

Read Genesis 49:24a. He was a fighter. He triumphed.

Now watch this because Jacob begins to describe God three ways to Joseph:

Read Genesis 49:24b.

1. The mighty one of Jacob

God is described as the Mighty One. That is the Shaddai. He is all powerful. Jacob tells Joseph that he has strength because the Mighty One, the Shaddai has provided it.

2. The shepherd

The shepherd is the provider and the protector. The Lord is my shepherd; I shall not want. He provides for me. He has the table. He anoints my head.

3. The stone of Israel

He is the rock. He never moves. He never changes. He is the same yesterday, today, and forever. We are supposed to build our house on the rock.

Do you view God that way? As the Mighty One. The Shepherd. The Rock.

Read Genesis 49:25a. God is going to give you all the blessings from above, from below. He is going to take care of you, whatever your needs are.

Read Genesis 49:25b-26a. He says I am going to bless you from your mother and your father. Who is that? God. God is always going to provide for you. He always will.

Read Genesis 49:26b. He says, "Joseph, you get all the blessings. So much that you get the double portion."

Now for the last son, Benjamin.

Read Genesis 49:27. Wow. What would you do if you were Benjamin? For them, a wolf wasn't necessarily bad. But represented something that was able to gain victory. To go out and get the enemy. He gains the victory. What tribe did the first king of the nation of Israel come from? Saul was from the tribe of Benjamin. It was a small tribe. When the nation was divided into two kingdoms. The southern kingdom has two tribes, Benjamin and Judah. And the northern kingdom has the other ten tribes. But after the division of the nation. Benjamin just kind of went in with Judah because the southern kingdom was known as Judah, not Judah and Benjamin.

Read Genesis 49:28. Jacob says, "This is exactly what I was supposed to tell these boys. What was appropriate for each of them."

Forgive One Another
Genesis 49:29-50:26

Open your Bibles to Genesis 49. In Genesis we have really seen God's great promise. And that is the Messiah and the Savior. Beginning with Adam and Eve, and it seems so long ago, the promise of the seed of a woman to crush the head of the serpent. Then to Abraham, Isaac, Jacob, and even down to Judah we have seen the promise. This book closes with the deaths of Jacob and Joseph. And now we will see once again the issue of forgiveness. Because Joseph's brothers are afraid that their father, Jacob, will die, what is Joseph going to do to them after what they had done to him?

In our relationships, many times, we hurt one another. In our marriages, in our friendships, people we work with, even in the church body. Sometimes that happens. We say or do things that hurt other people. We are misunderstood, we are wrong. Sometimes people do us wrong. We realize that we are fallen people who live in a fallen world. We have the natural bent to do wrong. But how do we deal with this? What are we supposed to do when others hurt us? When we are wronged? Well, the whole idea is forgiveness. 1 Peter 4:8 says, "Let love cover over a multitude of sins." Sometimes in our lives, when people do us wrong, the best thing is to overlook it. Let it go. Ephesians 4:32 says, "Be kind, tenderhearted, forgiving one another even as God in Christ Jesus has forgiven you." In this lesson, as we conclude our study in Genesis, we are going to see forgiveness and what we are supposed to do.

After Jacob's death, the brothers are wondering, 'Will Joseph now get them back for what they did to him so early in his life?' Joseph is in a very powerful position in Egypt. He can do anything he wants to. What will he do? Has he really forgiven them?

If you remember last time, Jacob has been blessing all the sons.

Read Genesis 49:28. So he blessed the twelve sons. And we saw that some of the statements were very short and vague. And others gave much more details. And the truth is that how we live now affects not only our family and friends right now but future generations as well. Who you are today is the result of past actions and lifestyle, and who you are now will influence your future.

Read Genesis 49:29-30. This is the charge. Jacob says, "I want you to promise to take me back to the cave of Machpelah in Canaan when I die. I want to be resurrected in the land that God has given to our family."

Read Genesis 49:31-32. Everybody is buried there except Rachel, who is buried in Bethlehem because she died on the way after giving birth.

Read Genesis 49:33. This is the last of the three patriarchs. And he has now died. He died at the age of 147. Abraham was a man of faith. Isaac was a man of courage. And Jacob is the father of the nation. Jacob has died. And there is sadness. And no matter what you think, every time there is a death, there is sadness. Because we remember that we are fallen people who have disobeyed God. There is a hole in our lives, because the person that we loved, that person that we cared about, that person that touched our lives is gone. There is sadness. But there is also an aspect of joy. Because the truth is - death is not the end. We have the hope of eternal life which is from the Messiah, our savior Jesus Christ.

Read Genesis 50:1. You know Joseph loved his father. They were separated for such a long time. Joseph was the favorite. And his father loved him very much.

Read Genesis 50:2. Embalming was typical for Egyptians. It really was a marvel of its day. It was an elaborate process. And we aren't sure exactly what they did.

Read Genesis 50:3. Did you see just how important Joseph was to the Egyptians? Joseph is a hero. He had saved the Egyptian's lives. They wept for 70 days. Now, they would normally weep for the Pharaoh for 72 days. But they really are weeping for Jacob. They just barely knew Jacob. I think it was all to honor Joseph. Now, here is the plan...

Read Genesis 50:4-5. Basically when the time of mourning was over, Joseph goes to speak to the Pharaoh and asks him if it would be all right to go back to the land of Canaan to bury his father as he promised.

Read Genesis 50:6. Go do whatever you need to do. Keep your promise. I think the Pharaoh trusts Joseph. Joseph is a man of character and truth. Whether he is working for Potipher, or in prison, or serving the Pharaoh, He does whatever he is supposed to do. Because he really does this not for his masters, but for his God. And that is the key. You see, sometimes we get wrapped up in this world if we just remember that we actually represent the living God and that one day we will give an account of ourselves. Romans 14:11-12 "Each one will give an account to God." if we realize that what we do, what we say, and how we say it, and where we go – we are accountable to God. We represent Him. We are living for Him. We are serving Him.

Read Genesis 50:7. Now, realize that when they head to Canaan, it isn't a small group. I think there was a huge caravan of Egyptians. All of the brothers, the family members, servants of Pharaoh, elders of the household etc.

Read Genesis 50:8. So only the little children and the family's herds, stayed in Goshen and didn't go back to Canaan. So Pharaoh probably wasn't worried about Joseph coming back, because they left their kids.

Read Genesis 50:9. Can you imagine this scene? This huge caravan of people, chariots etc.

Read Genesis 50:10. So they stopped on the East side of the Jordan River and mourned for a week. Now watch what happens...

Read Genesis 50:11. Abel-mizraim means the mourning of the Egyptians. The locals looked out and said, "Look at all those Egyptians over there. It must be something really sad because they are all mourning. Some famous Egyptian must have died." It wasn't an Egyptian at all; it was a famous Hebrew who died.

Read Genesis 50:12-13. The author is saying the same thing over and over so that we don't miss it. Same field, same cave, bought by the same guy. They did what they promised. A lot of times in the Bible, this one issue keeps coming up. Do you do what you promise? It's so easy to say 'Yes, I will' and then we don't. We live in a society of convenience. And if it is convenient, we will do it, but if not, we won't. But we need to be people of character who keep our word. That's a key in relationships. And it is a key in our testimony. The best way for you to hurt a relationship is to don't follow through on what you say you will do. Because then the people in the relationship can't trust you. And in a fallen world, one of the things that they look at is – the consistency of people. Are we faithful to do what we say?

Read Genesis 50:14. He did what he said. He buried his father as he had promised and returned to Egypt.

Now, the easiest thing that Joseph could have done when he saw his brothers bowing before him the first time they came for food - would be not to give them anything. But you love your father, and you find out that he is still alive. And you love your brother, and you find out that he is also still alive. So you finagle things around in order to get your little brother Benjamin there so that you can see him again. And then, eventually, the whole family comes down. But now, your father, Jacob, is gone. And your father is the head of this whole thing who keeps it together. And you have the chance if you want to, especially since you are a very powerful leader in Egypt, to get your brothers back. You can call those brothers into the royal hall and say, "You thought you were going to get away with treating me like a slave, didn't you? You thought everything would be, easy come, easy go. Well, I have been waiting for this moment. Dad has died. And now I am going to take care of you! He could have done that. He had the power to do so. And some would say he even had the right to do that.

Now, picture it from one of the brothers' viewpoints. You have grown up, maybe have a wife and kids. And you remember what you did. And when you finally found out it was Joseph, he took off that headdress thing and said, "I am your brother, Joseph, who is alive." You have never slept really well since then. And you have wondered what he is going to do one of these days. Is he just waiting to get us back one day? I mean, he said, "God brought me down here to preserve you all," But I don't know if I really believe that or not. And all Joseph has to do is have one bad day, and we're toast. He could kill us all. So, the brothers began to worry about it.

Read Genesis 50:15. They knew they had done wrong. 'What if Joseph wants to get us back?' But what do you know of Joseph? Does he seem to be the kind of person that wants revenge? No. He is a man of character. So watch what they do.

Read Genesis 50:16-17. They sent a message to him. Too afraid to face him face to face. And they said, "Dad said before he died for you to forgive us." Now, do you think that is true? If it is true, then Jacob knew the entire story. They lied to their father about Joseph's whereabouts for years. Did we ever see in the Bible passage that they actually told their father, Jacob, the truth? No. And if this message isn't true, then they just made up a story to save themselves. Which one do you think it is? Well, look at Joseph's response... He wept. Do you know what I think Joseph is saying by this action? How could they think I would get them back after all that I have done for them? I mean, never once since I revealed myself to them have I done them wrong. I have never tried to get them back. How could they actually think I would be the kind of person that gets even? How could they believe that?

Read Genesis 50:18. What was the dream years ago that Joseph had? That his brothers would bow down before him. Do you realize that this is the sixth time that is recorded in which they bowed down before him? And they are bowing down, pleading for their lives, offering themselves as servants. And with Joseph's answer, there are three keys to forgiveness.

The first one is in verse 19.

Read Genesis 50:19.

1. You don't have to be afraid because I am not the one who will get you.

I am not the judge. It is God who judges. Not us. When people do us wrong, you aren't the one to get them back. You're not the judge. Vengeance belongs to who? God. We should never say, "I am going to get them back." Because when you do, you are actually taking God's place. You are saying that you are the judge.

Now look at the second truth dealing with forgiveness.

Read Genesis 50:20.

2. God is the one who is sovereign, working behind all events. Even when somebody does us wrong.

Joseph is saying, "You did me wrong, but God took your evil and meant it for good." And so when people do us wrong, we can say, "God is sovereign and in control and allowed this, and He is working in this, and God can take this and use it for good." He is working to fulfill His plan.

And finally, there is a third truth dealing with forgiveness.

Read Genesis 50:21.

3. You always return evil with good.

You never repay evil with evil. If somebody does you wrong, don't do them wrong back.

And there is a fourth truth found in the Scriptures. In Ephesians.

4. We can forgive others because we are forgiven in Jesus Christ.

To forgive means to cancel the debt. To let it go.

Now, every time we see Joseph, he does right. They threw him in prison; he was the best prisoner you could have. They raised him up to #2 in Egypt; he was the best worker you could ever find. His brothers did him wrong, and he forgives them totally and loves them. He was a great man, but he was going to die. And it is sad.

Read Genesis 50:22. Abraham lived 175. Isaac lived 180. Jacob lived 147. Joseph lived 110.

Read Genesis 50:23. He got to see his grandchildren. How many of you are grandparents? Isn't it great to see your children's children?

Read Genesis 50:24. Here in this verse he tells his brothers that he is going to die but remember the Abrahamic covenant. God will one day take our family back to the land that He promised.

Read Genesis 50:25. He, too, wants to be buried in the Promised Land.

Read Genesis 50:26. May we be faithful to God, relying on Him for guidance. God is with us.

THANK YOU, LORD!

For giving us this wonderful book that we have studied. All the wonderful lessons, truths, principles, and applications that You have given to us. And now that You have equipped us, may we go out and teach others what we have learned in Genesis. May we tell others about salvation found in Jesus Christ. Lord, use us for your glory.

About the Author

David R. Bradley currently serves as the pastor of First Baptist Church in Valdez, Alaska. David has also served with the North American Mission Board of the Southern Baptist Convention as a chaplain with the U.S. Navy, U.S. Marines, and U.S. Coast Guard. He and his wife, Cynthia, have also served with the International Mission Board of the Southern Baptist Convention as career missionaries to Chile.

As a pastor, he has goal to help the church to:

1. Proclaim the Gospel message to the local community and the world. - II Corinthians 5:20

2. Equip the Believers to do the work of the ministry, to build up the body of Christ. - Ephesians 4:12

3. Teach the Word of God in order that Believers may understand the truths and make application in their lives. - II Timothy 2:15

4. Lead the assembled Believers to worship The Lord and fellowship with each other through: song, prayer, giving, teaching, and praise. - Hebrews 10:24-25